Counseling as an Art: The Creative Arts in Counseling

(Second Edition)

Samuel T. Gladding, PhD

COUNSELING AS AN ART (SECOND EDITION)

10 9 8 7 6 5 4 3 2 1

American Counseling Association
5999 Stevenson Avenue
Alexandria, VA 22304

Director of Acquisitions
Carolyn Baker

Director of Publishing Systems
Michael Comlish

Copyeditor
Wendy Lieberman

Library of Congress Cataloging-in-Publication Data

Gladding, Samuel T.
    Counseling as an art : the creative arts in counseling / Samuel T. Gladding.
— 2nd ed.
        p.   cm.
    Includes bibliographical references and indexes.
    ISBN 1-55620-202-4 (alk. paper)
    1. Counseling.   2. Arts—Therapeutic use.   I. Title.
BF637.C6G533   1998
158' .3—dc21

                                                   97-29494
                                                    CIP

To Jim Cotton, Robbin McInturff, Mariam Cosper, Laurie Smith, and the other helping professionals at Adult and Child Developmental Specialists in Birmingham, Alabama, who taught me the art of good counseling.

Contents

CHAPTER 1

History, Rationale, and Benefits of Using the Arts in Counseling 1

CHAPTER 2

Music and Counseling 15

CHAPTER 3

Dance and Movement and Counseling 33

CHAPTER 4

Imagery and Counseling 49

CHAPTER 5

Visual Arts and Counseling 63

CHAPTER 6

Literature and Counseling 81

Preface

Counseling is a creative process that focuses on helping clients make appropriate choices and changes. Effective counselors are aware of the multidimensional nature of the profession and are able to work with a variety of populations by using appropriate interventions. One key aspect of counseling that promotes the best within the helping arena is the use of the creative arts. By their very nature, the arts foster different ways of experiencing the world. They are enriching, stimulating, and therapeutic in their own right. When employed in clinical situations, they help counselors and clients gain unique and universal perspectives on problems and possibilities.

In the second edition of this book I have concentrated on how the creative arts can be used independently and complementarily to enhance the counseling process on primary, secondary, and tertiary levels. The following creative arts are specifically examined:

1. music,
2. dance and movement,
3. imagery,
4. visual arts,
5. literature and writing,
6. drama and psychodrama, and
7. play and humor.

These arts share much in common. They are all process oriented, emotionally sensitive, socially directed, awareness focused, and applicable in numerous forms for working with clients over the life span. In addition, they enable persons from diverse cultural backgrounds to develop in ways that are enjoyable as well as personally and socially enhancing.

Mental health providers such as counselors, social workers, psychologists, creative arts therapists, marriage and family therapists, psychiatric nurses, pastoral care specialists, and psychiatrists will find the contents of these pages useful because of the pragmatic nature of the material covered. The material presented here comes from a variety of educational and treatment-focused work settings. Due to their systematic format, chapters 2 through 8 may be especially helpful; they present readers with a great deal of information in a relatively uniform manner. These chapters contain the following:

1. introductory background about the specific art form;
2. the premise behind using the art form discussed;
3. the general practice of employing the art in counseling settings;
4. the unique use of the specific art with special populations such as children, adolescents, adults, elderly persons, groups, families, and cultural minorities;

5. a summary;
6. art-related exercises; and
7. references.

In addition, the first and last chapters of this book contain information on the history and rationale behind using artistic methods in general as well as material about current trends in the employment of the arts in counseling. These chapters enable readers to obtain a global view of the field and how it is developing. Overall, practitioners will find this book "user friendly" and the ideas disclosed extensively field tested. By carefully reading this book, you as a clinician will become better informed so that you may enhance your skills and effectiveness. The creative arts have much to offer the healing and helping professions.

Acknowledgments

Writing a book is similar to group work. Many people share valuable information with you and give you important feedback. The group that has helped me put together this second edition of *Counseling as an Art: The Creative Arts in Counseling* contains some of the same individuals who helped me with the first edition as well as a few new group members.

First, I want to thank Carolyn Baker and the American Counseling Association (ACA) Media Committee for accepting my proposal for a second edition of this text. Carolyn kept me on task in a timely and professional manner. Next, I want to thank Dr. Richard Hayes for encouraging and supporting me to write this book initially. Without Richard's advocacy, I doubt this work would have ever been written. I also want to thank the reviewers and editor of the first edition of this text, Drs. Howard S. Rosenblatt, Stephen G. Weinrach, JoAnna White, and Elaine Pirrone. They were honest and straightforward in their appraisal of the manuscript and offered constructive thoughts that made this work far better than it would have been otherwise. In addition, I want to express my appreciation to Wake Forest University students—Michele Kielty, Debbie Newsome, Mary Beth Edens, Regan Reding, and Deborah Tyson, in particular—for contributing ideas and thoughts on counseling and the creative arts. Michele was a meticulous proofreader, as well.

Finally, I am grateful to clients and colleagues over the years who have shared creative ideas with me and helped me to focus more on the importance of the arts in counseling. I especially appreciate the support of my wife, Claire, and our children, Ben, Nate, and Tim. They have humored me with jokes and good will while this book was in process. I am truly a fortunate individual to be surrounded with so much that is so good and artistic.

About the Author

Samuel T. Gladding is professor of counselor education, director of the counselor education program, and assistant to the president at Wake Forest University in Winston-Salem, North Carolina. His academic degrees are from Wake Forest (B.A., M.A.Ed.), Yale (M.A.), and the University of North Carolina at Greensboro (Ph.D.).

Before assuming his current position in 1990, he held academic appointments at the University of Alabama at Birmingham and Fairfield University (Connecticut). He was also an instructor of psychology at Rockingham Community College (North Carolina) and director of children's services at the Rockingham County Mental Health Center. He is a licensed professional counselor in North Carolina, a National Certified Counselor, and a former member of the Alabama Board of Examiners of Counselors.

Gladding is the author of a number of publications on counseling, including *Counseling: A Comprehensive Profession* (1996), *Group Work: A Counseling Specialty* (1995), *Family Therapy: History, Theory, and Practice* (1998), and *Community and Agency Counseling* (1997). He is the former editor of the *Journal for Specialists in Group Work* and the Association for Specialists in Group Work (ASGW) newsletter, *Together*. Gladding is past president of the Association for Counselor Education and Supervision (ACES), ASGW, Chi Sigma Iota (counseling academic and professional honor society international), and Southern ACES. He is also the former vice-president of the Association for Humanistic Education and Development (AHEAD).

Dr. Gladding is the recipient of the Chi Sigma Iota Thomas J. Sweeney Professional Leadership Award, the AHEAD Joseph W. and Lucille U. Hollis Outstanding Publication Award, and the ACES Outstanding Publication Award. He is also a Fellow in ASGW. Gladding is married to the former Claire Tillson and is the father of three children. He enjoys the arts, jogging, and humor on a daily basis.

1
History, Rationale, and Benefits of Using the Arts in Counseling,

I am taken back by your words—
To your history and the mystery of being human
 in an all-too-often robotic world.
I hear your pain
 and see the pictures you paint
 so cautiously and vividly.
The world you draw is a kaleidoscope
 ever changing, ever new, encircling and fragile.
Moving past the time and through the shadows
 you look for hope beyond the groups you knew as a child.
I want to say: "I'm here. Trust the process."
But the artwork is your own
 so I withdraw and watch you work
 while occasionally offering you colors
 and images of the possible.

(Gladding, 1990, p. 142)

COUNSELING IS A PROFESSION with the common purpose of making human experience constructive, meaningful, and enjoyable. It is like art in its emphasis on creativity, structure, uniqueness, enactment, and originality. This is a book on the uses of the "creative arts" in counseling. A creative art is an art form, either verbal or nonverbal, that sensitizes or encourages the involvement of clients into the counseling process. In such a process, clients recover from traumatic experiences or grow and develop in functional and healthy ways. In either case, they change for the better.

Cultivation of the arts is enriching for counselors because it sensitizes them to beauty and creates within them a greater awareness of possibilities (Jourard & Landsman, 1980). Traditional arts range from those that are primarily auditory or written (e.g., music, drama, and literature) to those that are predominantly visual (e.g., painting, mime, dance, and movement). Many overlaps exist between these two categories, and in most cases two or more art forms are combined in counseling, such as literature and drama or dance and music. These combinations work because "music, art, dance/movement, drama therapy, psychodrama, and poetry therapy have a strong common bond" (Summer, 1997, p. 80).

This book concentrates on the contents and possibilities of specific arts in counseling and therapeutic settings. The processes and outcomes of employing the arts in this manner will be addressed, too, although it should be pointed out that both of these dimensions are related to specific client populations. Just as becoming a painter takes talent, sensitivity, courage, and years of devotion, a similar process is at work in counseling—the actual practice differs from a knowledge of theory (Cavanagh, 1982). In this text the ingredients needed to enrich counseling through using the arts will be emphasized, but the effective implementation of these skills and processes will only come with practice on the part of the counselor.

The Nature of Creativity

Before examining the creative arts in counseling, it is crucial to explore the nature of creativity itself. There are two reasons that this examination is prudent. First, by knowing something about the nature of creativity, counselors may understand and better appreciate the creative process, especially in regard to the arts. Second, counseling by its very nature is a creative endeavor. Although the arts have much potential to help counselors assist clients in development, like other aspects of counseling, such as basic helping skills, the arts are limited in what they can do unless the counselor knows how to creatively use them.

Creativity is an overused word that is sometimes talked about without being defined. "It is a lot like kissing and counseling in that it is so "intrinsically interesting and satisfying that few bother to critically examine it" (Thoresen, 1969, p. 264), yet a definition of creativity and the underlying dynamics of it are important to understand.

At its core, creativity "is the ability to produce work that is both novel (i.e., original or unexpected) and appropriate (i.e., useful or meets task constraints)" (Sternberg & Lubart, 1996, p. 677). In counseling and other helping professions, creativity usually results in the production of a tangible product that gives a client insight, such as a piece of writing or a painting, or a process that the clinician formulates, such as a new way of conducting counseling that leads to client change. Creativity is a worldwide phenomenon that knows no bounds in regard to ethnicity, culture, gender, age, or other real or imagined barriers that separate people from each other (Koestler, 1964). In addition, creativity can be preventative as well as remedial.

Overall, creativity is a nonsequential experience that involves six steps (Witmer, 1985). First, there is preparation, which is the phase of gathering enough data and background information to make a new response. Next, there is incubation, in which the mind is allowed to wander away from a task or problem. Then comes ideation; ideas are generated but not judged. Following this type of divergent thinking, illumination takes place when there is a breakthrough in one's thinking, a kind of enlightenment. After illumination, evaluation takes place, during which convergent and critical thinking occur. A part of evaluation is fine-tuning and refining thoughts or behaviors that have not been thoroughly thought through. Finally comes verification/production, during which an original idea becomes a new or refined product or action. In this last step, one's life changes forever, for it is impossible to see or be in the world again as one was before the novel idea came into existence.

Although these general aspects about creativity are pertinent to counseling, the profession itself, through its theories, has even more specific ways of viewing creativity (Gladding, 1995). For example, the psychoanalytic viewpoint is that creativity is a positive defense mechanism, known as sublimation. From a gestalt perspective, however, creativity is an integrative process in which people who are more congruent with themselves and their environments try new behaviors. Imagery theorists, on the other hand, would argue that creativity is a matter of envisioning mental pictures and implementing these pictures into reality.

Regardless of how it is seen, creativity is valued in society and in the culture of counseling. Through creativity new, exciting, and productive ways of working and living are formulated and implemented.

History of the Creative Arts in the Helping Professions

Since the vital aspects of what creativity and a creative art are have been explained, the ways in which creative arts have impacted counseling can now be examined in an informed manner. Many of the creative arts, such as drama, music, and dance, have had long and distinguished associations with healing and mental health services. Various art forms have been employed since ancient times to help prevent distress and remediate internal and external strife. Some of their most notable contributions to mental health services are chronicled here according to broad time periods.

Ancient Cultures and the Arts

The ancient Egyptians, as early as 500 B.C., encouraged the mentally ill "to pursue artistic interests and attend concerts and dances" (Fleshman & Fryrear, 1981, p. 12). The idea was that through such activities feelings could be released and persons made whole again. Likewise, the ancient Greeks "employed drama and music as a means to help the disturbed achieve catharsis, relieve themselves of pent-up emotions, and return to balanced lives" (Gladding, 1985, p. 2). The connection and importance of music in the lives of the Greeks is symbolized in the Greek god Apollo, who was both the god of music and the god of medicine. "The Greek philosophers Plato and Aristotle often talked about the effects of music and its importance to the health of the whole person" (Peters, 1987, p. 25). They advocated the careful control of music to promote many moods from relaxation to excitement (Grout, 1973).

The early Hebrews used music and lyrical verse in helping to develop integrated and healthy relationships, too. For example, for those who were emotionally volatile, such as King Saul, music served a calming function. Music was employed, also, to remind these people of the covenant relationship they shared with Yahweh (God) and each other. The psalms, for instance, played a major part in worship and in creating a sense of community through religious rituals.

Similarly, the ancient Roman philosophers encourage the public to use the arts to achieve health and happiness. Lucretius, Cicero, and Seneca "all spoke in different ways of the healing power of 'discourse.' Poetry, Lucretius said, could disperse the 'terrors of the soul'" (Coughlin, 1990, p. A6). A further belief among the Romans was that the study of humane letters could alleviate pain. Finally, music, cymbals, flutes, and other sounds were used by the Romans to dispel melancholy thoughts as well as to promote wellness (Peters, 1987).

Overall, ancient world healers saw power in the arts. They encouraged their followers to experience these forms of creativity vigorously, for they believed that such a procedure would have a significant impact on them.

In the Middle Ages (at least in Europe), magic and superstition replaced the arts in many quarters as the primary way to treat the emotionally disturbed. Yet even in these "Dark Ages," the traditions and actual works of music, art, and literature were preserved in monasteries and were considered in the Judeo-Christian tradition a relevant part of the process of healing (Coughlin, 1990; Flake, 1988). An interesting example of the use of the arts in the service of health is the treatment of the disorder known as "tarantism," which arose in southern Italy during this period and was believed to be caused by the bite of a tarantula. Healers thought that the only cure of this disease was music accompanied by the performance of a dance known as the "tarantella" (Coughlin, 1990)

In contrast to this period in European history was the use of music, dance, painting, and literature as healing forces in African, Native American, and Asian cultures (Fleming, 1986). For example, African music developed into a form with strong, driving rhythms and choral singing, which helped bind communities together. In addition, Asian, African, and Native American art in the form of paintings, jewelry, masks, and architecture flourished and helped give cultures and people in these geographical areas a distinctiveness and freedom unknown in Europe during the Middle Ages. It was during this time period in the Americas that the arts became an integral part of Native American healing (Dufrene & Coleman, 1994). The use of metaphor and healing stories became especially powerful.

The Arts in More Modern Times

During the European Renaissance (starting in the 1500s), the use of the arts was emphasized in preventative and remedial mental health services, as it had been with ancient cultures such as the Greeks. For example, in the 16th century "an Italian named Vittorino de Feltre emphasized poetry, dance, and games" in the education of children and suggested the alternation of study and play in working with children (Flake, 1988). In the 1600s, "writers such as Robert Burton, author of *The Anatomy of Melancholy* (1621), talked about the role of the imagination in both psychological illness and health" (Coughlin, 1990, p. A9). One of his premises was that individuals who were more imaginative and more creative were more likely to be healthy. They could respond to both comedies and tragedies and thus keep a better balanced and more realistic perspective on life.

The integration of health and the arts was exemplified in the work of 17th century physicians such as Tommaso del Garbo, who advised his patients that one way to avoid the plague was to keep a positive mindset and to listen to music (Peters, 1987). His belief in the healing power of music was apparently a part of the culture of the day, as plays such as those written by Shakespeare reflect. Likewise, the poetry of meditation in 17th century England arose at this time with an emphasis on health and wholeness. Poets such as Robert Southwell, John Donne, and George Herbert practiced methodical meditation to become more sensitive to the images within themselves, which they then expressed in verse (Martz, 1962). Thus, concentration led to art, which led in turn to further exploration and discovery of the self.

By the time of the industrial revolution in England (18th century), the use of the arts in the service of healing had expanded. Reformers such as Philippe Pinel in France, Benjamin Rush in the United States, and William Tuke in England stressed the humane treatment of mental patients. A form of counseling known as "moral therapy" was begun. In this approach to treatment, mental patients were sent to country retreats where they received individual attention including occupational training and special times of involvement in the arts including selected reading, music, and painting (Fleshman & Fryrear, 1981). It was in this type of an environment that Vincent Van Gogh, the famous Impressionist painter, spent part of his life as an adult. Overall, this approach proved to be beneficial but was quite time consuming and expensive. Thus, it was relatively short lived.

Despite the brief lives of some forms of art treatment, the power and impact of the arts continued. Music, for instance, was seen as an adjunct to the practice of medicine in many cultures throughout the world (Heller, 1985).

In the 20th century, the use of the arts in counseling has increased significantly. One of the reasons is the work of Sigmund Freud. It was Freud who first probed into the influence of the unconscious through the exploration of dreams and humor. His systematic way of treatment made it possible for others to emulate many of his methods, such as the inducement of catharsis. More importantly, Freud set the standard for incorporating artistic concepts into his therapeutic work. "Freud found the fiction of Dostoyevsky, Sophocles, and Shakespeare, the sculpture of Michelangelo and Leonardo. . . to be the inspiration for his theories. It was not his formal medical training, as much as his readings of *King Lear*, *Hamlet*, *Oedipus Rex*, and *The Brothers Karamazov*, that formed the cornerstone of his theories" (Kottler, 1986, p. 35).

The work of Carl Jung (1964), particularly his examination and use of universal archetypes such as mandalas, also made the arts more attractive to researchers and innovators in counseling. Mandalas are symbols of completeness and wholeness, such as circles. As Jung stated, "The psychological work of art always takes its materials from the vast realm of conscious human experience—from the vivid foreground of life" (Jung, 1933, p. 157). Throughout his life Jung continued to draw and paint, portraying his dreams in writings and through illustrations that he sometimes carved in wood and stone. "He felt that psychological health was a delicate balance between the demands of the outer world and the needs of the inner world. To him, the expressive arts represented an important avenue to the inner world of feelings and images. He came to see the unconscious mind. . . as a source of health and transformation" (Allan, 1988, p. 20–21). Thus, through the influence of Jung, art and creativity became more valued as ways of understanding human nature in our culture.

In addition, the creative genesis of Jacob Moreno (1923), the founder of psychodrama, fostered the use of enactment to work through pain and achieve balance. Moreno originated numerous psychodrama techniques to help clients become more self-aware and make insightful breakthroughs. All of his innovations have an artistic dimension, but among the most notable are these:

1. creative imagery, in which participants imagine pleasant or neutral scenes to help them become more spontaneous;
2. sculpting, during which participants nonverbally arrange the body posture of group members to reflect important experiences in their lives with significant others;

3. monodrama, during which participants play all the different parts of themselves; and
4. role reversal, during which participants literally switch roles with others (Blatner, 1988).

Overall, a major reason for the growth of the arts in counseling during the 20th century has been the powerful personalities who have advocated for them. In addition to the theorists already mentioned, the writings of Abraham Maslow, Rollo May, Arnold Lazarus, Virginia Satir, Bunny Duhl, Peggy Papp, and Cloé Madanas have emphasized the importance of counseling as an artistic endeavor or a profession that can make a difference through the use of the arts. Research emphasizing the results of specific "artistic" strategies and interventions has also resulted in increased acceptance of artistic components in helping relationships.

Another important reason the use of the arts and artistic methods have achieved prominence in counseling is due to many of the events following World War II. For example, veterans of the war were often in need of extended care for the traumas of combat. In addition to the traditional "talk therapies," mental health practitioners began developing new approaches to working with the impaired. These included the use of some arts, such as drawing or painting, music, and literature. In this creative atmosphere, clients were helped to identify and work through pent-up emotions. Interest in the arts as an adjunct to traditional mental health practices thus gained new recognition and acceptance. In addition, professional arts therapy associations were formed. Some of these, such as the American Dance Therapy Association, have advocated using the arts in the service of counseling in an even more professional way.

Thus, out of the development of theories and the treatment of clients following the second world war, arts therapies attracted more interest and gained more acceptance as unique and valuable disciplines. In the 1960s, universities began designing degrees in the "arts therapies," for example, dance and the visual arts. From the graduates of these programs came new enthusiasm and energy to develop standards and guidelines for practice. By the late 1990s, most arts therapy associations either registered or certified their members as qualified practitioners. Multiple attempts have been made by these associations to have arts therapists licensed in some states (S. Kleinman, personal communication, April 3, 1997).

Paralleling the growth of professional associations was a surge in the publication of periodicals dealing with the arts in counseling, such as *The Arts in Psychotherapy*. Likewise, the 1980s heralded an increased effort at sharing knowledge among mental health professionals interested in the arts. The National Coalition of Arts Therapy Associations (NCATA) was established in 1979. It held interdisciplinary conferences for arts therapists in 1985 (New York) and 1990 (Washington, D.C.). The emergence of NCATA signaled a formal and systematic attempt to foster communication between art therapy groups and individuals interested in these groups. NCATA also focused on being an inclusive voice to achieve legislative recognition for creative arts therapists (Bonny, 1997).

Rationale for Using the Creative Arts in Counseling

Along with the increased growth of creative arts in counseling has come the formulation of a rationale for using them in the helping process. Numerous reasons exist for using the creative arts therapeutically besides the fact that they have an historical precedent. First, the arts are a primary means of assisting individuals to become more completely in touch with themselves, that is, promoting the connectedness between their minds and bodies. Often people who become mentally disturbed, such as those with anorexia or depression, have distorted views of their bodies or do not acknowledge or use their bodies in productive ways. They estrange themselves from reality and therefore prevent healing forces within themselves from coming into action. This is a phenomenon that Carl Rogers (1957) described as "incongruence," and it prevents growth and development. Many of the arts, such as dance and music, have the potential for helping individuals become more integrated and more aware of their total selves.

A second reason for using the arts in counseling involves energy and process. Most creative arts are participatory and require the generation of action. This active involvement helps give individuals new energy and is reinforcing. It leads somewhere. In many cases the input-output energy cycle is similar to that of a marathon runner. Initially, a runner uses energy to cover mileage at a set pace. Later, after considerable physical pain, he or she experiences what is known as a runner's high, a feeling of renewal and energy that allows the person to pick up the pace. After such an event there is an analysis of what happened and how what was learned can influence the future. This type of reflecting and talking, regardless of the activity, but especially with arts activities, can lead to new and usually improved functioning of the person(s) involved.

A third reason for incorporating the arts in counseling is focus. There is an old African American saying to "keep your eye on the prize." The arts, especially those that involve vision, allow clients to see more clearly what they are striving for and what progress they are making toward reaching their goals (Allan, 1988; Lazarus, 1977). Other nonvisual arts such as those dealing with sound also encourage this type of concentration.

Yet a fourth rationale for using the arts in counseling is creativity. To be artistic as a counselor or to use the arts in counseling "enlarges the universe by adding or uncovering new dimensions" (Arieti, 1976, p. 5), while enriching and expanding people who participate in such a process. Thus, counseling as an art and the use of the arts in counseling expands the world outwardly and inwardly for participants. Better yet, the artistic side of counseling allows and even promotes this expansion in an enjoyable and relaxed manner.

A fifth reason for including artistic components in counseling is to establish a new sense of self. Awareness of self is a quality that usually increases with age (Erikson, 1968; Jung, 1933). Nonetheless, this ability to become more in contact with the various dimensions of one's self can be sped up and highlighted through the use of the arts in counseling. The visual, auditory, or other sensory stimuli used in sessions give clients a way to experience themselves differently in an atmosphere where spontaneity and risk taking are encouraged within limits. Clients are able to exhibit and practice novel and adaptive behaviors. Thus, clients gain both confidence and ability through sessions, and the arts assist them to "become" continuously (Allport, 1955).

A sixth reason for including the arts in counseling involves concreteness. In using the arts, a client is able to conceptualize and duplicate beneficial activities. For example, if writing poetry is found to be therapeutic, the client is instructed to use this method and media when needed (Gladding, 1988). By doing so, the client lays out an historical trail so that he or she can see, feel, and realize more fully what he or she has accomplished through hard work and inspiration. Such a process allows the memories to live again and lead to other achievements.

Insight is another reason for the employment of the arts and artistic methods in counseling. Two types of insight are most likely to result. The first is primarily that of the participants in counseling, that is, the counselor and client. In this type of insight, one or both of these individuals comes to see a situation in a different light than when counseling began. For example, the client may see his or her situation as hopeless but not serious, or serious but not hopeless (Watzlawick, 1983). This type of focus makes a difference, for it is what people perceive that largely determines their degree of mental health or alienation (Ellis, 1988).

In the second type of insight, mental health professionals gain new sensitivity into how they need to collectively develop. For example, they may recognize "that art often leads to science" and that balance is needed between scientific and artistic endeavors if the profession is to avoid becoming mechanical (Seligman, 1985, p. 3).

A final reason for using the arts in counseling centers on socialization and cooperation. Johnson and Johnson (1994) have compiled an extensive amount of information that shows that cooperative tasks result in the building of rapport and the establishment of greater self-esteem and prosocial behavior. The arts are a useful means to promote these two developments and have been shown to provide a common ground for linking people to one another in a positive manner (Menninger Foundation, 1986).

The Creative Arts in a Multicultural Context

The creative arts are multicultural. This fact could be listed in the preceding section as a rationale for using them. Yet the importance of being aware of culture and the creative arts warrants its own separate space. It is crucial that counselors and other helpers are aware and prepared to work in the rapidly changing, multicultural world.

In regard to cultures, counseling, and the creative arts it should be noted that different cultures and clients within these cultures have preferred ways of expressing creativity and artistic ability. Counselors are challenged to help clients discover what works best for them, when, and even why. The counselor providing a resource of materials and examples for clients to use in sessions can prompt this type of awareness and the positive experiences that go with it. Furthermore, the awareness can be promoted by the counselor's being attuned to culturally preferred ways of dealing with problematic situations (Rossiter, 1997).

In different cultural settings, the creative arts may do any of the following:

- draw people out of self-consciousness and into self-awareness by having them express themselves in a symbolic manner
- call attention to the process of expression as well as the universal and unique nature of strategies employed in such a procedure
- provide a set of concrete experiences clients can carry with them to help them relate to others and themselves
- help clients develop new ideas and interests to use in relating to themselves and others outside of counseling
- bring clients together cognitively, behaviorally, and mentally by giving them experiences that link them with their past, their present, and their future
- help clients appreciate the beauty and wisdom of cultural backgrounds
- promote positive feelings and affect that can be tapped when celebrating and coping with life's highs and lows
- engender hope, confidence, and insight in persons who have never realized their potential for living life to the fullest

Numerous studies show the impact of the creative arts in different cultures, such as those by Omizo and Omizo (1989) with Hawaiian children; Constantino, Malgady, and Rogler (1986) with Latino children; Appleton and Dykeman (1996) with Native American children; and Woodard (1995) with African American children. The point is that there are multiple ways of using the creative arts in helping clients from different cultures and circumstances (Ishiyama & Westwood, 1992).

Advantages and Limitations of the Creative Arts in Counseling

In addition to the arguments just made, numerous pragmatic advantages to using the arts in counseling exist. Several will be mentioned here, along with the limitations of employing the arts in counseling.

Advantages

A major advantage of using the arts in counseling involves playfulness. Almost all great leaders from Freud to Gandhi have had a sense of playfulness about them that helps them temper their reactions to serious moments and gain a clearer perspective on life (Erikson, 1975). As a group, the arts are known for their playfulness. There is a winsome quality about those involved with the arts that enables them to appreciate and create a type of cosmos out of chaos. This light-heartedness in the midst of serious tasks is enabling.

A second benefit of using the arts in counseling is that it promotes a collegial relationship (Arnheim, 1990). Many counseling theorists, including those who are existentialists, person-centered, Adlerian, or gestalt advocate this type of partnership. In this kind of encounter, professional barriers are broken down, and the ability of clients and counselors to more clearly understand and address present difficulties is enhanced.

A third advantage of including the arts in counseling is that such action usually promotes communication (Arnheim, 1990). Artists from Picasso to Stevie Wonder have talked about the "universal language" of artistic expression and the ability of the arts to convey information in a simple but direct way. Sometimes a picture or a movement is worth a thousand words. By sounding off musically, visually, or dramatically, clients are often able to help their counselors understand their predicaments better. Art can help outsiders, such as counselors, look on something that they have never been a part of and make them feel as if they had always been a part of it (Christenberry, 1991). As a result, these counselors become more sensitive and effective helpers.

A fourth benefit of incorporating the arts in counseling is that they enable clients to recognize the multiple nature of themselves and the world. This task of discovery may seem simple, but just like in the adventures of Carlos Castenada's (1972) character Don Juan, the complexities of life are not always easily learned or understood. Thus, clients who have been struggling for identity may discover through their immersion in the arts during counseling that the depth and richness of lives is much greater than they initially envisioned.

A fifth advantage of using the arts in counseling is their perceived objectivity. They are seen as neutral or even fun and therefore are not resisted. "The use of the arts. . . is a natural spin-off from the use of displacement material in other areas. Therapists, educators, theologians, and parents have used displacement materials for generations to help people focus on problems that they are too involved in emotionally to see clearly" (Guerin, 1976, p. 480),

A sixth advantage of using the arts in counseling is that these forms of expression allow, and even encourage, nonverbal clients to participate meaningfully in counseling relationships (J. White, 1991). People who have been victimized or traumatized may be unable to verbally convey the events they have experienced. By using the arts, however, they may say creatively and profoundly what is uppermost in their minds. The arts also encourage concrete thinkers and those of limited mental abilities to expand their horizons.

Finally, the inclusion of the arts in counseling gives the counselor one more tool to use in promoting diagnoses, understanding, or dialogue in the professional relationship. When encountering extremely resistant or reluctant clients, every means should be employed to bring about a mutually satisfactory outcome. The theoretical and technical aspects of the arts in counseling can make such a difference.

Limitations

The disadvantages of using arts in counseling must also be recognized, for they can cause complications if they are not acknowledged and dealt with properly. Not every counselor or client is a suitable candidate for such procedures.

One of the chief limitations of using the arts in counseling is that clients who are artists themselves may not benefit from such an approach. In fact, according to Fleshman and Fryrear (1981), "for artists, the use of the arts in therapy may be counterproductive" (p. 6). The reason for this phenomenon is that artists support themselves through creative expression, and to be asked to perform in a therapeutic setting may seem too much like work. In such situations, the use of arts in counseling becomes an obstacle to therapeutic progress.

A connected reason is that many artists (and some clients) may view counseling and activities associated with it as being nonartistic. Therefore, they may be less inclined to work on problems if the format is not highly structured and primarily cognitive in nature. For these individuals, using the arts in counseling may be distracting and frustrating.

A third reason that the arts are not always welcomed in counseling relates to popular misperceptions about the arts, especially links between creative arts and mental health. In the 17th century an Italian physician, Ceare Lombroso, linked creativity with mental illness. Even though such a connection is totally unfounded, the perception still remains and encourages a reluctance on the part of many to participate in activities that are of a creative nature.

On the opposite side of this reluctance, but with the same results, is the tendency of clients to avoid artistic enterprises because of an irrational fear that they will become too involved (Ellis, 1988). Such a response is typical of someone with loose ego boundaries and with obsessive-compulsive behavior habits, but it is also a feeling found in many other people. Some artists, such as Mozart, are reported to have worked at the expense of their health and that of their families. People who avoid the arts in counseling fear being placed in a situation with potential liabilities as well as possibilities.

A fifth drawback to including the arts into one's repertoire of skills is that the actual techniques used may become arts and crafts, which is a much more mechanical and structured activity than procedures used in the creative arts (Gladding, 1985). It should be stressed that arts and crafts as typically practiced in therapeutic settings have limited goals and are often seen as "busy work." Few problem-solving skills and innovative factors are used in arts and crafts as opposed to the creative arts. For example, crafts in counseling are usually associated with putting things together, such as assembling a basket, whereas creative arts promote the production of something new and different. Crafts usually do not require much thinking. Instead, they instruct the participant to follow directions. The creative arts, on the other hand, involve the full use of one's imagination and often bring to the forefront latent talents and abilities.

A sixth limitation of using the creative arts in counseling is that by so doing clients may become too introspective, passive, or overcritical of themselves or situations. Such a posture leads to paralysis and inhibits growth born out of involvement. It is just the opposite of active mental and physical involvement that Siegel (1986) described as an essential part of self-healing.

A seventh drawback to the use of the creative arts in counseling is that they may be employed in nontherapeutic ways. Many art forms promote the expression of feelings and help persons get beyond the mere intellectual acknowledgment of situations. In helping clients recognize and express their feelings—especially the "big four," anger, sadness, joy, and fear (Meier & Davis, 1997)—the release of emotions must be therapeutically channeled if they are to realize more fully their own humanity (Warren, 1984). Catharsis in and of itself is of limited usefulness and may actually be detrimental to the health and well-being of individuals.

A final drawback to using the arts in counseling is that they may be employed in nonscientific ways. The arts and sciences share four common attributes: "honesty, parsimony, duality, and insight" (Burke, 1989, p. 27). Honesty implies genuineness, authenticity, and openness of one's work. Parsimony is conciseness and straightforward simplicity. Duality is the ability to be simultaneously sensitive and tough-minded. Finally, insight, as alluded to before, deals with the ability to understand old material in a new way. Whenever the arts are used in counseling without adherence to this common bond with science, practitioners face the danger that the results will not be therapeutic.

Summary

Counseling at its best employs an artistic quality that enables individuals to express themselves in a creative and unique manner. It is an activity that may be enhanced through encouraging some clients to participate in creative experiences, especially artistic expressions such as painting, writing, dancing, or playing. These activities, if carried out in a nonmechanical manner, help persons become more in tune with their emotions and form new relationships with themselves and others (Frank, 1978). The arts sensitize clients to untapped aspects of themselves and thus promote an awareness of uniqueness and universality. Ancient and modern civilizations have recognized this quality about the arts, and the tradition of using the arts in counseling is a long and distinguished one.

The creative arts in counseling are as a group process oriented, empowering, authentic, parsimonious, multicultural, and insight focused. They energize individuals and help connect them with positive aspects within and outside of themselves while fostering a new sense of self. By engaging in the playful, cooperative, and communicative dimensions of art, individuals recognize more clearly the complexity and simplicity of their lives. Similarly, counselors benefit from their involvement with the arts by being able to work with a greater variety of clients in therapeutic ways. Furthermore, engaging in creative processes enriches them personally and professionally.

Although those who are professional artists, irrationally minded, and mentally unstable may not be appropriate for therapeutic treatment using the arts, many individuals are excellent candidates. It is to the advantage of everyone that professional helpers learn how to use the arts in counseling.

References

Allan, J. (1988). *Inscapes of the child's world*. Dallas, TX: Spring.

Allport, G. W. (1955). *Becoming: Basic considerations for a psychology of personality*. New Haven: Yale University Press.

Appleton, V. E., & Dykeman, C. (1996). Using art in group counseling with Native American youth. *Journal for Specialists in Group Work, 21*, 224–231.

Arieti, S. (1976). *Creativity: The magic synthesis*. New York: Basic Books.

Arnheim, R. (1990). The artist as healer. *Arts in Psychotherapy, 17*, 1–4.

Blatner, A. (1988). *Acting in: Practical application of psychodramatic methods* (2nd ed.). New York: Springer.

Bonny, H. L. (1997). The state of the art of music therapy. *Arts in Psychotherapy, 24*, 65–73.

Burke, J. F. (1989). *Contemporary approaches to psychotherapy and counseling*. Pacific Grove, CA: Brooks/Cole.

Castenada, C. (1972). *Journey to Ixtlan: The lessons of Don Juan*. New York: Simon and Schuster.

Cavanagh, M. E. (1982). *The counseling experience*. Pacific Grove, CA: Brooks/Cole.

Christenberry, W. (1991). *Of time and places*. Albuquerque, NM: University of New Mexico Press.

Constantino, G., Malgady, R., & Rogler, L. (1986). Cuento therapy: A culturally sensitive modality for Puerto Rican children. *Journal of Consulting and Clinical Psychology, 54*, 639–645.

Coughlin, E. K. (1990). Renewed appreciation of connections between body and mind stimulate researchers to harness healing power of the arts. *Chronicle of Higher Education*, pp. A6, 9.

Dufrene, P. M., & Coleman, V. D. (1994). Art and healing for Native American Indians. *Journal of Multicultural Counseling and Development, 22*, 145–152.

Ellis, A. (1988). *How to stubbornly refuse to make yourself miserable about anything—yes, anything!* Secaucus, NJ: Lyle Stuart.

Erikson, E. H. (1968). *Identity: Youth and crisis*. New York: Norton.

Erikson, E. H. (1975). *Life history and the historical moment*. New York: Norton.

Flake, C. L. (1988). A systems approach: The foundation of a quality environment. In M. H. Brown (Ed.), *Quality environments for young children*. Champaign, IL: Stipes.

Fleming, W. (1986). *Arts & ideas* (7th ed.). New York: Holt, Rinehart and Winston.

Fleshman, B., & Fryrear, J. L. (1981). *The arts in therapy*. Chicago: Nelson-Hall.

Frank, J. D. (1978). *Effective ingredients of successful psychotherapy*. New York: Brunner/Mazel.

Gladding, S. T. (1985). Counseling and the creative arts. *Counseling and Human Development, 18*, 1–12.

Gladding, S. T. (1988, April). *Counseling as an art: The use of the expressive arts in counseling*. Paper presented at the convention of the American Association for Counseling and Development, Chicago, IL.

Gladding, S. T. (1990). Journey. *Journal of Humanistic Education and Development, 28*, 142.

Gladding, S. T. (1995). Creativity in counseling. *Counseling and Human Development, 28*, 1–12.

Grout, D. J. (1973). *A history of Western music* (2nd ed.). New York: Norton.

Guerin, P. J., Jr. (1976). The use of the arts in family therapy: I never sang for my father. In P. J. Guerin, Jr. (Ed.), *Family therapy: Theory and practice* (pp. 480–500). New York: Gardner.

Heller, G. N. (1985, November). *Ideas, initiatives, and implementations: Music therapy in America, 1789–1848*. Paper presented at the joint conference of the National Coalition of Arts Therapy Associations, New York.

Ishiyama, F. I., & Westwood, M. J. (1992). Enhancing client-validating communication: Helping discouraged clients in cross-cultural adjustment. *Journal of Multicultural Counseling and Development, 20*, 50–63.

Johnson, D. W., & Johnson, F. P. (1994). *Joining together* (5th ed.). Englewood Cliffs, NJ: Prentice-Hall.

Jourard, S. M., & Landsman, T. (1980). *Healthy personality* (4th ed.). New York: Macmillan.

Jung, C. G. (1933). *Modern man in search of a soul*. New York: Harcourt, Brace & World.

Jung, J. C. (1964). *Man and his symbols*. Garden City, NY: Doubleday.

Koestler, A. (1964). *The act of creation*. New York: Macmillan.

Kottler, J. A. (1986). *On being a therapist*. San Francisco, CA: Jossey-Bass.

Lazarus, A. (1977). *In the mind's eye*. New York: Rawson.

Martz, L. L. (1962). *The poetry of meditation*. New Haven, CT: Yale University Press.

Meier, S. T., & Davis, S. R. (1997). *The elements of counseling* (3rd ed). Pacific Grove, CA: Brooks/Cole.

Menninger Foundation. (1986). *Art therapy: The healing vision*. Topeka, KS: Author.

Moreno, J. L. (1923). Das Stegif Theatre, Berlin: Gustav Kiepenheur. (1947). The theatre for spontaneity. *Psychodrama Monographs, 4*. New York: Beacon House.

Omizo, M. M., & Omizo, S. A. (1989). Art activities to improve self-esteem among native Hawaiian children. *Journal of Humanistic Education and Development, 27*, 167–176.

Peters, J. S. (1987). *Music therapy: An introduction*. Springfield, IL: Thomas.

Rogers, C. R. (1957). The necessary and sufficient conditions of therapeutic personality change. *Journal of Consulting Psychology, 21*, 95–103.

Rossiter, C. (1997, May). *Where we're coming from: Cultural understanding through poetry therapy.* Paper presented at the annual conference of the National Association for Poetry Therapy, Cleveland, OH.

Seligman, L. (1985). The art and science of counseling. *American Mental Health Counselors Association Journal, 7,* 2–3.

Siegel, B. S. (1986). *Love, medicine, and miracles.* New York: Harper & Row.

Sternberg, R. J., & Lubart, T. I. (1996). Investing in creativity. *Arts in Psychotherapy, 31,* 677–688.

Summer, L. (1997). Considering the future of music therapy. *Arts in Psychotherapy, 24,* 75–80.

Thoresen, C. E. (1969). Relevance and research in counseling. *Review of Educational Research, 39,* 264.

Warren, B. (1984). Introduction. In B. Warren (Ed.), *Using the creative arts in therapy* (pp. 3–8). Cambridge, MA: Brookline.

Watzlawick, P. (1983). *The situation is hopeless, but not serious.* New York: Norton.

Witmer, J. M. (1985). *Pathways to personal growth.* Muncie, IN: Accelerated Development.

Woodard, S. L. (1995). Counseling disruptive Black elementary school boys. *Journal of Multicultural Counseling and Development, 23,* 21–28.

2

Music and Counseling

The music of counseling varies in time
from the soft sound of crying
to laughter's staccato
Often the melody becomes unbound
in deep feeling voices
and words rich in hope.
Within each session is a symphony
leading to inner harmony
and possible new movements.

(Gladding, 1991)

Music is a universal, multicultural experience that is most simply described as "the appreciation of sound" (Beaulieu, 1987, p. 13). It is a creative act that involves listening sensitively to the cacophony of rhythm and rhyme that occur spontaneously and purposefully in nature and responding in an active or passive way. On its most basic level, music is an essentially nonverbal medium (Vanger, Oerter, Otto, Schmidt, & Czogalik, 1995). Music has been used in various ways since the beginning of time to communicate and express feelings. Indeed, many civilizations and their people are defined by the types of music they develop and the part that music plays in transmitting social values and status. Some popular music is significant in creating a sense of cultural identity, for example, among the Yoruba of southwestern Nigeria (Coughlin, 1990). Other music is connected with a period of time, or with a group of people.

Music sets up an atmosphere that is either for better or worse (S. Liebmann, personal communication, 1986). It can elicit a wide range of mental, emotional, physical, and spiritual responses. Research indicates that music can create and alter moods, facilitate the expression of emotions, and reduce stress and anxiety. Music can also be used to capture attention, elicit memories, communicate feelings, and create a sense of community (Mandsager, Newsome, & Glass, 1997).

Many populations who have been the victims of abuse have developed distinct musical forms, such as African-Americans' creation of spiritual gospels and the blues, to provide an outlet for their individual and collective expressions of pain (Moreno, 1987). Other groups have created different sounds that express the essence of their experiences and perceptions. In the United States the great diversity of sound includes rock and roll, bluegrass, jazz, country and western, big band, and reggae music. Internationally, an even wider variety of sound exists.

"Corporations such as MUZAK have made a business out of supplying background music to positively influence and regulate people's moods and behaviors in offices, businesses," and other environments (Peters, 1987, pp. 31–32). The influence of music in daily life is truly phenomenal. Even though people may not always remember lyrics, they seem to be influenced by "the beat, the rhythm, (and) the sound" of music they listen to regularly (White, 1985, p. 67). For many ordinary people "music is the most significant experience in life" (Storr, 1992, p. 168).

The importance of music to human health has long been recognized. Throughout history, music has been used therapeutically. "The field of music therapy is based largely on claims of the sedative results music produces and the psychological impact of the musical experience" (Hanser, 1988, p. 211). Documentation worldwide shows that music has played a major role in the healing and nurturing of people from ancient cultures (Mandsager et al., 1997; Moreno, 1988b). "Homer recommended it to stave off negative emotions, and Pythagorus and Plato said a daily dose could improve one's general well-being" (Miller, 1991, p.1E). Shamans have used "hypnotic and rhythmic music" (Moreno, 1987, p. 335) to help their patients achieve emotional highs—a tradition that continues today in most cultures.

A healthy integration of sacred and secular music in fostering positive outcomes can be found today through the musical combinations of those who perform the blues and performers of religious music. Many blues performers have made this type of music their orientation to life after struggling to perform in the confines of churches. Their satisfaction with this arrangement has generally proven beneficial to them as well as their audiences.

Overall, music "allows feelings to be revealed that may not be defined in words" (Yon, 1984, p. 106). In essence, music "is a form of communication analogous to speech in that it has cadences and punctuation" (Aldridge, 1989, p. 93). For example, new age music, which makes use of long themes and slow tempi, expresses a sentiment and affect that cannot be translated into a verbal equivalent. Therefore, music has been seen as a therapeutic ally to verbal approaches to counseling. It links people together and gives them a common denominator with which to relate (Bonny, 1987; Rosenblatt, 1991).

Music and medicine were at one time strong allies because of their similar emphasis on wholeness. Indeed, in some countries, such as France, this connection is still strong and "psychomusical techniques are regarded as excellent and privileged means of exploring dreams and ideas, the conscious and the unconscious, the effective and emotional worlds of the individual, and for provoking catharsis" (Owens, 1986, p. 302). In hospital settings, music may take one's mind off unpleasant experiences and promote spontaneous interactions. Overall, music is used worldwide to promote positive mental health, especially in psychiatric hospitals. According to William L. Schurk, sound-recording archivist at Bowling Green State University, music is "not a lonely art form" (Rosenblatt, 1991, p. B7). Rather, it involves vocal, physical, social, and emotional responses. Music activities are numerous. "Applications include improvising, recreating, composing, listening, [and] game or play activities" (Bonny, 1997, p. 70).

Premise of the Use of Music in Counseling

Although all the creative arts help foster a link between the inner world of the person and outside reality, music "enhances this process by requiring time-ordered and ability-ordered behavior, evoking affective response and increasing sensory input. Music also requires self-organization and provides an opportunity for socialization" (Wager, 1987, p. 137). Thus, music serves multiple purposes in helping individuals become more aware, able, confident, and social.

The extent of music's healing power in counseling is related to how deeply involved with it people are. Music is both a passion and a diversion, and its uses in counseling are geared accordingly. Among persons for whom it is a central part of life (i.e., a passion), identity is strongly influenced by their shared values with select performers, writers, and other listeners. Thus, they are usually quite willing to participate in counseling activities that involve music. In this type of situation many of the words, sounds, and feelings these people embrace as their own actually originated with someone else and have been borrowed and incorporated by these persons. Since their identity is wrapped up in music, they are eager to be exposed to musical experiences, and counselors are usually more successful in working with these clients than with those for whom music is only a diversion. By being aware of the lyrics and melodies that clients have adopted and other complementary music, counselors who employ music set up conditions that foster increased communication and understanding (White, 1985).

In addition to centering music in counseling around the interests and tastes of clients, a musical approach may take the form of writing, performing, or listening to certain types of sounds selected by counselors. The idea behind this activity is to foster therapeutic expression by clients through initially unfamiliar music-related experiences. For example, a client may play a new instrument in a predetermined way and make discoveries about his or her abilities never before imagined (Moreno, 1985). Similarly, "ethnic music" (i.e., music identified with a particular culture or subculture) may motivate "otherwise unresponsive mainstream music therapy clients into musical experiences through the exotic appeal of unfamiliar musical styles and approaches to music making" (Moreno, 1988a, p. 17). Even for clients who are unfamiliar with "classical music" this genre can have a powerful effect. When carefully chosen and played softly, classical music "can be a tremendous aid in producing an atmosphere conducive to creative activity" (Nadeau, 1984, p. 68).

A key in deciding on what music activity, if any, to choose is based on the goals of counseling (whether preventive or remedial) and the personalities of all involved. For example, some individuals prefer classics such as Beethoven, Bach, and Brahms, and others opt for popular rock, such as the lyrics and melodies of groups known as Bread, No Doubt, U2, and Foreigner. Still other individuals prefer energetic African- or Japanese-oriented group rhythms performed on drums or traditional Indian and Far East music, which is helpful in stimulating imagery and fostering meditation (Moreno, 1988a).

Individual need is another crucial variable to consider in music-oriented counseling. For example, trauma victims need calmer types of music than those who are not so physically or psychologically distressed (McDonnell, 1984). Likewise, aerobic and exercise groups need and prefer rock, pop, and new age music (Gfeller, 1988). In regard to needs and music, it is helpful to realize that some clients need to be actively involved in making music (e.g., depressed individuals), but for others simply listening to music may be most beneficial (e.g., anxious or manic persons).

Finally, the decision about music activities is rooted in genuine sharing and self-disclosure about whether both parties in the counseling process are open to exploring this means of help. If the participants reach sharing and consensus, musical pieces used are likely to produce positive results because an atmosphere of trust and expectation is created. These qualities, along with the skills of counselors and courage of clients to participate, ultimately dictate how powerful the musical experience will be. Well-chosen music done in collaboration with the client has the capacity to calm, relax, and help the client feel secure (Hodas, 1994; Owens, 1986). There is no substitute for personalizing the process.

Practice of the Use of Music in Counseling

The degree to which counselors and clients relate to each other when music is a part of counseling is dependent on whether music is used as therapy or in therapy (Bruscia, 1987). When employed as therapy, the counselor is likely to take an active role, whereas during use in therapy the counselor's involvement may vary considerably.

Music Therapy

Music as therapy is usually known as "music therapy." It is "taught and practiced in 23 countries at 132 locations" (Bonny, 1997, p. 71). Music therapy is formally defined as "a goal-directed process in which the therapist helps the client to improve, maintain, or restore a state of well-being" (Bruscia, 1987, p. 5). As such, the process is goal-directed and carried out under the supervision of specially trained mental health providers. It may take one of many forms, but music therapy has five main elements, which according to Peters (1987, pp. 6–8) are these:

1. It is prescribed.
2. It involves the use of musical or music activities, for example, "singing, playing musical instruments, listening to music, composing or creating music, moving to music, or discussing lyrics and characteristics of songs or instrumental compositions" (Peters, 1987, p. 6).
3. It is directed or supervised by specially trained personnel.
4. It is received by clients from newborns to geriatrics.
5. It is focused on achieving definite therapeutic goals (e.g., physical, psychological, or socioemotional).

In music therapy, clients improve their level of musical functioning while simultaneously accomplishing objectives related to new or improved behaviors in the areas of motor skills, academics, communications, social interactions, or emotions. The number of musically related activities (e.g., singing, playing in a rhythm band, playing "name that tune") that can be employed to accomplish these goals is extensive (Schulberg, 1981). A main task for the music therapist is to be versatile and creative. Therefore, music therapists must be fluent and expressive in the language of music. "Technical musical skills needed by the music therapist include keyboard, guitar, and vocal skills; the ability to arrange, compose, and improvise simple songs and accompaniments; proficiency in playing a variety of melodic and percussive nonsymphonic instruments and conducting skills" (Peters, 1987, p. 12). Overall, music therapists must be specialists in music and human behavior, but must be generalists in their ability to apply this knowledge in various situations (Michel, 1976).

To become professional music therapists, individuals graduate from specifically designed college curricula with a minimum of a B.M. in music therapy (Maranto & Bruscia, 1989). Educational standards are established and approved by the American Music Therapy Association (AMTA), which is the integrated organization formed from its predecessors the National Association for Music Therapy (NAMT) and the American Association for Music Therapy (AAMT). AMTA requires a specific number of course-work hours as well as supervised internships for individuals to successfully complete approved programs of study to become music therapists.

Music in Counseling

Counseling that includes music in its overall structure is not nearly as encompassing or direct as music therapy, but it involves activities such as listening, performing, improvising, and composing that are beneficial for clients. Each activity has a population that profits from its use.

Listening to sounds in a deep and appreciative way is an art. Such listening helps individuals to relax and learn and directs their attention away from life stressors (Crabbs, Crabbs, & Wayman, 1986). Listening to music can help clients alter their moods by either reducing their anxiety or arousing their emotions. Listening also promotes the process of making music out of life and understanding more fully the rhythm or lyrics of songs. The latter case is sometimes referred to as "audiotherapy" (Lazarus, 1989).

According to Hindu tradition, listening can occur on four levels. "The first is the level of meaning. The second is the level of feeling. . . . The third is an intense and constant awareness or presence, and the fourth is known as the 'soundless sound'" (Beaulieu, 1987, p. 13). Each of these levels is self-explanatory, except for soundless sound. It is really the rhythmic, punctual moments of silence within a composition of sound that make such a work predictable, safe, and enjoyable (Bonny, 1987).

In addition to the four levels of listening, such an activity holds the power to stir up emotions in the unconscious. Song selection by clients is a kind of "projective technique" that reveals the needs of the unconscious for certain types of stimuli (Brodsky & Niedorf, 1986). By tracking the theme and tempo of music chosen, therapists can ascertain more clearly the emotional level at which clients are operating and thereby plan effective treatment interventions. They can also understand more readily what unique musical prescriptions, if any, might work for their clients (Hanser, 1988).

One way to help clients listen more intensely to music and the meanings they derive from it is to ask clients to bring in audiotapes or CDs that reflect their emotional states. They may then be asked what part of the music speaks to them the most, for example, the rhythm, the melody, the lyrics (if there are any), or some combination of the three. At times the counselor can also provide music, and clients are asked to listen to music the counselor selects. They respond by drawing, moving, or closing their eyes and imagining. In both client- and counselor-initiated listening activities, the music provides a springboard from which material is processed on either a verbal or nonverbal level.

Performing music is a very personal experience with a powerful potential. It involves the musician, the instrument, and sometimes an audience. Through performing, individuals use music "as a means of communication, identification, socialization, and expression" (Siegell, 1987, p. 185). They introduce themselves in a way that is impossible to duplicate otherwise. Sometimes the music that is performed is relatively simple, such as becoming "a sound" within a group experience. At other times, it is elaborate and involves harmonizing many notes in a clear and distinct way. For example, I once had a client who played out his life on a guitar for almost an hour.

Music was performed by employees of French mental hospitals as early as the 17th century for the treatment of melancholy. In the 19th century, music was elevated to an active form, as psychiatric patients organized choruses and orchestras (Owens, 1986). In the early part of the 20th century music was considered an "occupational therapy" and focused on resocialization rather than healing. Nevertheless, throughout the history of musical performances, patients from a variety of sites including mental hospitals and outpatient centers have benefited. Performing activates people to the realities of self, instruments, time, and others. "The tempo of the song, the tone quality of the singer, and the lyric content all provide indications of the feelings being expressed" (Goldstein, 1990, p. 120).

Improvising with music is best represented in American jazz. In improvising, musicians follow a plan to be playful as well as artful in their work with others. In a jazz band, for example, there are at least two parts: a "rhythm section" and a "front line." "The rhythm section lays down the beat of the music. The front line instruments are responsible for the melodic lines and their interplay" (Barker, 1985, p. 132).

When working with clients who are musically inclined, improvisation can be accomplished concretely by asking individuals to do variations on a musical theme. In these cases—and in others in which clients understand musical improvisation—individuals can play with their instruments and alter melodies (i.e., making them faster, slower, or more pronounced). The results of such transactions can then be discussed or in some cases left alone. In the latter situation, the process of creating and developing a relationship is seen as therapeutic in and of itself (Nordoff & Robbins, 1977).

Composing music is a creative act that puts composers in closer touch with their feelings. "It can be used as a way of promoting many of the healing qualities inherent in creative acts" (Schmidt, 1983, p. 4). It is empowering because it gives its composer an opportunity to arrange notes in a way that is unique and personal. Composing can also be self-enhancing in that it requires perseverance and discipline that become part of a person's self-concept after the event has occurred. The client who played a guitar piece that represented his life was exhausted at the end of the hour from the intensity of the experience. However, he was quite satisfied with himself. He had put his feelings into sound by not only writing them down but also playing them in a way that expressed the essence of himself.

Composing music need not always involve recognizable instruments. Instead, clients can be asked to tap, snap, click, bang, or hum to represent different emotions (Mandsager et al. 1997). A musical group of the 1960s, the Mamas and the Papas, had a popular record titled "You've Got to Make Your Own Kind of Music," which perhaps stresses the individualization of people, especially clients, in using themselves to create harmony both within and without. Composition promotes this creative emphasis, thereby proving useful to counselors who use music in treatment.

In actual practice, counselors may request or encourage musically inclined clients to compose a piece of music through which they can represent themselves, whether they write it down or not. At the next session clients literally make music first and then talk about the experiences of composing and performing afterwards. In some cases, musically inclined counselors may compose and play music to represent themselves to clients. Such a process, whether unilateral or reciprocal in nature, assists clients in realizing the universal power that a musical composition can generate.

Music in Counseling With Specific Populations

Children

Children, especially preschoolers and those in elementary school, seem to love music and spontaneously sing, listen, or play music-like instruments such as those found in "rhythm bands." The natural affinity of children for music can be used by counselors to promote fun, learning, good feelings, and bonding among children from diverse backgrounds (Crabbs et al., 1986). Music may also be used to help foster changes in children who are developmentally delayed (Aldridge, Gustorff, & Neugebauer, 1995).

Music is often a primary ingredient in teaching guidance lessons. One technique that works is the use of music to express feelings (Gerler, 1982). In this approach, a counselor and music teacher work together to devise a game in which children are "teamed in groups of four and instructed to create musical ways to express feelings" (p. 63) without words or lyrics. In the case of fourth graders who carried out this task, one feeling was assigned to each group, and they were directed to devise two or three musical ways to express this emotion. Responses ranged from forming a "hum and sniffle quartet" to represent sadness to using two pianos to convey an angry musical conversation.

Besides cooperative ventures with music teachers, counselors can work on their own to find and use music that gives their students experiences involving singing, composing, or playing an instrument (Bowman, 1987; Harper, 1985; Newcomb, 1994). Sometimes all three of these types of musical expression can be combined; however, usually one modality, such as singing or composition, is used more than others. Children find singing fun and often remember main ideas of lessons through incorporating them into songs (Crabbs et al., 1986). When songs are used in guidance classes the following procedure is helpful:

1. Introduce the words of a song as a poem.
2. Chant the words in rhythm.
3. Practice chanting words for 3 or 4 minutes per class period until students memorize them.
4. After students know and understand the words, play the song (prerecorded music is fine to use).
5. Keep a double-spaced copy of the words before the children when they sing, with the verses separated from the refrain.

Outside of guidance classes, singing is also beneficial, especially for children who may have suffered trauma. This is because "singing is natural behavior for humans, and it is used as a self-help technique, a means of developing feelings of rapport with others, and a method of self-affirmation in many, if not most, cultures" (Mayers, 1995, p. 497). Singing a song repetitively, either alone or in a group of other children, can be ritualistic and hypnotic as well. It can alter breathing patterns and help in general relaxation.

In composition, children are encouraged not only to write but to sing their songs. "It is not necessary to teach the child to engage in this activity, only to direct the songwriting toward a therapeutic end. Children are capable of determining what they need, what words will be calming, what tune fits the mood" (Mayers, 1995, p. 497). Through composing and writing their own songs, children learn to be more independent as well as creative. They also learn to be less anxious and feel a sense of empowerment. Mayers reported that children as young as 4 and 5 years can compose songs that are helpful to them in dealing with their situations.

Music is employed with children in other therapeutic ways as well. For example, Hodas (1993) has created a music tape titled *Stretch Yourself? Songs for Coping* that contains a variety of selections counselors can use with children who are having difficulty dealing with different forms of adversity. The song selections encompass a wide variety of topics including sexual abuse, physical illness, suicide, the effects of war, and gender issues. Thus, songs must be chosen with care. A well-chosen song can be quite powerful in helping children recognize situations and deal with them appropriately and constructively .

Another way of breaking through children's shells of isolation therapeutically with music is by playing familiar sounds to them, such as internal body sounds (i.e., a stomach growling or a heart beating) or having them listen to neighborhood sounds (Baker, 1982). Once rapport is established in this manner, rhythmic activities and rhythm instruments such as sticks and tambourines can be used to engage these children and gradually draw them into social relationships with other children and adults.

Adolescents

Music is popular with teenagers. Many adolescents either play in a band or identify with major musical figures. For some, music is quite inspirational because it evokes "images of movies. . . in which movie characters triumphed over adversities" (Gfeller, 1988, p. 41). The fact that the television channel MTV is largely viewed by an audience under 30 years of age (and even the existence of such a channel) is further evidence of the importance of music in the lives of this age group. The rhythm and words of Alanis Morissette, Mariah Carey, and The Fugees speak to adolescent youth in unique and powerful ways.

For young adolescents, "music therapy is helpful in bridging the gap between nonverbal and talking therapy. It aids in mastery and sublimation of thoughts and feelings, and it helps to facilitate ego development through success-oriented experiences" (Wells, 1988, p. 47). For older adolescents, participating in music therapy activities gives them a firsthand experience of the relationship between effort made and skill achieved in music performance. Adolescents in juvenile delinquency programs benefit from music therapy activities because they become increasingly aware of that connectedness between hard work and achievement (Johnson, 1981). They may also realize that playing a socially desirable music instrument such as the piano or guitar increases their acceptance among peers (Cassity, 1981).

In addition, adolescents are often interested in song writing and may wish to express themselves lyrically (Roscoe, Krug, & Schmidt, 1985). A song is generally considered to be a poem set to music (Mayers, 1995). To foster a preventative and therapeutic process, music therapists and counselors skilled in music can work with adolescents using a number of song-writing techniques "including changing the words to familiar songs, filling in the blanks of edited familiar songs, vocal improvisation, adding new verses to known songs, parodying familiar songs, and using natural rhythms of speech as a starting point" (Goldstein, 1990, p. 119). Counselors who are musicians themselves may also use original music they have written to help adolescents explore difficult areas such as gender issues and sexuality (Hodas, 1991).

Adults

Besides offering adults sounds to relax by, research suggests that music enhances physical endurance, especially if "movement is rhythmically coordinated with a musical stimulus" (Thaut, 1988, p. 129). Therefore, adults who are athletes or who regularly exercise can enhance their efforts by coordinating their physical movement with certain sounds. These positive effects occur because music either distracts people's perceptions by causing them to selectively focus on pleasant stimuli, or it physically inhibits negative feedback transmissions (i.e., fatigue) because of the pleasurable electrosensory reactions it generates. Regardless, music is a prime ingredient in helping people physically and mentally maintain health or rehabilitate.

Another important function music plays in the lives of adults is by enhancing experiences for them. Prepared childbirth is often linked with relaxing and soothing music that makes delivery, recovery, and bonding stronger. The type of exhilaration that results makes intrapersonal and interpersonal relationships better. It promotes growth to the fullest (Maslow, 1968). Other marker events in the lives of adults are equally enhanced through music. As Virginia Perry wrote about a workshop she attended in which each session was introduced by music: "He sings, and I forget myself. We move, one through another, vibrating the resonances of soul. These connected hearts and voices remain beyond time and place" (personal communication, July 19, 1991).

Elderly Clients

Playing or making music with elderly persons has several goals, including the promotion of social interaction, the enhancement of self-worth, the encouragment of self-expression, and the recall of past events (Bruscia, 1987; Osborn, 1989). Ways of conducting sessions vary, and they may be carried out in a formal or in an improvised manner. When such times are formally conducted, members of these groups follow more of a schedule, and their personal or interpersonal gains may become secondary to the achievements of the group as a whole. If the sessions are less formally conducted, on the other hand, more creativity and interaction may occur with less music.

In reminiscing or in present-oriented self-social groups, music may be the key to encouraging the discussion of past or present feelings and thoughts about events, such as learning, romance, loss, and family life. Typically, music is initially played that revolves around a particular theme, such as the importance of home or family. However, such an activity only takes place after the group as a whole has warmed up by participating in a brief sing-along of familiar songs that include their own accompaniment of clapping and foot-tapping.

In a maximum-participation group, members select their own music and theme. In less democratic groups, much of the selections are made by the leaders with particular foci in mind. Songs as current as Barbra Streisand's "The Way We Were" and early American ballads like "My Old Kentucky Home," are used to set a tone and a mood that encourages talk and interaction after the singing has stopped.

Music may also be used with elderly clients to help them achieve better functioning in their movements. Rhythmic music, for example, acts as a stimuli for helping elderly patients with gait disorders improve the flow of their walk (Staum, 1983). In this process, the beat of the music serves as a cue for individuals in anticipating a desired rate of movement.

Families and Couples

Music by itself may be beneficial to families or couples because of its ability to evoke feelings and promote cooperation. Feelings are often rekindled by playing music associated with earlier developmental stages (Gladding & Heape, 1987). If a family or couple has experienced content-ment or positive affect at a previous stage, the music of that time may ignite memories that help individuals within these systems remember specific behaviors that were helpful in achieving harmony. Such events once triggered can aid the family or couple in getting "unstuck" from be-havioral stalemates and positively reinforcing each other.

A similar method initiated by the counselor may be used in marital counseling. In such a situ-ation, the counselor prescribes a song in which the lyrics represent issues brought forth by the couple. For example, Paul Simon's "Train in the Distance" is a song about yearning to live in a better time (J. Chapman, personal communication, November 19, 1994). The last verse of the song speaks powerfully to this point: "What is the point of this story? What information per-tains? The thought that life could be better is woven, indelibly, into our hearts and our brains." Using that lyric as a cue, the couple is then asked to listen to the song at home using it as either a springboard or a metaphor from which to initiate discussion of relevant thoughts, feelings, and issues (V. Perry, personal communication, February 20, 1996).

Music may also help families and couples if it is created by them. In such an exercise, persons within these units make up sounds or play instruments that represent themselves as individuals. Then they combine the sounds and either try to establish a rhythm or work at interjecting their sounds so that the entire group feels good about the beat. In such situations cooperation is vital, and those who are so engaged may translate this facilitative climate to other relationships.

Groups

Most people in groups wish to be in concert with themselves and humanity. They are also look-ing to see where they fit in with others. Music provides an avenue for clients to assess themselves and others. Music can be especially powerful in a group at its beginning or end. Select music can help set an upbeat or sedate tone when clients first enter the group room. Likewise, during ter-mination, music can help instill in clients a sense of closure and can promote integration (Plach, 1996). A number of song books, such as *Rise Up Singing* (Blood & Patterson, 1992), con-tain a wealth of songs about subjects ranging from faith to friendships; they can be used to intro-duce music into a group, especially one that contains people from a wide range of cultural backgrounds.

Hodas (1994) reported using music in a mixed group of European American and African American male adolescents to help the group handle anger, learn coping skills, and appreciate universal truths about human nature. In this group, a variety of songs, some of which were even violent, were played. The group members came to realize through the music that when wrongs occur in society actions other than revenge can be taken.

Clients With Illnesses

Music functions in several therapeutic ways in regard to ill clients. Music can serve to promote closeness within families through group singing, lyric analysis, and reminiscences (Gilbert, 1977; Miller, 1991). This type of bonding enhances the quality of life for family members both inside and outside of the hospital and helps them establish better communication patterns and firmer support systems (Fagan, 1982). In the process, anxiety and tension are lessened and inti-macy is promoted (Bailey, 1984; Slivka & Magill, 1986). In addition, religious faith may be in-creased through the playing and singing of religious music if the family is so inclined.

"Music has the capacity to touch and bring to the surface emotions that have been repressed for years" (Rider, 1987, p. 117). Some chronic diseases such as cancer, rheumatoid arthritis, and coronary difficulties correlate with negative feelings such as anxiety, hostility, and depression. Select music, particularly violin, flute, and piano, can help clients in these and other tension-filled situations to relax more. Compositions cited in the literature as anxiety-reducing include the "Largo" movement from Dvorak's New World Symphony, "Largo" from Dvorak's Symphony No. 5, and Brahms' First Symphony (Mandsager et al., 1997).

Music can also encourage healing by promoting catharsis and a refocusing of thoughts. For instance, Clarkson (1994) recounted the case of a young man with autism who, after several years of music therapy, began to communicate again. Likewise, music therapy seems to be helpful in the recovery of breast cancer patients as they work to find and form new identities (Aldridge, 1996). In the process of making music, patients bring feelings into consciousness without any immediate verbal labels being attached to their emotions. This active intervention uses patients' strength and creativity to cope and maintain coherence in the midst of what might otherwise be chaotic transition.

Teachers

Music can be used to punctuate and emphasize points in the teaching of a variety of material. For instance, in an abnormal psychology course or a mental health center song lyrics may highlight important concepts and provide concrete examples (Potkay, 1974; Schiff & Frances, 1974). One thinks for example of Don McLean's song "Starry, Starry Nights" about the life of Vincent Van Gogh and how the melody and words of this work depict the difficulty of mental instability. In a similar fashion, the lyrics of Janis Ian's "At Seventeen" portray some of the transitions adolescents experience in forming their identities and establishing relationships with the opposite sex. The possibilities of using music as a background to understand thoughts and emotions throughout the life span and in different cultures is limited only by the imagination of the instructor and his or her knowledge of different types of music.

Music in Counseling With Other Creative Arts

Music may be combined with a number of creative arts to produce an effect it could not have alone. For instance, familiar sedative music plus imagery is more effective in reducing state anxiety among college students than just music alone (Russell, 1992). In counseling, music is most often connected with the creative arts of poetry, movement and dance, play, and autobiography and story telling.

Music and Poetry

Poetic lyrics add to the rhythm message of music, although their impact varies (White, 1985). For example, adolescents are often detrimentally influenced by the lyrics of rock songs that are sexually explicit or exploitive in nature (Ray, Soares, & Tolchinsky, 1988). Such has been the case with some of the recordings of 2 Live Crew and other rap artists and with some of the music produced by heavy metal artists (Took & Weiss, 1994). On the other hand, lyrics and music may be combined in a prosocial way, such as those by popular rock music artists like Whitney Houston and her song "The Greatest Love of All," Don Henley and "Heart of the Matter," or Bette Midler and "From a Distance." Likewise, country performers such as Matraca Berg and Clint Black sing about growth through pain and convey a positive view of change in such songs as "I Must Have Been Crazy" and "Walkin' Away." These works sensitize listeners to words that promote the best within and between persons, and they provide "a nonthreatening device to stimulate. . . interaction" (Mazza, 1986, p. 297). It is important that counselors who use lyrical music listen carefully to the words and the melody of songs before advocating that clients try using the recordings therapeutically.

When music and lyrics are packaged together, the way they are expected to be handled therapeutically should be made clear. For example, an inspirational tape, such as Nancy Day's (1989) *Survivor*, which focuses on surviving and recovering from sexual abuse, may be one that counselors want clients to hear at specific times of the day when clients are likely to feeling discouraged or depressed. Likewise, *If You Believe in You*, an audiotape by Dan Conley (1994), that describes the mixture of feelings derived from divorce, contains materials that should be used selectively. By "prescribing" music in this manner, counselors increase the chances of clients being therapeutically influenced. Developmental stages of people and families along with gender, ethnicity, age, and roles must be considered in the process (Gladding & Heape, 1987). Some music and lyrics are more appropriate for certain populations at specific times in their lives.

Music and Movement and Dance

Movement and dance and music complement each other. The action involved in moving to music, whether as a formal dance or not, allows clients the freedom to express themselves in a way not possible in stillness. The awareness that follows can help individuals realize they are exerting themselves in ways they would never have imagined. The beat of the music makes such expression possible. Once clients have chosen new creative actions or danced in a set pattern, their awareness of self is never the same again.

Music and Play

Music is used in play in a number of ways, but primarily to set a tone or mood for an activity. One of the more integrative ways of fusing music and play together is "music play therapy" (Moreno, 1985). In this approach, a nondirective orientation is taken just as in play therapy, but the playroom is supplied with musical instruments instead of toys and traditional play therapy materials. Children with whom this approach is tried gradually become tired of randomly playing instruments and commit themselves to the playing of a tune either by themselves or with the counselor. In so doing, a structure is established to which these children become committed. This active setup can be manipulated for the overall benefit of the children.

Another way music and play may be combined is through "improvised musical play" (IMP), an intervention technique using improvised music and lyrics to encourage social play between developmentally delayed and nondelayed children in mainstream settings (Gunsberg, 1988). In such situations teachers will make up simple songs using familiar tunes to describe what is occurring with the children, such as "Everyone is clapping their hands and being active." This encourages continuous interaction of the children and sustains "social play episodes lasting more than three times the expected duration" (Gunsberg, 1988, p. 178).

Music and Autobiography and Story Telling

A final way of using music with other creative arts is to do what is normally a literary task in sound or with sound in the background (Watkins, 1990). A musical autobiography is one interesting literary task that can be done with sound. In this creative endeavor, participants represent their lives through sound. For instance, someone who has spent a lifetime living by the ocean may splash a hand in water with a certain rhythm; someone who has lived in an arid region may clap rocks together in a unique way. Completing a music autobiography may also involve connecting bits of lyrical music together. The effect is particularly powerful if there are verses and a refrain, similar to what the rock singer Billy Joel did with his song "We Didn't Start the Fire."

In story telling, music may be used to enhance the background of the presentation. For instance, Painter (1989) recommended using classical music such as Handel's "Concerto for Harp and Orchestra in B-flat Major, First Movement," Bach's "Suite for Harp, First Movement," Mozart's "Adagio and Rondo in C Minor," or Wagenseil's "Concerto for Harp and Orchestra, Second Movement," as background music to stories being told to young children. Such pieces set a mood and stir up emotions that would not occur without such an accompaniment. Although Painter (1989) prefered the emotional nuances offered by classical music, other forms of music such as "Dixieland, swing, marches, ballet, solo instrumental, western, folk melodies, polkas, and novelty music" (p. 3) may also work to create an atmosphere for a story or the character in a story. *Schwann's Record and Tape Guide*, which is updated quarterly, is a resource for searching out musical selections to accompany stories.

Summary

Music has a long history as a healing art. Throughout human history, music has soothed or inspired individuals. It has been a major impetus in the prevention and treatment of major disorders and minor problems. It has allowed persons to communicate in a universal, nonverbal way that has promoted identity, bonding, creation, and discovery.

In this chapter the multiple ways music is employed in counseling have been examined. Some professionals are "music therapists," and there are also counselors who use music in their therapeutic practice. Both types of individuals are helpful, but the background and emphasis of these two groups differ. In music therapy, practitioners place greater emphasis on certain procedures with specific difficulties and populations. Individuals who obtain the designation of music therapist are more skilled in music than counselors who occasionally use music therapeutically. Regardless of the counselor's designation, four ways that music may be employed in counseling are through listening, performing, improvising, and composing.

The choice of music in counseling depends upon the needs of clients. Because music is so universal, it is appropriately used with children, adolescents, adults, elderly persons, people who are ill, and students. The various ways this medium can be employed are limited only by the creativity and skills of practitioners. Music is often combined with poetry and with movement and dance, which enhance its overall impact. In summary, music is a universal and versatile art that is of major importance to counselors who wish to promote catharsis, creativity, and communication abilities in a variety of clients and situations.

=== **Exercises** ===

1. On a daily basis, for at least a week, at specific times of the day, notice how you are feeling. With materials that are immediately available, such as pencils, pans, or books, "make music" by tapping, banging, or even humming in a way that best represents your mood. Record your sessions whenever possible and process these experiences with a colleague regularly. How could you use what you learned in this exercise with clients?

2. At the beginning of a group, ask participants to bring in records, CDs, or tapes that express some of their feelings. Emphasize to the whole group that there is no right or wrong music for this task. As each group member introduces himself or herself have them use the music they brought in any way they so choose. After introductions, discuss the variety of sounds and words within the group and what diversity, as well as sameness, can contribute to growth.

3. When working with clients who primarily relate in a nonverbal manner, ask them to listen to a variety of music you have selected (from as many different sources as possible). Have them respond as they wish, such as by drawing or dancing. Limit this exercise to about 15 minutes, and then process what happened with these clients during the rest of the counseling session. Repeat the exercise as needed to help clients become more comfortable in expressing themselves in multiple ways.

References

Aldridge, D. (1989). A phenomenological comparison of the organization of music and the self. *Arts in Psychotherapy, 16,* 91–97.

Aldridge, D., Gustorff, D., & Neugebauer, L. (1995). A preliminary study of creative music therapy in the treatment of children with developmental delay. *Arts in Psychotherapy, 22,* 189–205.

Aldridge, G. (1996). "A walk through Paris": The development of melodic expression in music therapy with a breast-cancer patient. *Arts in Psychotherapy, 23,* 207–223.

Baker, S. B. (1982). The use of music with autistic children. *Journal of Psychosocial Nursing and Mental Health Services, 20,* 31–34.

Bailey, L. M. (1984). The use of songs in music therapy with cancer patients and their family. *Music Therapy, 4,* 5–17.

Barker, P. (1985). *Using metaphors in psychotherapy*. New York: Brunner/Mazel.

Beaulieu, J. (1987). *Music and sound in the healing arts: An energy approach*. New York: Station Hill.

Blood, P., & Patterson, A. (Eds.). (1992). *Rise up singing: The group singing songbook*. Bethlehem, PA: Sing Out.

Bonny, H. L. (1987). Music: The language of immediacy. *Arts in Psychotherapy 14*, 255–261.

Bonny, H. L. (1997). The state of the art of music therapy. *Arts in Psychotherapy, 24*, 65–73.

Bowman, R. P. (1987). Approaches for counseling children through music. *Elementary School Guidance & Counseling, 21*, 284–291.

Brodsky, W., & Niedorf, H. (1986). "Songs from the heart": New paths to greater maturity. *Arts in Psychotherapy, 13*, 333–341.

Bruscia, K. E. (1987). *Improvisational models of music therapy*. Springfield, IL: Thomas.

Cassity, M. (1981). The influence of a socially valued skill on peer acceptance in a music therapy group. *Journal of Music Therapy, 18*, 148–154.

Clarkson, G. (1994). Creative music therapy and facilitated communication: New ways of reaching students with autism. *Preventing School Failure, 38*, 31–33.

Conley, D. (1994). *If you believe in you* (audio recording). New Rochelle, NY: Treehouse.

Coughlin, E. K. (1990, December 5). Yoruba music. *Chronicle of Higher Education*, p. A10.

Crabbs, M. A., Crabbs, S. K., & Wayman, J. (1986). Making the most of music: An interview with Joe Wayman. *Elementary School Guidance & Counseling, 20*, 240–245.

Day, N. (1989). *Survivor* (audio recording). Pittsburgh, PA: Author.

Fagan, T. S. (1982). Music therapy in the treatment of anxiety and fear in terminal pediatric patients. *Music Therapy, 2*, 13–23.

Gerler, E. R., Jr. (1982). *Counseling the young learner*. Englewood Cliffs, NJ: Prentice-Hall.

Gfeller, K. (1988). Musical components and styles preferred by young adults for aerobic fitness activities. *Journal of Music Therapy, 25*, 28–43.

Gilbert, J. P. (1977). Music therapy perspectives on death and dying. *Journal of Music Therapy, 14*, 165–171.

Gladding, S. T. (1991). *Harmony*. Unpublished manuscript.

Gladding, S. T., & Heape, S. (1987). Popular music as a poetic metaphor in family therapy. *American Journal of Social Psychiatry, 7*, 109–111.

Goldstein, S. L. (1990). A songwriting assessment for hopelessness in depressed adolescents: A review of the literature and a pilot study. *Arts in Psychotherapy, 17*, 117–124.

Gunsberg, A. (1988). Improvised musical play: A strategy for fostering social play between developmentally delayed and nondelayed preschool children. *Journal of Music Therapy, 25*, 178–191.

Hanser, S. B. (1988). Controversy in music listening/stress reduction research. *Arts in Psychotherapy, 15*, 211–217.

Harper, B. L. (1985). Say it, review it, enhance it with a song. *Elementary School Guidance & Counseling, 19*, 218–221.

Hodas, G. R. (1991). Using original music to explore gender and sexuality with adolescents. *Journal of Poetry Therapy, 4*, 205–220.

Hodas, G. (1993). *Stretch yourself? Songs for coping* [With user's guide]. Philadelphia, PA: Second Chance.

Hodas, G. R. (1994). Reversing narratives of failure through music and verse in therapy. *The Family Journal, 2*, 199–207.

Johnson, E. (1981). The role of objective and concrete feedback in self concept treatment of juvenile delinquents in music therapy. *Journal of Music Therapy, 18*, 137–147.

Lazarus, A. A. (1989). Multimodal therapy. In R. J. Corsini & D. Wedding (Eds.), *Current psychotherapies* (4th ed., pp. 502-544). Itasca, IL: Peacock.

Liebmann, M. (1986). *Art therapy for groups*. Cambridge, MA: Brookline.

Mandsager, N., Newsome, D., & Glass, S. (1997, February). *Music as metaphor*. Paper presented at the conference of the North Carolina Counseling Association, Greensboro.

Maranto, C. D., & Bruscia, K. (1989). The status of music therapy education and training. *Arts in Psychotherapy, 16*, 15–19.

Maslow, A. H. (1968). *Toward a psychology of being* (2nd ed.). New York: Van Nostrand Reinhold.

Mayers, K. (1995). Songwriting with traumatized children. *Arts in Psychotherapy, 22*, 495–498.

Mazza, N. (1986). Poetry and popular music in social work education: The liberal arts perspective. *Arts in Psychotherapy, 13*, 293–299.

McDonnell, L. (1984). Music therapy with trauma patients on a pediatric service. *Music Therapy, 4*, 55–63.

Michel, D. E. (1976). *Music therapy: An introduction to therapy and special education through music.* Springfield, IL: Thomas.

Miller, M. E. (1991, July 16). A dose of sound to ease cancer's pain. *News & Observer*, (Raleigh, NC), pp. 1E, 6E.

Moreno, J. J. (1985). Music play therapy: An integrated approach. *Arts in Psychotherapy, 12*, 17–23.

Moreno, J. J. (1987). The therapeutic role of the blues singer and considerations for the clinical applications of the blues form. *Arts in Psychotherapy, 14*, 333–340.

Moreno, J. J. (1988a). Multicultural music therapy: The world music connection. *Journal of Music Therapy, 25*, 17–27.

Moreno, J. J. (1988b). The music therapist: Creative arts therapist and contemporary shaman. *Arts in Psychotherapy, 15*, 271–280.

Nadeau, R. (1984). Using the visual arts to expand personal creativity. In B. Warren (Ed.), *Using the creative arts in therapy* (pp. 61–86). Cambridge, MA: Brookline.

Newcomb, N. S. (1994). Music: A powerful resource for the elementary school counselor. *Elementary School Guidance and Counseling, 29*, 150–155.

Nordoff, P., & Robbins, C. (1977). *Creative music therapy.* New York: John Day.

Osborn, C. (1989). Reminiscence: When the past eases the present. *Journal of Gerontological Nursing, 15*, 6–12.

Owens, G. (1986). Music therapy in France. *Arts in Psychotherapy, 13*, 301–305.

Painter, W. M. (1989). *Musical story hours: Using music with storytelling and puppetry.* Hamden, CT: Library Professional.

Peters, J. S. (1987). *Music therapy: An introduction.* Springfield, IL: Thomas.

Plach, T. (1996). *The creative use of music in group therapy.* Springfield, IL: Thomas.

Potkay, C. R. (1974). Teaching abnormal psychology concepts using popular song lyrics. *Teaching of Psychology, 9*, 233–234.

Ray, L., Soares, E. J., & Tolchinsky, B. (1988). Explicit lyrics: A content analysis of top 100 songs from the 50's to the 80's. *Speech Communication Annual, 2*, 43–56.

Rider, M. S. (1987). Treating chronic disease and pain with music-mediated imagery. *Arts in Psychotherapy, 14*, 113–120.

Roscoe, B., Krug, K., & Schmidt, J. (1985). Written form of self-expression utilized by adolescents. *Adolescence, 20*, 841–844.

Rosenblatt, J. (1991, February 6). From rock 'n' roll to zydeco: Eclectic archives of popular music at Bowling Green State University, *Chronicle of Higher Education, 37*, pp. B6–B7.

Russell, L. A. (1992). Comparisons of cognitive, music, and imagery techniques on anxiety reduction with university students. *Journal of College Student Development, 33*, 516–523.

Schiff, M., & Frances, A. (1974). Popular music: A training catalyst. *Journal of Music Therapy, 11*, 33–40.

Schmidt, J. A. (1983). Songwriting as a therapeutic procedure. In *Music Therapy Perspectives.* Washington DC: National Association for Music Therapy.

Schulberg, C. (1981). *Music therapy source book.* New York: Human Sciences.

Siegell, M. (1987). Review of the book: *Music and trance: A theory of the relations between music and possession, Arts in Psychotherapy, 14*, 183–185.

Slivka, H. H., & Magill, L. (1986). The conjoint use of social work and music therapy in working with children of cancer patients. *Music Therapy, 6*, 30–40.

Staum, M. (1983). Music and rhythmic stimuli in the rehabilitation of gait disorders. *Journal of Music Therapy, 20*, 69–87.

Storr, A. (1992). *Music and the mind.* New York: Free Press.

Took, K. J., & Weiss, D. S. (1994). The relationship between heavy metal and rap music and adolescent turmoil: Real or abstract? *Adolescence, 25,* 613–623.

Thaut, M. H. (1988). Rhythmic intervention techniques in music therapy with gross motor dysfunctions. *Arts in Psychotherapy, 15,* 127–137.

Vanger, P., Oerter, U., Otto, H., Schmidt, S., & Czogalik, D. (1995). The musical expression of the separation conflict during music therapy. *Arts in Psychotherapy, 22,* 147–154.

Wager, K. M. (1987). Prevention programming in mental health: An issue for consideration by music and drama therapists. *Arts in Psychotherapy, 14,* 135–141.

Watkins, B. T. (1990, September 19). In nontraditional, interdisciplinary study at Columbia College, artists get a chance to broaden their horizons, hone creativity. *Chronicle of Higher Education,* pp. A17, A20.

Wells, N. F. (1988). An individual music therapy assessment procedure for emotionally disturbed young adolescents. *Arts in Psychotherapy, 15,* 47–54.

White, A. (1985). Meaning and effects of listening to popular music: Implications for counseling. *Journal of Counseling and Development, 64,* 65–69.

Yon, R. K. (1984). Expanding human potential through music. In B. Warren (Ed.), *Using the creative arts in therapy* (pp. 106–130). Cambridge, MA: Brookline.

3

Dance and Movement and Counseling

Dance Street began before I was born
    and I don't know where it will end
Could be it will trail on forever
    perhaps it shall suddenly stop.
The street began in downtown Richmond
    made of bricks, entitled "Dance,"
        for a man who bore the burden
            of fighting for a dream and beliefs.
When war ended
    he built again
        cared for the "cause" but more its people,
Moving with courage in the midst of strife
    he left an ancestral legacy
        for the dance of life.

(Gladding, 1991)

DANCE AND MOVEMENT are important dimensions of life. They are developmental and cross-cultural types of expression (Beaudry, 1997). In the United States, classical ballet (e.g., Swan Lake), modern dance groups (e.g., Dance Theater of Harlem), Broadway productions (e.g., *A Chorus Line*), and specific recording artists (e.g., Michael Jackson) often give us pleasure through their grace, motion, and breathtaking performances. In a similar manner, people world-wide are often moved by different stimuli to take action on their own behalf or that of someone else. From ancient communities to modern time, individuals have recognized and revered the nature of movement in the healing and helping process.

Indeed, living "is movement, from the motion of the tides to the life cycle of the human being. The way we move broadcasts our relationship to life. It is the bridge between what goes on inside and what we show the world" (Hendricks, 1982, p.165). Yet despite the importance society places on dance and movement, these two action-oriented artistic forms are often neglected aspects of counseling.

It is ironic that such is the case, for "healers were movers until the age of the mind-body dichotomy, and ancient communities recognized and honored the healing power of movement" (Hendricks, 1982, p.165). In many ancient cultures dancing was considered as important as eating and sleeping and was directly associated with healing (Levy, 1988). Indeed, "dance was one of the [primary] ways in which people experienced their participation in a community" (Stark & Lohn, 1989, p. 107). In societies that still follow an oral tradition, dance serves "as an instrument of consciousness and as a vehicle for mediating unknown forces, relenting pent-up emotions and promoting individual transformation and communal inclusiveness" (Beaudry, 1997, p. 52).

The language of counseling is actually filled with dance and movement words and phrases such as: *being in step* or *out of step* with others, *heading in the right/wrong direction, leaning* toward a point of view; moving together like *poetry in motion*, and *tap-dancing around the issues* (Carkhuff, 1983). In addition, numerous counselors have backgrounds in and currently participate in dynamic endeavors that require coordinated movement and abilities, such as gymnastics, swimming, aerobics, dance, and jogging.

Because a sit-and-talk model of helping is more conservative, expected, and easy to implement, counseling sessions are most often sedentary in nature. This staid model of reflecting and talking has dominated traditional counseling theory and practice in the 20th century (Gladding, 1996). Thus, through their educational experiences, counselors are usually not exposed to dance and movement in the therapeutic process, and they often fail as practitioners to make the most of the individual and collective abilities of their clients (Kottler, 1986).

Premise of the Use of Dance and Movement in Counseling

The use of dance and movement in counseling has been found to benefit clients in one or more of five areas:

1. resocialization and integration within a larger group system;
2. nonverbal creative expression for emotional expression;
3. total self- and body-awareness and enhanced self-esteem;
4. muscular coordination, broader movement capabilities, and tension release; and
5. enjoyment through relaxation (Ritter & Low, 1996, p. 249).

As an approach in therapeutic settings, dance and movement are premised on several theoretical assumptions. The first comes from the psychoanalytic literature, where there is the implicit belief that the initial awareness of self is through the body (Freud, 1923). It is further assumed that body movement (as a representative aspect of the unconscious) may inform the conscious mind of feelings and repressed influences that affect a person's life (Feder & Feder, 1981). "Movement conveys truth" and "is the direct printout from the unconscious" (Hendricks, 1982, p. 166). In this tradition, dance and movement promote awareness and further "the physical and psychic integration" of persons (Krueger & Schofield, 1986, p. 327). These avenues of expression help clients heal their fragmentation and alienation from themselves and others (Beaudry, 1997; Levine, 1996).

A second premise on which dance and movement in counseling is based is bodywork. There are many forms of bodywork, including "various forms of massage, rolfing, bioenergetics, yoga, Tragerwork, Lomi bodywork, and acupressure. They are all designed to help people dissolve psychophysical blocks in the body. Some are more physical in nature (massage), and others focus more on psychological blocks (bioenergetics). Direct manipulation of the body often triggers memories of old traumas and injuries or can produce a flood of feelings" (Weinhold, 1987, p.7). By working one's body through dance and movement, avenues of awareness that were previously closed begin to open up. Body work seeks to help people become more integrative (Brownell, 1981). It is especially effective with persons who are closed to talking about their feelings.

A third rationale for incorporating dance and movement in the therapeutic process is based on developmental theory. Human behavior is initially dominated by physically oriented experiences. In infancy, movement is a primary way of communicating. "The bodily interaction between mother and infant is, in a sense, the first dialogue. In harmonious relationships this physical give and take becomes a smoothly flowing piece of choreography, a perfect symbiotic dance" (Mohacsy, 1995, p. 33). Regardless of how rhythmic interpersonal relationships are, people pass through a number of different physical stages in life, each of which is characterized by distinct movement patterns.

A fourth rationale for dance and movement in counseling is based on gestalt therapy, which has recognized the potency of movement for many years. Fritz Perls and others involved in the formulation of gestalt therapy stressed that body movement is a primary method of experiencing feelings and promoting psychological growth (Meier & Davis, 1997; Perls, Hefferline, & Goodman, 1951). Perls probably overstated his case when he said, "Lose your mind and come to your senses." Nevertheless, this adage has value in reminding clients that through using all aspects of themselves they will make progress in working through personal issues. In movement and dance the expressions of choice and change become visibly more clear.

Finally, the use of movement and dance in counseling is founded on social psychology and the interpersonal theory of Harry Stack Sullivan, which emphasize that personality is formed in relationship to others. The basis of movement and dance is to "establish or reestablish a sense of relatedness to self and to others" (Stark & Lohn, 1989, p. 107). In rhythmic movement people feel a "heightened sense of oneself (a flow of energy, a feeling of aliveness, and sense of well-being), [which facilitates] bonding and empathic response in the body with others" (Stark & Lohn, 1989, p. 107). Thus movement and dance are connecting arts that unite people with themselves and others.

Practice of the Use of Dance and Movement in Counseling

Dance and movement occur in many ways, and their impact is multidimensional. In their purest form, dance and movement are initially expressed in physical movements. Indeed, the body is seen as the manifestation of one's personality, and any spontaneous movement is viewed as an expression of personality (Bunney, 1979). Therefore, the way people move—from being "light on their feet" to being "mechanical and slow"—is an indicator of who they are and how they are generally functioning (L. F. Armeniox, personal communication, February 5, 1994).

The therapeutic emphases of dance and movement are not just physical, however. Rather, dance and movement therapy have three main goals: physical, psychological, and social (Fleshman & Fryear, 1981). "Physical goals may include releasing physical tension through activities and broadening one's movement repertoire. Psychological goals might include channeling one's self-expression in a meaningful way and helping a client adjust to reality. Social goals may involve getting a client to join a group interaction and to develop social relationships with others" (Gladding, 1985, p. 10).

The extent to which these goals are highlighted and how depends on the education and skill of counselors. Some professionals are specifically taught ways to use dance and movement therapy; others employ this emphasis at select times and in limited ways. Different aspects of each tradition will be examined, and populations with which movement and dance may best be employed will be explored.

Dance and movement therapy has been officially defined by the American Dance Therapy Association (ADTA) as "the psychotherapeutic use of movement as a process that furthers the emotional, cognitive, and physical integration of the individual" (ADTA Web site, 1997). Dance and movement therapy effects changes in feelings, cognitions, physical functioning, and behavior. Yet dance and movement, although they have much in common, are also seen as distinct specialty areas.

Marian Chace at St. Elizabeth's Hospital in Washington, D.C., is considered to be the founder of modern dance and movement therapies (Sandel, Chaiklin, & Lohn, 1993). She started her dance therapy work in the early 1940s and was a professional dancer before beginning her work as a dance therapist. Other pioneers that followed or were contemporaries of Chace included Mary Whitehouse, Blanche Evan, Liljan Espenak, Alma Hawkins, and Trudi Shoop.

Together, dance and movement therapists acknowledge "the intrinsic life forces in all people, the healing power of shared rhythms and expressed feelings" (Hendricks, 1982, p. 166). They believe in a reciprocal influence between a person's emotions and body movement. Changes in body movement can bring about positive changes in a person's psychic life, and vice versa (S. Kleinman, personal communication, April 3, 1997). Despite these similarities, professionals in the fields of dance and movement therapy maintain many distinctions

Dance Therapy

Dance therapy is the use of dance and movement as psychotherapeutic (healing) tools (Levy, 1988). Professionals who specialize in this area (i.e., dance and movement therapists) have met educational and performance standards set up by the ADTA. The term *dance* is used by dance therapists to stress the "expressive movement and the integrating aspects of the rhythmic use of body movement" (Duggan, 1981, p. 229). Thus, dance therapy connotes the artistic nature of performance through movement and the use of music to promote rhythm and fluidity in this process. "Through dance one becomes more fully alive—physically, emotionally, intellectually, and spiritually. It opens a path toward one's higher self—a way to transcend the mundane" (Fisher, 1989, p. 15). Music therapy is closely associated with dance therapy.

Movement Therapy

In movement therapy practitioners place less emphasis on performance and outside stimuli and more on a concentration of the inner senses. Through this approach people are trusted to act as they feel and are encouraged in various ways to become more connected with their inner selves (Jacobs, Harvill, & Masson, 1994). Thus, the action associated with movement therapy is usually spontaneous, unrehearsed, and relatively brief. "The process of the mover [how the mover moves] is the focus of movement therapy" (Hendricks, 1982, p. 167). Drama and enactment techniques are closely allied with movement therapy.

Dance and Movement in Counseling

As previously noted, few traditional counseling theories have basic rationales that emphasize dance or movement as primary ways of clarifying or resolving problems. Nevertheless dance and movement therapies consider such psychologically based authorities as Sigmund Freud, William James, Gordon Allport, Wilhelm Reich, Carl Rogers, Abraham Maslow, Alfred Adler, and Harry Stack Sullivan to have been influential in the development of their specialty. For example, Liljan Espenak, a pioneer in dance therapy, based much of her work on integrating Adlerian concepts with the discipline of dance therapy. These Adlerian concepts included aggressive drive, inferiority feelings, social feelings, life style, and first memory. The nonverbal emphases of other theorists has been especially valued by dance and movement therapists. The following examples illustrate how theories of counseling and psychology are used separately or together.

First is gestalt therapy. It has two primary foci centered on movement. One is simply "body language" in which the counselor and eventually the client concentrate on what different parts of the body are doing in conjunction with a client's verbalizations. A client may state that he or she is calm and relaxed, while simultaneously making a kicking motion. The incongruence of these messages is pointed out, and the client is confronted with the inconsistency of verbal and nonverbal signals (Gladding, 1995). In the process, clients are encouraged to examine and own personal feelings and behaviors more directly.

A second focus of gestalt therapy is the movement encouraged with the technique of "becoming a dream" (in which enactment of a dream event is carried out). In this process each part of a dream (e.g., people, event, and mood) are considered to be projections of one's self, often representing contradictory roles (Perls, 1969). Therefore, dreamers are asked to become each part of their dream and to invent dialogue and interactions between the various components regardless of how absurd such a process may seem. Through this technique opposite sides are expressed and become clearer. Through this type of dream work the dream becomes the "royal road to integration" (Perls, 1969, p. 66).

In addition to the emphasis on movement in gestalt therapy, social learning theory and family therapy focus on what many within these approaches call the "dance": regular rhythmic interactions that enhance or impede one's overall functioning. Social skills and competencies through such a dance are emphasized with these perspectives. Thus, selective dances are shaped and reinforced using the plethora of techniques derived from these traditions. The way individuals and family members generally relate to significant others in their lives determines how rigid, spontaneous, or healthy their lives will be (Napier & Whitaker, 1978). For example, in a social situation a husband and wife may constantly put each other down or compliment and encourage each other. As a result of these actions their behavior will either be positive (spiraling up) or negative (spiraling down).

Among atheoretical approaches, there are a number of effective generic movement and dance experiences. Many of these approaches are associated with groups. For example, a movement activity that creates greater awareness for group members about the nature of conflict is known as "home spot." In this nonverbal experience, individuals are asked to join hands or put their arms around each others' shoulders. Then they are to pick out a spot in the room to which they wish to take the group, without telling anyone. Finally, they try to begin moving the group toward the spot they have selected (Jacobs et al., 1994). The ongoing group dynamics are the primary focus of the exercise as group members struggle with issues of power and persuasion in a 2- to 5-minute time span.

Overall, movement (and dance) are actively practiced as a part of counseling for these reasons:

- They get people moving around and keep them from becoming fatigued from sitting too long in one spot.
- They provide a change in format and an opportunity to renew interest and energize.
- They give individuals "a chance to experience something rather than simply discuss it" (Jacobs et al., 1994, p. 172).
- They help participants remember what they experience more vividly than words alone.
- They involve all people in a counseling experience or the total person that is the client in a way not possible otherwise (Jacobs et al., 1994).

Dance and Movement in Counseling With Specific Populations

Professional dance and movement therapists (and those who use these modalities in counseling) "work with all ages and populations—in psychiatric hospitals, prisons, geriatric residence programs, adolescent halfway house settings, special education programs, and private practice" (Hendricks, 1982, p. 166). A representative sampling of the settings and techniques employed is presented in the material that follows; however, movement and dance are constantly being created and implemented. Thus, those who prefer these active art-based ways of working with clients must be innovative in their endeavors.

Children

A primary characteristic of many children is abundant energy, so the use of dance and movement with them is often accepted with enthusiasm. The idea of movement activities with children focuses on self-awareness. For instance, directed dance and movement therapy may help abused children exercise control over personal space and regain a sense of control and ownership of their own bodies (Goodhill, 1987). Movement and dance also help children gain an awareness of others. Several types of movement exercises can engage children and promote different aspects of their mental and physical health quite concretely (Chiefetz, 1977).

Walking

In this activity children walk in a circle at their normal pace and cadence. After they have a feel for how they walk, they are asked to walk faster than usual and then to walk in slow motion. Walking is then linked to feelings so that the children walk as if they were tired, happy, or sad. After this experience, children are instructed to act as if they were walking on or through different terrain including a desert, a mountain, mud, ice, water, and even silly substances such as peanut butter, whipped cream, yogurt, and corn flakes. After the walk is completed (usually by pretending to walk through a grassy meadow) children and their leaders talk about what the experiences were like.

Locomotion

The idea of this exercise is to have children see how many different movements they can make to get from one place to another (e.g., jumping, running, and skipping). They can then combine movements and even do the same movements with a partner. Afterwards, the feelings involved with these movements are processed.

Robot

In "robot," children pretend they can only move or talk like a robot does. They become stiff-limbed and monotone. Halfway into the exercise they become human again. After the exercise they work with their facilitators and talk about the robot-to-human experience.

In addition to the above exercises for physically functional children, movement and dance can have a therapeutic effect on children who are born with disabilities. One of the most dramatic examples of this impact is the use of movement with children who are born blind. In such cases, "the dance and movement therapist's highly developed communicative mode emphasizes sound, rhythm, and touch and helps the blind child find pleasure and safety in the natural expression of moving together" (Kalish-Weiss, 1988, p. 108). Such experiences, which must be tailored for each child, are truly the essence of art.

Dance therapy treatment may be equally positive in outcome, as illustrated in the use of this process on a 12-year-old girl with motor abnormalities, mild mental retardation, and emotional problems (Lasseter, Privette, Brown, & Duer, 1989). The result of 1-hour, twice-a-week sessions of dance treatments over 18 weeks was markedly improved motor development and enhanced self-esteem.

Adolescents

Dance and movement can be used preventatively and therapeutically with adolescents. Preventative dance and movement focus on helping adolescents explore "the radical changes in body image and awareness [they are undergoing] and the transient feelings of depersonalization this engenders" (Emunah, 1990, p. 103). Dance and movement also lead to the expression of creativity within adolescents in healthy and actualizing ways (May, 1975).

Therapeutically, dance and movement allow adolescents to express their conflicts in an active, behavioral form that is often easier for them than it is to verbalize what they are experiencing. Thus, adolescents who are angry or confused can show their feelings in a safe and dynamic form by enacting them through dance and movement that can be accompanied by music. With severely disordered clients, such as those with anorexia nervosa, body boundary exercises are used: clients attend to the tactile differences "between their bodies and other objects in the environment" (Kaslow & Eicher, 1988, p. 180). Other movement- and dance-related exercises such as muscle relaxation, deep breathing, and centering, are also helpful to this population, regardless of the problems they present.

Adults

Many adults participate in some form of dance or movement activity as a way to stay healthy and fit. Jazzercise and jogging are two of the more recent movement trends that have captured the attention of a large number of individuals. Jazzercise, which is valued for its group-support dynamic and upbeat tempo, is a popular musically oriented way to exercise. Jogging is equally popular and as a movement experience has been used in group counseling settings to help participants become psychologically as well as physically healthier (Childers & Burcky, 1984). In addition, many professional athletic teams hire dance specialists to help their players learn agility and coordination essential to teamwork and individual performance. Overall, dance-related activities are embraced by both men and women. These activities help them become more aware of how "in step" they are with themselves and others.

The use of bodywork with men has proven effective (Brownell, 1981). Although many forms of bodywork exist, it is defined here as any nonverbal activity in which men actively participate. It makes use of prop, and gestalt-type experiences to help these individuals become more aware of their bodies and emotions. The result is that many men release repressed feelings such as fear, anger, hurt, or joy.

Women benefit from bodywork, too. Through this method, they come to a clearer understanding of their own boundaries and are thus able to be more caring for themselves. Self and nonself distinctions gained through bodywork facilitate better intra- and interpersonal relationships. Likewise, dance therapy can help women reconcile the gap between inner experiences and external self-image and thereby facilitate a fuller integration of self (Meyer, 1985).

Elderly Clients

The use of creative movement and dance with elderly persons is an unexpected but pragmatic reality. Movement and dance activities have been associated with a number of improvements in older adults including memory, alertness, reality orientation, judgment, personal insight, and acceptance (Ashley & Crenan, 1993). Older adults have the ability and willingness to engage in a number of activities, including simple dances, which benefit them physically and mentally. The exact nature of exercises chosen for members of aging populations depends on the physical well-being of participants as well as the space and time available. Movement can include a number of activities that focus on such things as breathing (e.g., blowing soap bubbles), hand dances, nonlocomotor actions (e.g., bending a body part), enactment with props (e.g., moving a scarf to the flow of music), and exercises on the floor or in a chair (Fisher, 1989).

Even though elderly clients are not as flexible in their movements, the main limitation to working with this age population is the creative abilities of the dance and movement therapist or counselor. Dances, including aerobics, have proven useful to people in this age range (Atterburg, Sorg, & Larson, 1983; Lindner, 1982). The main emphasis of any movement or dance, however, should be on improving participants' self-esteem, physical well-being, and sense of accomplishment.

General Population

Jacobs (1992) has devised a number of movement techniques to use in counseling with people of various ages. Among these general processes are the following, appropriate for clients over the life span.

Evaluation of Progress

In this experience, clients are asked to stand up and position themselves according to how much progress they have made during counseling. A line is drawn representing where counseling started, and a goal line is also drawn, with clients placing themselves in between. Such a procedure may be especially powerful for clients who have become resistant to counseling or who are concrete thinkers and need to visualize their progress.

Feeling Pulled

The idea behind "feeling pulled" is that clients often have forces in their lives that impede their progress in reaching goals. Therefore, in this experience a client is asked to start moving toward his or her goals with the counselor holding onto his or her arm and pulling him or her back-wards. The right amount of tug is agreed to by the client. The counseling session then turns to identifying what forces with what levels of power are inhibiting the client.

Circles

When clients do the same thing over and over, they fail to make progress. In circles, clients are asked to walk around in the same direction a number of times to get a better feel for what doing the same thing again and again is like. This realization hopefully leads to insight and new direc-tions for the therapy.

Movement Between Chairs

The premise behind movement between two chairs is that clients sometimes need to experience their vacillation in regard to decisions they have discussed but failed to make. In movement be-tween chairs, clients are asked to simply move continuously between two or more chairs that represent decisions they could make. They are not to speak, unless at the end of bouncing back and forth between chairs (which should go on a minimum of 2 to 3 minutes) they have some-thing new to say.

Jacobs (1992) also stated that counselors need to move either closer or farther away from clients at times to illustrate the dance going on in the therapeutic setting. In such cases, coun-selors should move with caution and inform clients of what they are doing either before or dur-ing the time they are moving.

Groups

When individuals enter a group, they often feel a great deal of tension. The other people are strangers, and everyone sometimes feels ill at ease in knowing what to say or do. The ability of people to feel relaxed in the group and for the group to provide a structure that is supportive, safe, and predictable crucial if members of the group and the group as a whole are going to func-tion well (Sandel & Johnson, 1996). In these situations some movement can help alleviate ten-sion, break down barriers, and energize the group as a whole.

One way of promoting the formation of a group is called "train station," which comes from Playfair (an organization dedicated to putting fun back into the workplace—2207 Oregon Street, Berkeley, CA 94705, phone 510-540-8768, fax 510-540-7638, e-mail Playfair1@aol.com). In train station, the group is divided in two. Half of the group is designated to be the greeters and the other half the passengers. The group is then given the following instructions: Each greeter has just received a phone call from their best friend from early childhood. It has now been a num-ber of years since they saw each other, but the former best friend is to arrive in a few hours at the train station in the city where the greeter now lives. The greeter is so excited that after agreeing to meet the friend, he or she hangs up the phone without thinking to ask what the person who called looks like. Lacking this information, the greeter goes to the train station at the designated hour and decides that the best strategy to employ in this situation is to run with enthusiasm to-ward the group of passengers now arriving. Thus with arms waving, the greeters as a group move in slow motion toward the passengers, who all display similar behaviors. As each greeter gets to a passenger looks are exchanged but then both realize the person who they are exchanging glances with is not the right person; thus, both look away and toward another person in the immediate area who also turns out not to be the right person. This activity continues until all the greeters and passengers have passed each other, after which participants are given a chance to voice how they experienced the exercise. They are then informed by the leader of the group that nothing they ever do in the group will be nearly as embarrassing.

Another exercise suggested by Mintz (1971) to help a group experience a good beginning is known as the "hand dialogue." In this exercise, two individuals are partners. They are seated and then instructed to improvise dances with their hands with one person initially leading and the other following. They put their hands together and may chose to keep their eyes open, but they are encouraged to close their eyes to get the full impact of this nonverbal experience. Participants may use their fingers, palms, or both in doing their dance. Likewise, they may use the front or back of their hands. The leader then instructs them to switch their positions of being either a leader or a follower after they have "danced" for about 60 to 90 seconds in one position. Talking is reserved for after the dance has finished—time is set aside for discussions between pairs and then the group as a whole about feelings and emotions associated with what they have been through and how such affect is expressed nonverbally.

A similar type of movement dance that comes at the start of many groups, but can be implemented during the working stage of the group as well, is "shadows." This exercise involves one person imitating another in a follow-the-leader style. Sometimes it is done in silence, but it is not unusual to have shadows occur to music. The type of music chosen can help encourage interaction and break down inhibitions. After the event, participants talk about their experience in groups of two, four, eight, and then in the group as a whole. Again, this type of movement opens individuals up for more awareness and gives them a common experience as a basis for sharing.

Families

As alluded to earlier, the complex way individuals in families relate to each other is often referred to as the "family dance" (Napier & Whitaker, 1978). In healthy families "the partners do not need to hold on tightly. . . because they know they are. . . moving to the same rhythm" (Lindberg, 1975, p. 104). On the other hand, dysfunctional family members cling closely to one another and hesitate to let their members change, much less leave home (Haley, 1978). Thus, the results of family dances are either positive or negative. Healthy families move to resolve common problems and move toward a final dissolution of themselves as a functional, working unit. Unhealthy families, on the other hand, take steps to hinder the growth of persons within the family unit by keeping them developmentally delayed and "stuck" in nonproductive patterns.

Three family dance and movement exercises can assist families in distress. Family choreography is an excellent example that involves the whole family in a physical and mental experience. Enactment and paradox are two more artistic-based ways to help families move in harmony.

In family choreography, different members of the family stage a moment in time in the family's life. Then specific movements are given to each player and repeated until members of the family get a feel for the multiple interconnectedness of their lives. This approach is well illustrated in the work of Papp (1982), in which married couples were assisted in acting out their patterns of behavior in this manner. The exercise resulted in a change in the couples' present actions and a potential metaphorical memory trace of what movements could be positive in the marriage.

In enactment, the counselor directs the family members to do a "dance movement" they are stuck in, such as resolving arguments, and to show him or her what happens. This type of direction takes the involuntary nature away from the action in which the family is stuck and places it in the hands of the counselor. Therefore, even if the family does not resolve their disputes, their relationships with each other change. They have to try another (hopefully positive) way of settling their disputes because of the power they have given the counselor to direct their old, non-productive patterns.

Finally, in paradox, a type of reverse enactment takes place. The counselor basically tells the family they cannot do something, such as change, or he or she instructs the family to "go slow." The results are either that the family obeys and moves differently under the counselor's direction or they rebel and change to resist the counselor's instructions. Change in patterns and movement within the family are the end product.

Dance and Movement in Counseling With Other Creative Arts

Dance and movement have many common elements with other creative arts. "Shape, space, time, and force are used by dancers, artists, and musicians alike" (Fisher, 1989, p. 51). On a specific level, dance is usually associated with the creative art form of music. After all, music provides a rhythmic background that can heavily influence the types and frequency with which persons engage in dance. Other art forms that have an influence on dance and movement are drama and art.

Dance and Movement and Music

"In many cultures the root word for music and dance are the same. It would be inconceivable for people in some parts of the world to remain motionless while music is played, or to move together rhythmically except with the support of music" (Chace, 1967, p. 25). The natural connectedness between dance and music is exemplified in the society of the United States in a number of ways, including the following two sentences of a newspaper story about a college basketball team preparing to play in the annual National Collegiate Athletic Association (NCAA) tournament. "Some call the NCAA Tournament the 'big dance,' others the 'grand ball.' In either case, Wake Forest is ready to face the music" (Collins, 1991, p. 27).

Regardless of how it is portrayed, the linkage of music with movement is one that occurs frequently when dance and movement are accompanied by rhythm and sound. One example is an intergenerational program between kindergarten children and residents of a geriatric facility—Project TOUCH (Mason-Luckey & Sandel, 1985). In this situation, children and their elder partners sing certain songs and move accordingly. Thus, in expressing feelings about fantasy and hope the group sings "Bluebird Through My Window" while standing in a circle holding hands. As the song is sung, a designated "bluebird" flies through the spaces (frames) made by the arms and finally lands within the circle and designates another person to become the bluebird.

Another example of music and dance pairing up is in the use of both to help homeless children learn problem-solving strategies (Straum, 1993). Although the combination did not produce significant results compared to more verbal methods, it did foster good participation and helped children to stay on task.

Dance and Movement and Drama

Dramatic activities that can be used as adjuncts to dance therapy have been outlined by Johnson and Eicher (1990). According to these practitioners, dramatic techniques are effective with adolescents in dance therapy because they mediate the threat of intimacy members of this population feel. Basically the techniques work internally "by decreasing the ambiguity of emotional and feeling states" and externally "by providing a safer container for the aggressive drives stimulated by the intimate environment" (Johnson & Eicher, 1990, p. 163). Thus, drama techniques such as labeling feelings, freezing action, and defining linear space help unsure adolescents feel safe within themselves and secure with others.

Other successful dramatic activities include these exercises:

1. Adverbs—One member of a group leaves the room and the others decide on an adverb (a word ending in "ly," e.g., "warmly"). When the member returns, he or she asks designated members to act out a task in a way that reflects the chosen adverb and tries to guess what it is.
2. Chair Game—Group members decide on a famous person while one member of the group is gone. When that person returns, he or she is treated like the famous person by others in the group until he or she guesses that person's identity.
3. Areas—The room is marked off into different feeling areas such as "sad," "bored," "happy," and "angry." Each member of the group spends time in these areas and tries to embody that emotion. Then members reassemble and talk about how each experience felt.
4. Environments—The group breaks into two teams, and each creates an environment for the other, such as the surface of the moon or a tropical jungle. After going through or participating in the environment, the teams reassemble and talk about the experience and how it relates to their lives.

Overall, dramatic techniques such as those above get adolescents moving in many directions and interacting with different people in novel ways. Therefore, after adolescents participate in dance therapy experiences, they are usually not intimidated and in fact may welcome opportunities to be more expressive and creative.

Dance and Movement and Art

In the case of working with persons with eating disorders, for whom perception of self is greatly distorted, dance and movement are sometimes combined with projective drawings (Krueger & Schofield, 1986). The idea in this treatment is to help clients with these goals:

- to immediately visualize the movement experience they just had,
- to give them a way to symbolize and objectify this experience in a drawing,
- to depict current developmental issues that have arisen because of what they have been through,
- to provide a concrete means (i.e., the drawing) to bridge the transition between nonverbal and verbal means of expression, and
- to measure progress and change.

Drawings are usually made at the end of each dance and movement therapy session, and the individual and overall impact of such drawings are analyzed by practitioners for patterns and symbols that will help create insight.

Art and movement are also combined in the treatment of chemically dependent individuals. In this inpatient work, "concrete art and movement tasks are applied to parallel" (Potocek & Wilder, 1989, p. 99), each of the first four steps of Alcoholics Anonymous (AA). For example, in Step 1, in which addicts admit they are powerless over alcohol, participants construct with chairs the walls of a pit while despondent, self-absorbing music plays in the background. They take turns climbing over the walls and sitting in the pit in the midst of a darkened room. While there, they draw their feelings on a large brown piece of paper on the floor. In all of the four steps are similar movement and art exercises with the intent of promoting abstract thinking and making intangible emotions clear.

Summary

Dance and movement are physically demanding and energizing art forms. Their use in counseling varies, but in general they are employed to help clients become more aware of their bodies, boundaries, and interpersonal relationships. They provide integrative ways of helping individuals of all ages and stages in life become more whole. They free people to move in ways that talk alone does not allow. Dance differs from movement in its emphasis on performance and music, but both stress that clients become actively involved in the therapeutic process.

Some counseling theories such as psychoanalysis, gestalt, and social learning approaches advocate and employ dance and movement techniques. With children, these procedures will be more active than they will be for older adults. Families and groups also use dance and movement, especially choreography, in ways that are unique and innovative. Overall, dance and movement can be combined with a number of other creative arts, such as music, drama, and drawing to enrich and enliven counseling sessions and to promote change and growth.

═══ Exercises ═══

1. Focus on your most physically active time of life. What did you learn from your body that now effects your practice as a counselor, for instance, that you are more verbally direct when you are fatigued or that you need a specific amount of exercise to feel mentally alert? Discuss your need or lack of need for movement with a colleague and notice how much structured or spontaneous physical activity plays a part in the life of your clients.

2. A dance is usually described as movement that is structured and usually performed on some level in public. What types of dances do you observe among clients and nonclients you know? How do such dances either get to the heart of issues or side-step important issues?

3. Lead a "milling around" exercise with a group of trusted friends or colleagues. In this exercise, individuals simply walk around and participate with others as instructed by the leader—by making or not making eye contact, by touching or not touching each other with shoulders or elbows. The idea is to assess how comfortable each member feels moving in a certain manner. The entire exercise is brief (about 2 to 5 minutes) and is processed with the group leader for as long as needed afterwards.

References

Ashley, F. B., & Crenan, M. (1993). Dance: The movement activity for the elderly. *Nursing Homes, 42,* 50–51.

Atterburg, C., Sorg, J., & Larson, A. (1983). Aerobic dancing in a long-term care facility. *Physical and Occupational Therapy in Geriatrics, 2,* 71–73.

Beaudry, I. D. (1997). Reconfiguring identity. *Arts in Psychotherapy, 24,* 51–57.

Brownell, A. J. (1981). Counseling men through bodywork. *Personnel & Guidance Journal, 60,* 252–255.

Bunney, J. (1979). Dance therapy: An overview. In P. B. Hallen (Ed.), *The use of the creative arts in therapy* (pp. 24–26). Washington, DC: American Psychiatric Association.

Carkhuff, R. R. (1983). *The art of helping* (5th ed.). Amherst, MA: Human Resources Development.

Chace, M. (1967, November). Music in dance therapy. *Music Journal, 25,* 25, 27.

Chiefetz, D. (1977). Activities. In B. Zavatsky & R. Padgett (Eds.), *The whole word catalogue 2* (pp. 176–180). New York: Teachers & Writers Collaborative.

Childers, J. H., Jr. & Burcky, W. D. (1984). The jogging group: A positive-wellness strategy. *AMHCA Journal, 6,* 118–125.

Collins, D. (1991, March 12). "Big dance" awaiting deacons. *Winston-Salem Journal,* p. C1.

Duggan, D. (1981). Dance therapy. In R. J. Corsini (Ed.), *Handbook of innovative psychotherapies* (pp. 229–240). New York: Wiley.

Emunah, R. (1990). Expression and expansion in adolescence: The significance of creative arts therapy. *Arts in Psychotherapy, 17,* 101–107.

Feder, E., & Feder, B. (1981). *The expressive arts therapies.* Englewood Cliffs, NJ: Prentice Hall.

Fisher, P. P. (1989). *Creative movement for older adults.* New York: Human Sciences.

Fleshman, B., & Fryear, J. L. (1981). *The arts in therapy.* Chicago: Nelson-Hall.

Freud, S. (1923). The ego and the id. *The standard edition, 19* (pp. 12–60). London: Hogarth.

Gladding, S. T. (1985). Counseling and the creative arts. *Counseling and Human Development, 18,* 1–12.

Gladding, S. T. (1991). *Dance street.* Unpublished manuscript.

Gladding, S. T. (1995). *Group work: A counseling specialty* (2nd ed.). Englewood Cliffs, NJ: Prentice Hall.

Gladding, S. T. (1996). *Counseling: A comprehensive profession* (3rd ed). Englewood Cliffs, NJ: Prentice Hall.

Goodhill, S. W. (1987). Dance and movement therapy with abused children. *Arts in Psychotherapy, 14,* 59–68.

Haley, J. (1978). *Leaving home.* New York: McGraw-Hill.

Hendricks, K. T. (1982). Transpersonal movement therapy. In G. Hendricks & B. Weinhold (Eds.), *Transpersonal approaches to counseling and psychotherapy* (pp. 165-187). Denver, CO: Love.

Jacobs, E. (1992). *Creative counseling techniques: An illustrated guide.* Odessa, FL: Psychological Assessment Resources.

Jacobs, E. E., Harvill, R. L., & Masson, R. L. (1994). *Group counseling* (2nd ed.). Pacific Grove, CA: Brooks/Cole.

Johnson, D. R., & Eicher, V. (1990). The use of dramatic activities to facilitate dance therapy with adolescents. *Arts in Psychotherapy, 17,* 157–164.

Kalish-Weiss, B. I. (1988). Born blind and visually handicapped infants: Movement psychotherapy and assessment. *Arts in Psychotherapy, 15,* 101–108.

Kaslow, N. J., & Eicher, V. W. (1988). Body image therapy: A combined creative arts therapy and verbal psychotherapy approach. *Arts in Psychotherapy, 15,* 177–188.

Kottler, J. A. (1986). *On being a therapist.* San Francisco, CA: Jossey-Bass.

Krueger, D. W., & Schofield, E. (1986). Dance and movement therapy of eating disordered patients: A model. *Arts in Psychotherapy, 13,* 323–331.

Lasseter, J., Privette, G., Brown, C., & Duer, J. (1989). Dance as a treatment approach with a multidisabled child: Implications for school counseling. *The School Counselor, 36,* 310–315.

Levine, S. K. (1996). The expressive body: A fragmented totality. *Arts in Psychotherapy, 23,* 131–136.

Levy, F. J. (1988). Introduction. In F. J. Levy (Ed.), *Dance movement therapy* (pp. 1–16). Reston, VA: American Alliance for Health, Physical Education, Recreation and Dance.

Lindberg, A. M. (1975). *Gifts from the sea*. New York: Pantheon.

Lindner, E. C. (1982). Dance as a therapeutic intervention for the elderly. *Educational Gerontology, 8*, 167–174.

Mason-Luckey, B., & Sandel, S. L. (1985). Intergenerational movement therapy: A leadership challenge. *Arts in Psychotherapy, 12*, 257–262.

May, R. (1975). *The courage to create*. New York: Norton.

Meier, S. T., & Davis, S. R. (1997). *The elements of counseling* (3rd ed.). Pacific Grove, CA: Brooks/Cole.

Meyer, S. (1985). Women and conflict in dance therapy. *Women and Therapy, 4*, 3–17.

Mintz, E. E. (1971). *Marathon groups: Reality and symbol*. New York: Appleton-Century-Crofts.

Mohacsy, I. (1995). Nonverbal communication and its place in the therapy session. *Arts in Psychotherapy, 22*, 31–38.

Napier, A. Y., & Whitaker, C. A. (1978). *The family crucible*. New York: Harper & Row.

Papp, P. (1982). Staging reciprocal metaphors in a couples group. *Family Process, 21*, 453–467.

Perls, F. (1969). *Gestalt therapy verbatim*. Moab, UT: Real People.

Perls, F., Hefferline, R. F., & Goodman, P. (1951). *Gestalt therapy*. New York: Dell.

Potocek, J., & Wilder, V. N. (1989). Art/movement psychotherapy in the treatment of the chemically dependent patient. *Arts in Psychotherapy, 16*, 99–103.

Ritter, M., & Low, K. G. (1996). Effects of dance and movement therapy: A meta-analysis. *Arts in Psychotherapy, 23*, 249–260.

Sandel, S. L., Chaiklin, S., & Lohn, A. (Eds.). (1993). *Foundations of dance/movement therapy: The life and work of Marian Chace*. Columbia, MD: Marian Chace Memorial Fund of the American Dance Therapy Association.

Sandel, S. L., & Johnson, D. R. (1996). Theoretical foundations of the structural analysis of movement sessions. *Arts in Psychotherapy, 23*, 15–25.

Stark, A., & Lohn, A. F. (1989). The use of verbalization in dance and movement therapy. *Arts in Psychotherapy, 16*, 105–113.

Straum, M. (1993). A music/nonmusic intervention with homeless children. *Journal of Music Therapy, 36*, 256–262.

Weinhold, B. K. (1987). Altered states of consciousness: An explorer's guide to inner space. *Counseling and Human Development, 20*, 1–12.

4

Imagery
and
Counseling

In my mind there's a picture of Timothy
    and a vision of nonverbal memories.
Awakened to that awareness
    I walk lightly and with joy—
        a man having watched the birth of his son
            and vicariously experienced the labor.
White clouds blow in the cool March air
    but my sight is focused on a previous night
        when new movement came to life
            in the rhythmic cry of an infant.

(Gladding, 1991)

I MAGERY CAN BE DEFINED as "perception that comes through any of the senses—sight, smell, touch, taste, hearing, and feeling" (Kanchier, 1997, p. 14). Imagery is sometimes described as "seeing with the mind's eye" or "having an inner vision." It allows us to create and, in essence, symbolically experience imagined results of behavior before an activity is actually performed (Manz, 1992). The use of imagery is one of the most powerful of our human faculties. By using imagery, people can learn, rehearse, and solve problems (Myrick & Myrick, 1993). They can address present and future possibilities with creativity and confidence. Thus, imagery is a tool for working with and working through one's environment and circumstances. It is paradoxical: On one hand, imagery is passive, requiring little if any physical movement, but on the other hand, imagery is complex in that those who practice it usually deal with a number of complicated matters that they must arrange or rearrange.

Imagery has an extraordinarily rich history in the helping professions (Achterberg & Lawlis, 1984). Ancient Egyptians and shamans in many cultures used imagery to promote positive change in personal and interpersonal relationships. In more recent history, imagery has been associated with the process of learning (i.e., eidetic or photographic memory; Luria, 1968), relaxation techniques (Richardson, 1969), life meaning (Jung, 1956; Mills & Crowley, 1986), life enjoyment (Lazarus, 1977; Witmer, 1985), leadership (Neck, Stewart, & Manz, 1995), promotion of diversity (Russell-Chapin & Stoner, 1995), and clarification of feelings beyond facts (O'Neill, 1997).

Popular songs such as John Lennon's "Imagine," Smokey Robinson's "It Was Just My Imagination," and the Buckinghams' "Imagine You and Me," emphasize the significance of imagery in the life of people and its importance in promoting everything from peace to love relationships. Furthermore, the concept of "the dream" and envisioning a future is stressed in a variety of ways, such as the *South Pacific* song "Happy Talk," the "I Have a Dream" speech of Martin Luther King, Jr., the dream catcher idea in Native American Indian tradition, and the dream concept of life development for men elaborated on by Daniel Levison and associates. Almost all counseling theories and procedures depend to some extent on imagery (Gordon, 1978). It is a universal and natural modality for helping people engender, promote, or face change.

The two most dominant types of images are visual and auditory, but there are as many images as there are sensations, (e.g., sounds, touches, smells, tastes, and sights). "Imagery is the language of the unconscious and, as such, it serves as a tool for bringing unconscious material to conscious awareness" (Weinhold, 1987, p. 9). Sometimes images spontaneously appear in the mind's eyes without active, personal prompting (i.e., free-association daydreams; Klinger, 1987). At other times, images are "directed"; that is, they are amplified or creatively enhanced like scenes in a Hollywood or Broadway production. Counseling usually focuses on the elimination of unwanted spontaneous images that cause pain or distress and the promotion of directed images that help individuals relax and enjoy the inner and outer worlds in which they live (Witmer & Young, 1985, 1987).

Premise of the Use of Imagery in Counseling

A number of reasons exist for using imagery in counseling. A major one is related to what Bernie Siegel (1986) called a "'weakness of the body: it cannot distinguish between a vivid mental experience and an actual physical experience" (p. 153). Therefore, in helping people help themselves, imagery may work as powerfully as actual behavior. This type of mental practice is seen most graphically among athletes and actors who imagine a winning performance and actually perform better as a result.

A second rationale for using imagery in counseling is that it is an available resource that is already employed in some form by clients. All people carry mental pictures around in their minds, and tapping into these images has advantages (Ashen, 1977). For example, visual imagery can be employed as a fast way of learning new material or remembering experiences. A "visual matrix is the building block of the most delicate and sophisticated information. Music notation is displayed visually; blueprints for buildings are visual guides; maps for air and space travel are visual; and computers have been designed to give visual readouts to maximize information provided to the user" (Lankton & Lankton, 1983, p. 327). Thus, through visualization goals can be seen and individuals can gain a clearer picture of themselves and "imagineer" solutions to their concerns.

Auditory images such as voices are extremely valuable also. Milton Erickson, one of the leading pioneers in the family counseling and therapy field, used to tell his clients and students: "My voice will go with you." This assurance made it easier for individuals to leave his sessions. It helped those he worked with actually remember what they had heard him say. It is very common for persons to remember auditory experiences associated with specific situations. Research on self-instruction indicates that those who give themselves auditory commands before performing an action do their tasks more efficiently and quickly than those who are not prepared in this manner.

Tactile (touch), olfactory (smell), and taste (gustatory) sensations are valuable assets in the art of counseling, too. Sometimes clients describe their feelings in regard to one of these senses, such as "I just want to get a handle on it;" or "something is rotten in this relationship" or "I experienced the bitter taste of defeat." These expressions cue the counselor into the client's preferred ways of experiencing the world (Bandler & Grinder, 1975). Such information can then be used to find therapeutic solutions or images to help these individuals.

A third reason for using imagery, especially guided imagery, is that it is valuable for counselors and clients in "developing cognitive flexibility. It teaches people how to use their imagination as a tool for stimulating creativity and for loosening the tight grip of the so-called normal waking state of consciousness" (Weinhold, 1987, p. 9). Thus, former excuses for not taking action lose some of their power, and clients are seen as more capable than before. They have hidden mental resources that can be tapped and used to promote positive change. Their chances for breaking dysfunctional patterns are greatly enhanced, and their versatility in helping themselves in similarly magnified (Fisher, 1989).

A fourth premise for employing imagery in counseling is that many client problems are connected directly to their images of self and others. One of the most graphic examples of this phenomenon is eating disorders (Justice, 1994). Persons with disorders in eating almost inevitably have a distorted image of their body. However, concerns linked to images that individuals carry with them range from low self-concept and social ineptness to destructive game playing (Berne, 1964). Counselors who are "image conscious" and work with their clients from this perspective are much more likely to be effective than those who are not focused this way.

The final rationale for using imagery in counseling is that it promotes a holistic approach to working with individuals. Through imagery, many different aspects of one's personhood and environment can be examined and changed, if desired (Gawain, 1978). For instance, relationships, health habits, and talents may be assessed and modified appropriately by experiencing them in imagery form and then in real-life situations. The importance of imagery in counseling is well represented in the systematic and comprehensive perspective of Arnold Lazarus' multimodal therapy. In this approach, clients are assessed in regard to BASIC ID, an acronym in which each letter represents an area in life—behavior, affect, sensation, imagery, cognition, interpersonal relationships, and drugs or biology (Lazarus, 1989). By working with people from this broad base, counselors are better able to identify difficulties that can be corrected and help their clients become more integrated.

Practice of the Use of Imagery in Counseling

Imagery is used in many different ways in counseling. Sigmund Freud was among the first in the modern treatment of mental disorders to be concerned with imagery and its meaning, especially in dreams. It was Freud who emphasized the manifest (obvious) and latent (hidden) meanings of dreams and described dreams as the "royal road to the unconscious" (Freud, 1957). It was also Freud who insisted his patients lie on a couch when trying to access their images, a position that modern research supports as enhancing the quantity and quality of images produced, possibly due to its association with relaxation, sleep, and dreams and daydreams (Sheikh, Sheikh, & Moleski, 1985).

Mandala

Carl Jung expressed a great interest in symbols and images also, whether inside or outside dreams. He was particularly interested in images with universal qualities he called "archetypes" (e.g., the earth mother, the wise old man, the hero, rebirth). It was Jung's idea that certain images unite people with one another and with themselves. For instance, the mandala is a universal sign of wholeness and completeness that is embraced worldwide and that Jung thought was used in various forms as clients become healthier (Jung, 1968).

Outside of depth therapy, as espoused by these clinicians, imagery is embraced and used extensively by other counseling traditions, especially those based in humanistic and cognitive-behavioral theories. The most absurd way imagery is employed is in the humanistic, existential family therapy approach of Carl Whitaker. In his work Whitaker was known to fall asleep (leaving his co-therapist in charge), have a dream, and then share the images and experience of the dream with the family with whom he was working (Napier & Whitaker, 1978). The art of this process is found both in the content and process of what Whitaker did. He gave the family a different picture of who they were and one with which they could not rationally argue. At the same time he "unbalanced" the family unit by doing something unexpected and enabled them to think and interact in a manner that was different from their routine.

In gestalt therapy, fantasy and imagery are used in some novel ways as well. Dreams are seen as the road to integration (Perls, 1969). As such, gestalt therapists encourage their clients to recreate and relive their dreams in the present. This procedure requires clients to become all parts of their dreams, and in doing so they must ask themselves such questions as: "What am I feeling?" "What do I want?" "What is my dream telling me?" (Rainwater, 1979). By enacting, questioning, and becoming aware of the many variables within dreams, individuals who work from a gestalt perspective become more integrated as persons, because they recognize and accept the polarities within themselves that they have previously projected onto others. Thus, they are enabled to complete unfinished business in their backgrounds such as unacknowledged grief, anger, or loss (Gladding, 1991).

A similar way imagery is used in a holistic manner is exemplified by the humanistic psychologist Abraham Maslow (1991), who employed imagery to help people gain a greater sense of gratitude toward others and the blessings of life. Maslow advocated imagining the death of someone for whom a person cares and thinking as vividly as possible about what would be truly lost and about what one would be most sorry. After imagining in this way, thinking would shift to how to conduct a complete good-bye and how to best preserve the memory of the person. Another technique he proposed was imagining oneself to be dying and in the process vividly seeing and saying good-bye to persons one loves best. These techniques, Maslow stated, could prevent repetitive rumination or a sense of incompleteness, such as he suffered in regard to the loss of Alfred Adler with whom he had a slight argument shortly before Adler's death. Imagery of this type can promote health, too.

Imagery is used in several ways in cognitive-behavioral approaches. For example, in rational-emotive hypnotherapy (REH), emphasis is placed on "here-and-now" imagery of recent events and "regressive imagery" of remote events (Golden, 1986). In both cases, the use of imagery is emphasized as a way of understanding maladaptive thoughts and behaviors and devising strategies for changing them. Even more popular is rational-emotive imagery (REI), in which clients keep complete conscious control of their facilities (Maultsby, 1977, 1984). In this process clients are helped to create mental frames of reference for behaving rationally. They "imagine themselves thinking, emotionally feeling, and physically behaving exactly the way they want to think, feel, and act in real life. When people combine REI with physical practice, they learn new emotional as well as physical habits in the shortest possible time" (Maultsby, 1984, p. 196).

In behaviorally based treatment, clients are sometimes asked to "symbolically recreate a problematic life situation [and then] imagine it actually happening to them. When clients have conjured up an image of a situation, they are then asked to verbalize any thoughts that come to mind" (Wilson, 1989, p. 259). This particular technique is especially helpful during assessment to uncover thoughts associated with events of which clients may not be initially aware.

Another use of imagery in counseling is found in systematic desensitization (Wolpe, 1958). In this therapeutic method, clients are requested to construct a hierarchy of different situations that trouble them, starting with those that are mildly disturbing and working up to those that cause major concern. They are then instructed to clearly picture each situation as they work up the hierarchy with the counselor, and to simultaneously relax. The idea behind this method is that being relaxed and anxious are incompatible responses (i.e., reciprocal inhibition) and that clients can be taught to become relaxed in the presence of a situation that previously was bothersome. In other words, one emotion (relaxation or pleasure) is used to counteract another (anxiety) with imagery playing a major role in the process (Mckay, Davis, & Fanning, 1981).

Imagery may also be used to cope with physical pain by incorporating the pain into one's life rather than fighting it (Kleinke, 1991). This type of incorporation can occur through dissociation (imaging the hurt outside of the body), fantasy (fantasizing that one is suffering for a good cause), imagining numbness, and focusing on sensations (studying what the feelings are like).

Two major outcomes of counseling occur in image form if treatment has been successful. The first is a change in self-imagery from a negative to a positive—clients see themselves as more capable. The second change relates to coping images, which change from pictures of being out of control and helpless to images of being able and capable even in severe situations (Lazarus, 1989). Thus, clients modify their outlook of themselves and function in a more healthy way when they see themselves differently.

Imagery in Counseling With Specific Populations

A number of client populations can benefit particularly from the employment of imagery. Imagery may help in working with individuals suffering from posttraumatic stress disorder (Grigsby, 1987), career indecision (Skovholt, Morgan, & Negron-Cunningham, 1989), bulimia (Gunnison & Renick, 1985), difficulty in couple communications (Hendrix, 1988), and parenting problems (Skovholt & Thoen, 1987). Imagery may be used also in preventative and educational activities for children, such as enhancing self-esteem and reducing anxiety (Myrick & Myrick, 1993; Witmer & Young, 1987).

Counselors also benefit from using imagery, as demonstrated in the Counselor of Tomorrow project sponsored by the Association for Counselor Education and Supervision (ACES), in which a film using numerous images has helped professionals envision possible futures. Counseling conventions in recent years, such as the American Counseling Association World Conference of 1997, have even focused on minding counselor images and promoting counseling through the use of positive images.

Some specific examples of the ways imagery can be used in working with clients at different ages and stages of life are examined in the following material.

Children

Preschool children often feel they have little or no control over their lives, and they are often right. To empower such children, directed imaging can be used. One way it can be employed is through imagining games, during which a teacher or parent reads a passage to children from a structured exercise book, such as Richard De Mille's (1967) *Put Your Mother on the Ceiling* or Joseph Shorr's (1977) *Go See the Movie in Your Head*. The children then visualize the scene. These types of imagery games at their best create divergent thinking, motivate children, challenge them, and bring fun into the lives of those involved. They foster freedom in a constructive way not otherwise possible. When done properly, they are always interspersed with reality-based exercises. Thus, they help promote within young children an appreciation for imagery and reality.

For elementary-school–age children with low self-esteem, imagery is valuable in enhancing their self-concept. One way this can be done is by having children look at themselves through the eyes of a special person (Childers, 1989). In this exercise, children pretend to be artists, and in this role they draw special people into their lives that love them. After the drawings are finished (just one drawing per child), the children pretend to be the special people whom they have drawn and to see themselves through loving eyes. Then they reassociate back into their own bodies and bring back with them loveable feelings from the experience.

When using guided imagery with children in a school setting, Myrick and Myrick (1993, pp. 63–65) have suggested five guidelines to make the experience enjoyable and productive:

1. Create a scripted story. A script will help the counselor to select the right words for an activity as well as to concentrate on creating a proper mood.
2. Set the mood. Setting a mood consists of two parts. First is introducing the activity to students. Second is helping students find a comfortable and relaxed position for participating in the imagery exercise.
3. Speak softly and smoothly. By speaking in a relaxed and soothing way, students are able to concentrate on the imagery, not on the counselor.

4. Bring closure to the guided imagery experience. This can be accomplished in a number of ways, such as posing a final question or simply informing students that the imagery activity is about to come to a close.
5. Discuss the experience. If children are to benefit from an imagery activity they need to be able to share their experiences with others. A discussion of what occurred may be directed by the counselor asking specific questions, or it may take a more open-ended format. The important point is that children get to air their thoughts and feelings.

Overall, imagery is a powerful and potentially effective force in working with children. Most children do not have a hard time imagining, and by tapping into this creative force, counselors can use it to promote growth and health within members of this population.

Adolescents and Adults

Much of the inner lives of adolescents and adults involves imagery, too. For example, one summary of the literature reports that sexual fantasies are quite common in men and women from late adolescence through mid-life and are rivaled only by problem-solving daydreams (Pope, Singer, & Rosenberg, 1984). Sexual fantasies may be used therapeutically to enhance a couple's sex life and overall relationship in the treatment context devised by Masters and Johnson (1970) or in other forms of couple, or even individual, counseling. Likewise, problem-solving daydreams can be used to help adolescents and adults anticipate and productively respond ahead of time to developmental situations they expect to face.

With adolescents and adults, imagery exercises can be taught as a skill that can be used in the alleviation of depression (Schultz, 1984) and the modification of anger (Kaplan, 1994). In regard to depression, for example, people can be taught to image something that makes them angry and thereby gain control over the imaging process and the feelings associated with certain symbols. Similarly, they may learn "socially gratifying imagery" and positive imagery procedures and use these methods to temporarily or permanently combat depressive thoughts. The use of imagery as a visual art form, especially in combination with verbal directive techniques, powerfully produces "more extensive and long-lasting improvements" (Schultz, 1984, p. 143) than most other forms of treatment. It enhances "the effectiveness of verbal cognitions in altering unpleasant moods" (Kaplan, 1994, p. 139).

Imagery can be helpful in making transitions associated with immigration and living in a new culture, too. Toffoli and Allan (1992) found that guided imagery worked well with a group of adolescents enrolled in English as a second language; it provided these teens with an opportunity to finish some of the unfinished business they had before immigrating to Canada. In this experience, students not only had a chance to relax and tap into their thoughts and memories, but they also were given an "opportunity to draw, write, and talk about their former school experiences and to learn about those of their classmates" (Toffoli & Allan, 1992, p. 140). A secondary benefit of this 16-session activity was that those involved enjoyed it "even when painful or negative feelings" (Toffoli & Allan, 1992, p. 140) were tapped. Furthermore, language and writing skills improved during the process.

Overall, imagery sems to be highly correlated with the mental and physical health of adolescents and adults. "Imagery is receiving a tremendous resurgence of interest throughout the spectrum of the healing arts and is currently being researched in major medical centers and universities around the world in clinical situations ranging from the treatment of chronic pain to the management of patients with cancer" (Rossman, 1984, p. 232). The intensity of the public's interest in the positive and therapeutic use of imagery in health is reflected in the best selling status of Bernie Siegel's (1986) book *Love, Medicine & Miracles*.

Elderly Clients

Both free and guided imagery can be especially powerful tools in working with elderly persons. Guided imagery exercises can be used to help those who are aged take relaxed trips in time either to a place they long to go or back to a place they have enjoyed before (Fisher, 1989). These imaginary trips are followed with a process session; those who have traveled come back to the counselor or a group setting and share their experiences in verbal or nonverbal forms, such as talking or drawing.

Sometimes free imagery is used, too, in largely unstructured situations in which music may be played in the background and participants are asked to "dance in their minds" to the sound. After the experience ends, those that are mobile may actually act out what they envisioned, and the less physically agile move their limbs to the beat of the music while remaining seated.

Focused visual imagery can also improve the functioning of elderly clients who have mild cognitive impairments. For instance, Abraham, Neundorfer, and Terris (1993) found that 46 nursing home residents (aged 71–97 years) made a significant improvement in their cognitive abilities over a 24-week period when imagery experiences were used to help them. These researchers structured their focused visual imagery group around six themes—relaxation, protection (from anxiety and stresses that come with change), self-esteem, control (i.e., working out conflicts in symbolic form), energy (including strategies for increasing energy), and transition (e.g., dealing with aging, loss, and relocation).

Groups

Imagery works well in a number of different kinds of groups and during distinct group stages. Different imagery exercises have been suggested to enhance group process in the initial screening and follow-up processes and in the five-stage group model suggested by Tuckman and Jensen (1977) of forming, storming, norming, performing, and adjourning. In the forming stage, which is characterized by testing and dependency, group members may be given imagery tasks that are safe and connecting. Thus, they might describe themselves in the lines of a song or poem or by presenting their life to the group in historical photographs or a life road map. Likewise, in the adjourning stage, during which the focus is on closure and anticipation, group members may give each other good-bye gifts in the form of future visions for themselves and others.

Jacobs (1992) has suggested a number of projective fantasies in group settings that he has found productive. Among his favorites is one he calls "Common Object." In this fantasy members of the group are encouraged to imagine themselves as a common object, such as a piece of luggage. They are then asked to describe what their lives would be like and how they would feel if they were indeed that object. For example, as a piece of luggage a group member might have an active life of travel and feel both exhilarated and exhausted. When talking about the common object, members are encouraged to stay in the present tense. They actually end up talking about themselves in many ways and seeing their lives differently as a result of projection and fantasy.

Families

Family and couples work is wide open for the use of imagery, and it is often employed in this type of counseling. For example, in couple work imago (image) therapy is a method of using vision and enactment to help married people overcome obstacles to their relationship that are based on previous life experiences and expectations (Hendrix, 1988). This eclectic approach combines elements of psychoanalysis, transactional analysis, gestalt, cognitive therapy, and systems theory. It assists couples in seeing what they are doing and what they can do better. They are instructed to practice creating the new relationship they have envisioned.

Basically imagery can encourage the following types of activities in couples work: (a) the collection of initial information, (b) decision making, (c) clarification of power and intimacy issues, and (d) preparation for future events (Hoffman, 1983). Imagery enlivens counseling sessions and helps make interpersonal relationships more interesting and memorable.

In working with families as a whole, guided imagery can increase awareness and the process of differentiation from one's family of origin (Pare, Shannon, & Dustin, 1996). When guided imagery is combined with genogram work, individuals are able to access their conscious and unconscious thoughts regarding their families and themselves.

Clients Needing Career Counseling and Life Planning

The use of imagery, especially guided imagery and daydreams, has become more prevalent in career counseling and life planning since the 1960s (Skovholt et al., 1989). Some career-counseling material, such as Holland's (1985) Self-Directed Search, build an examination of occupational daydreams into the assessment process. It is the contention of certain theorists, backed up by theoretical, anecdotal, and empirical data, that although daydreams and fantasies do not guarantee a dream will come true, they are instrumental in helping individuals "contemplate new possibilities, try out new options, and make more informed life-planning decisions" (Skovholt et al., 1989, p. 288).

When guided imagery is used in career counseling and life planning it is a "structured activity in which the counselor provides guidelines to spur the imaginations of their clients" (Heppner, O'Brien, Hinkelman, & Humphrey, 1994, p. 79). Specific methods of how this process is carried out vary but when possible a concrete representation of fantasies, such as a projected life map, should be created. The use of guided imagery is somewhat suspect because of a lack of strong empirical data on its overall effects. Nevertheless, the benefits of guided imagery in career counseling include:

- flexibility,
- emphasis on the promotion of creativity and divergent thinking and the generation of more career options,
- safety and nonthreatening and inexpensive features,
- enjoyability and emphasis on considering nonrational aspects in decision making (Skovholt et al., 1989).

Imagery in Counseling With Other Creative Arts

Because imagery is often a picture in the mind of an event or a way of being, it helps to make the image more concrete. This way of representing imagery is best found in written, movement, musical, photographic, and artistic expression.

Written Expression of Imagery

One way to write about imagery is simply to keep a daily journal or log where dreams, daydreams, and guided fantasies are recorded. Along with recording these events it is important to note what reactions occurred in regard to the imagery. For example, there are some fantasies individuals are reluctant to give up and certain nightmares that make individuals sigh in relief when they awake.

In career counseling, written exercises can be used to help clients obtain a clearer picture of who they are and what they want to do vocationally. "Guided imagery can assist clients identify the kind of work and lifestyle they want" (Kanchier, 1997, p. 14), especially if it is combined with other career-counseling procedures. For example, in the Career Imagery Card Sort, clients are asked to sort 150 cards with career titles into five piles (Skovholt, 1981). During sorting, clients are asked to reflect on how the occupation matches up with their daydreams. Afterwards, clients pick an occupation of high interest to them based on their daydreams and are taken on a guided fantasy of a day in that specific occupation. After the exercise is processed, clients continue to keep track of their daydreams about careers and discuss these unsolicited fantasies with the counselor in future meetings.

Imagery and Movement

Imagery and movement can be combined in many creative ways. One of the most dynamic is choreography, in which images of a family or situation (past, present, or future) are enacted in a repetitive way. Family choreography (Papp, 1976) is an outgrowth of family sculpting; people in a family are arranged in "various physical positions in space that represent their relationships to each other at a particular moment in time" (Goldenberg & Goldenberg, 1996, p. 289).

Family sculpting can be compared to an image one would get from a photograph, whereas family choreography is like a videotape. Both processes are nonverbal, so participants get to experience and see themselves rather than talk about their situations. Because of this nonverbal quality a family and counselor are able to grasp members' experiences, boundaries, and alliances more easily and immediately.

Imagery and Music

Visualization is sometimes promoted by the use of background music. Eastern European trainers of athletes have used the "largo movements of baroque instrumental music, with their strong, regular bass-line rhythms of about sixty beats per minute" to help athletes envision winning performance (Siegel, 1986, p. 153). Any type of music will actually promote mental imagery as long as the listener finds it relaxing.

A combination of music therapy and guided imagery is reported to have helped a small group of women in exploring and healing personal inner wounds (Ventre, 1994). Likewise, guided imagery and music has worked in helping elderly clients with physical disabilities address a broad range of past, current, and impending future issues including bereavement, sexuality, and the aging process. Carefully selected taped classical music that ranged in length from 4 to 12 minutes was a main stimulus for creating images (Short, 1992). The key to working with clients in this way is the care shown in selecting and using the right combination of music and emphasis on symbolic images to achieve a desired effect.

Imagery and Pictures

The importance of concrete imagery to reinforce or supplement abstract imagery has received a good deal of attention. Popular songs such as a 1970s songs by Jim Croce, "Photographs and Memories," and Ringo Starr's "Photographs" underscore the perception of how photography can aid in the development of pictures in the mind. Indeed, photographs and drawings have generally been found to promote learning in children and adults in many situations (Alesandrini, 1985). The ACES Counselor of Tomorrow project mentioned previously uses photographs extensively in educating counselors about the future of the profession.

Photographs are helpful as supplemental material, too, especially to show children an example of what they can image. Instructing children and adults on how to form internal mental pictures of specifics is equally effective. A number of studies show that analogical (i.e., similar) and abstract (new and different) imagery can aid in learning and that the use of these verbal or written types of imagery should be more widely used.

In learning information and performing a new task, an analogical image would be most appropriate, but in representing something entirely new an abstract image would work well. An example of how such imagery can be used in counseling is found in the "mailbox" exercise I have devised. In this exercise, a client is instructed to photograph a mailbox from as many angles as possible and then bring the photographs to the next session mounted on poster board. When the assignment is completed the counselor and client discuss the task and examine the pictures. In this process the client usually discovers that just as a mailbox can be looked at from many angles so can other situations. A client is then freed by this analogy exercise to devise novel images for his or her own life. Basically, concrete abstract images that are related to earlier learning or completely novel can help clients become more mentally healthy by giving them a vision of situations and helping them master their environments.

Imagery and Drawing

Artistic expression of imagery can be displayed many ways. One is through having individuals draw in the air what they see in their minds. This technique, which may seem silly at first, helps clients put body movement to an image and reinforces their mental picture of it through simple motor movements.

Another way to express imagery is to have people draw out their visions through "lines of feelings" (a technique discussed in the chapter on the visual arts). The idea in this exercise is that by setting down their images concretely, clients are better able to conceptualize what they are feeling and can therefore take more positive steps to work on these matters. Another expression of imagery, especially for those who are artistically inclined, is to draw images in a freestyle way and then process the experience and drawing(s) with the counselor. A good example of clients doing self-portraits in this way is found in the work of Newton (1976), who worked with college students to have them depict themselves in various moods over time. From the sketches, clients were able to talk about other important areas of their lives.

Summary

Imagery is a popular concept in counseling and is becoming more used and appreciated as a powerful and effective helping tool. Just as an artist knows when and how to time his or her expressions to make the biggest impact, those who effectively use imagery in counseling are aware of what to do and when. They artistically apply their skills in a deft and dramatic fashion as a preventive and therapeutic force.

As this chapter has emphasized, almost all counseling theories make use of imagery. It is an extremely versatile art form. Furthermore, most of the other creative arts can be combined with imagery to make a more powerful impact on clients and assist them in more quickly resolving

---

$\equiv\equiv$ **Exercises** $\equiv\equiv$

1. Imagine that someone has asked you to demonstrate the most salient material you remember from reading this chapter. How would you do it? How could imagery help you complete this task even better?

2. Examine recent issues of the *Journal of Mental Imagery* and counseling periodicals such as the *Journal of Counseling and Development* and the *Journal of Counseling Psychology*. In what ways is imagery being used in helping? Are there predominant patterns for using imagery? Are there special populations for whom imagery is particularly effective according to the research?

3. What career images and senses are strongest for you when you reflect on yourself currently? What images about work did you have growing up? Are there wide differences between them and the realities of what work is actually like? Discuss this experience with a colleague.

---

their concerns. For populations ranging from children to those of advanced age, imagery is an art that counselors can draw on to help clients understand emotional situations and provide appropriate services to their clients.

References

Abraham, I. L., Neundorfer, M. M., & Terris, E. A. (1993). Effects of focused visual imagery on cognition and depression among nursing home residents. *Journal of Mental Imagery, 17,* 61–76.

Achterberg, J., & Lawlis, G. F. (1984). *Imagery and disease*. Champaign, IL: Institute for Personality and Ability Testing.

Alesandrini, K. L. (1985). Imagery research with adults: Implications for education. In A. S. Sheikh & K. S. Sheikh (Eds.), *Imagery in education* (pp. 199–221). Farmingdale, NY: Baywood.

Ashen, A. (1977). *Psycheye: Self-analytic consciousness*. New York: Brandon House.

Bandler, R., & Grinder, J. (1975). *The structure of magic*. Palo Alto, CA: Science and Behavior.

Berne, E. (1964). *Games people play*. New York: Grove.

Childers, J. H., Jr. (1989). Looking at yourself through loving eyes. *Elementary School Guidance & Counseling, 23,* 204–209.

De Mille, R. (1967). *Put your mother on the ceiling*. New York: Penguin.

Fisher, P. P. (1989). *Creative movement for older adults*. New York: Human Sciences.

Freud, S. (1957). The interpretation of dreams. In J. Strachy (Ed.), *The standard edition of the complete psychological works of Sigmund Freud* (Vol. 12). London: Hogarth.

Gawain, S. (1978). *Creative visualization.* San Rafael, CA: New World Library.

Gladding, S. T. (1991). *An image of Timothy.* Unpublished manuscript.

Golden, W. L. (1986). Rational-emotive hypnotherapy: Principles and techniques. In A. Ellis & R. Grieger (Eds.), *Handbook of rational-emotive therapy* (Vol 2, pp. 281–291). New York: Springer.

Goldenberg, I., & Goldenberg, H. (1996). *Family therapy* (4th ed.). Pacific Grove, CA: Brooks/Cole.

Gordon, D. (1978). *Therapeutic metaphors.* Cupertino, CA: META.

Grigsby, J. P. (1987). The use of imagery in the treatment of posttraumatic stress disorder. *Journal of Nervous and Mental Disease, 175,* 55–59.

Gunnison, H., & Renick, T. F. (1985). Using fantasy-imagery and relaxation techniques. *Journal of Counseling and Development, 64,* 79–80.

Hendrix, H. (1988). *Getting the love you want.* New York: Holt.

Heppner, M. J., O'Brien, K. M., Hinkelman, J. M., & Humphrey, C. A. (1994). Shifting the paradigm: The use of creativity in career counseling. *Journal of Career Development, 21,* 77–86.

Hoffman, L. W. (1983). Imagery and metaphors in couple therapy. *Family Therapy, 10,* 141–156.

Holland, J. L. (1985). *The Self-Directed Search: A guide to educational and vocational planning.* Odessa, FL: Psychological Assessment Resources.

Jacobs, E. (1992). *Creative counseling techniques: An illustrated guide.* Odessa, FL: Psychological Assessment Resources.

Jung, C. J. (1956). The structure of the unconscious. In C. J. Jung (Ed.), *Two essays on analytical psychology.* New York: Meridian.

Jung, C. J. (1968). *The structure and dynamics of the psyche.* New York: Pantheon.

Justice, R. W. (1994). Music therapy interventions for people with eating disoders in an inpatient setting. *Music Therapy, 12,* 104–110.

Kanchier, C. (1997, February). Using intuition in career decision making. *Counseling Today,* pp. 14, 16.

Kaplan, F. F. (1994). The imagery and expression of anger: An initial study. *Art Therapy, 11,* 139–143.

Kleinke, C. L. (1991). *Coping with life challenges.* Pacific Grove, CA: Brooks/Cole.

Klinger, E. (1987). The power of daydreams. *Psychology Today, 21,* 36–39, 42–44.

Lankton, S. R., & Lankton, C. H. (1983). *The answer within: A clinical framework of Ericksonian hypnotherapy.* New York: Brunner/Mazel.

Lazarus, A. A. (1977). *In the mind's eye.* New York: Rawson.

Lazarus, A. A. (1989). Multimodal therapy. In R. J. Corsini & D. Wedding (Eds.), *Current psychotherapy* (4th ed. pp. 503–544). Itasca, IL: Peacock.

Luria, A. (1968). *The mind of mnemonist.* New York: Basic Books.

Manz, C. C. (1992). *Mastering self-leadership: Empowering yourself for personal excellence.* Englewood Cliffs, NJ: Prentice-Hall.

Maslow, A. H. (1991). Experiential exercises for gratitude. *Journal of Humanistic Education and Development, 29,* 121–122.

Masters, W. H., & Johnson, V. E. (1970). *Human sexual inadequacy.* Boston: Little, Brown.

Maultsby, M. C., Jr. (1977). Rational-emotive imagery. In A. Ellis & R. Grieger (Eds.), *Handbook of rational-emotive therapy* (pp. 225–230). New York: Springer.

Maultsby, M. C., Jr. (1984). *Rational behavior therapy.* Englewood Cliffs, NJ: Prentice-Hall.

Mckay, M., Davis, M., & Fanning, P. (1981). *Thoughts and feelings: The art of cognitive stress intervention.* Richmond, CA: New Harbinger.

Mills, J. C., & Crowley, R. J. (1986). *Therapeutic metaphors for children and the child within.* New York: Brunner/Mazel.

Myrick, R. D., & Myrick, L. S. (1993). Guided imagery: From mystical to practical. *Elementary School Guidance & Counseling, 28,* 62–70.

Napier, A. Y., & Whitaker, C. A. (1978). *The family crucible.* New York: Bantam.

Neck, C. P., Stewart, G. L., & Manz, C. C. (1995). Thought self-leadership as a framework for enhancing the performance of performance appraisers. *Journal of Applied Behavioral Science, 31,* 278–302.

Newton, F. B. (1976). How may I understand you? Let me count the ways. *Personnel and Guidance Journal, 54*, 257–260.

O'Neill, B. (1997, May). *The unconstraining voice: The poetics of well being.* Keynote address at the annual conference of the National Association for Poetry Therapy. Cleveland, OH.

Papp, P. (1976). Family choreography. In P. J. Guerin, Jr. (Ed.), *Family therapy: Theory and practice.* New York: Gardner.

Pare, T. J., Shannon, B., & Dustin, T. (1996). The use of guided imagery in family of origin group therapy. *Canadian Journal of Counselling, 30*, 42–54.

Perls, F. (1969). *Gestalt therapy verbatim.* New York: Bantam.

Pope, K. S., Singer, J. L., & Rosenberg, L. C. (1984). Sex, fantasy and imagination: Scientific research and clinical applications. In A. A. Sheikh (Ed.), *Imagination and healing* (pp. 197–210). Farmingdale, NY: Baywood.

Rainwater, J. (1979). *You're in charge! A guide to becoming your own therapist.* Los Angeles: Guild of Tutors.

Richardson, A. (1969). *Mental imagery.* London: Routledge & Kegan Paul.

Rossman, M. L. (1984). Imagine health! Imagery in medical self-care. In A. A. Sheikh (Ed.), *Imagination and healing* (pp. 231–258). Farmingdale, NY: Baywood.

Russell-Chapin, L. A., & Stoner, C. R. (1995). Mental health counselors as consultants for diversity training. *Journal of Mental Health Counseling, 17*, 146–156.

Schultz, K. D. (1984). The use of imagery in alleviating depression. In A. A. Sheikh (Ed.), *Imagination and healing* (pp. 129–158). Farmingdale, NY: Baywood.

Sheikh, A. A., Sheikh, K. S., & Moleski, L. M. (1985). The enhancement of imaging ability. In A. A. Sheikh & K. S. Sheikh (Eds.), *Imagery in education* (pp. 223–239). Farmingdale, NY: Baywood.

Shorr, J. E. (1977). *Go see the movie in your head.* New York: Popular Library.

Short, A. E. (1992). Music and imagery with physically disabled elderly residents: A GIM adaptation. *Music Therapy, 11*, 65–98.

Siegel, B. S. (1986). *Love, medicine & miracles.* New York: Harper & Row.

Skovholt, T. M. (1981). *Career Imagery Card Sort.* Minneapolis: University of Minnesota.

Skovholt, T. M., Morgan, J. I., & Negron-Cunningham, H. (1989). Mental imagery in career counseling and life planning: A review of research and intervention methods. *Journal of Counseling and Development, 67*, 287–292.

Skovholt, T. M., & Thoen, G. A. (1987). Mental imagery in parenthood decision making. *Journal of Counseling and Development, 65*, 315–316.

Toffoli, G., & Allan, J. (1992). Group guidance for English as a second language students. *The School Counselor, 40*, 136–145.

Tuckman, B. W., & Jensen, M. A. C. (1977). Stages of small-group development revisited. *Group and Organizational Studies, 2*, 419–427.

Ventre, M. (1994). Guided imagery and music in process: The interweaving of the achetype of the mother, mandala, and music. *Music Therapy, 12*, 19–38.

Weinhold, B. K. (1987). Altered states of consciousness: An explorer's guide to inner space. *Counseling and Human Development, 20*, 1–12.

Wilson, G. T. (1989). Behavior therapy. In R. J. Corsini & D. Wedding (Eds.), *Current psychotherapies* (4th ed., pp. 241–282). Itasca, IL: Peacock.

Witmer, J. M. (1985). *Pathways to personal growth.* Muncie, IN: Accelerated Development.

Witmer, J. M., & Young, M. E. (1985). The silent partner: Uses of imagery in counseling. *Journal of Counseling and Development, 64*, 187–190.

Witmer, J. M., & Young, M. E. (1987). Imagery in counseling. *Elementary School Guidance & Counseling, 22*, 5–16.

Wolpe, J. (1958). *Psychotherapy by reciprocal inhibition.* Stanford, CA: Stanford University Press.

5

Visual Arts and Counseling

When all my clients have left the office
   I quietly turn off the overhead lights
   and watch a fading afternoon sun
      patiently spreading gold-tinged hues
     slowly across my cluttered desk
     and onto a wooden floor canvas.
That moment fills me with a sense of awe
   for quiet light and moving life.
Walking in shadows I picture past sessions
   and wonder if lives I so fleetingly touched
     will dare envision a personal art
      brushed in the beauty and grace of time.

(Gladding, 1975, p. 230)

T HE VISUAL ARTS ARE DEFINED as those processes within the realm of art that focus on visually representing reality. As such the visual arts including painting, drawing, photography, and sculpture. Knowledge of human history is often "a result of the work of the artist or artisans of particular times and cultures," (Nadeau, 1984, p. 62) and it is through works of art that the health of a society is gauged. It is through artistic experiences, too, that individuals experience more unified and meaningful lives, whether they are the creators or the observers (Maslow, 1991).

From prehistoric times, humans everywhere have tended to portray their world through visual means. Art exists "in every section of the world with a diversity that corresponds to the varieties of artistic experience" (McNiff, 1997, p. 38). Cave drawings, ancient Egyptian

Hieroglyphics

hieroglyphics, and impressionist paintings are but three examples out of dozens of the way the visual arts bring form to feeling and concreteness to perception. Hieroglyphics, in particular, is an excellent representation of how pictures of objects, such as animals, trees, and birds, were first visualized as words and writing.

"To Plato, the artist was one of those endowed by the gods with a 'divine madness'" (Esman, 1988, p. 13). Thus, the artist was both privileged and plagued. The first modern attempt to confirm or discredit the "divine madness" idea was done by the German psychiatrist and art historian Hans Prinzhorn (1922/1972) who attempted to scientifically study psychic forms of expression in art at the turn of the 20th century. In Prinzhorn's research, approximately 5,000 pieces of art were collected from psychiatric patients all over Europe. He suggested that "expression is a basic psychic need for all people" (McNiff, 1997, p. 39). However, because his collection of art came from the mentally disturbed, a link between artistic expression and mental instability was created or reinforced in the minds of many.

Much of Prinzhorn's influence was countered, however, by another of the early leading thinkers in the mental health field, William James, who was an artist before becoming a psychologist (Leary, 1992). James's artistic sensibility and experience "were critically important in the development of his psychological and philosophical thought" (Leary, 1992, p. 152). His background influenced the way he viewed human nature, which is one reason his view of human understanding has attracted the attention of many artists, humanists, scientists, and psychologists. James viewed art as a creative and productive human experience.

Regardless of the ideas surrounding them, the visual arts have been instrumental in fostering the growth of culture and the mental health of people. The visual arts have a lasting effect that often inspires and touches on universal themes, which arise from interpersonal encounters and individual struggles. Grace, beauty, harmony, balance, and rhythm are but a few of the underlying qualities expressed in visual art (May, 1953). Though it may be true that "the way we perceive visually is directly related to how we think and feel" (Rhyne, 1973, p. 242), it is likewise true that visual stimuli within art can influence our thoughts and emotions.

"Human life can. . . be likened to the work of any artist, who, facing empty canvas or shapeless clay, transmutes it into pleasing forms. At first, the picture or statue exists only as the artist's imaginative experience. When. . . done, [the] private image is transformed into a public perception" (Jourard, 1971, p. 92). It is both the perception and the product of visual art and human life with which this chapter deals.

Premise of the Use of Visual Arts in Counseling

The idea of using the visual arts in counseling and therapeutic settings is mainly the result of the pioneering work and writings of Margaret Naumburg, Edith Kramer, and Judith Rubin (Makin, 1994). Naumburg (1966), an educator, saw art as an essential component of education while simultaneously viewing it as a means of diagnosis and therapy. For Naumburg, art was symbolic of the person behind the work (Rubin, 1980). Her ideas were influenced by psychoanalytic theory. Naumburg's traditional psychoanalytic view stressed that "(1) art is yet another window to the unconscious, (2) insight is central to the process, and (3) treatment depends on obtaining the client's own interpretations of his or her own symbolic art images. Naumburg is responsible for the *therapy* in art therapy" (Orton, 1997, p. 256).

For Kramer (1971), art was more a means of controlling, managing, and integrating destructive impulses and conflictual feelings, especially in children. Kramer saw art as therapeutic in and of itself. In her view "the artistic process and products are ways to release conflict, reexperience it, rechannel it through sublimation, and resolve it" (Orton, 1997, p. 256).

On the other hand, Rubin has combined qualities of both her predecessors. She sees herself as an educator, and as such has emphasized creative thinking and flexibility as essential aspects of mental health. She has stressed growth in clients through artistic means. (Makin, 1994).

Regardless of the particular theoretical viewpoint a professional takes, the visual arts offer many mental health benefits for their users (Nadeau, 1984). First, they tap the unconscious and help individuals express their covert conflicts. Visual art is closer to the unconscious because visual perceptions are more archaic than cognitive or verbal expression (Freud, 1923). It is through such means that people realize and own the multitude of emotions that live within them. Art as a therapy "is an integrative approach utilizing cognitive, motor, and sensory experiences" (Tibbetts & Stone, 1990, p. 139).

A second advantage of the visual arts is that they symbolize feelings in a unique, tangible, and powerful way (Nichols & Schwartz, 1995). The visual arts, unlike talk therapies, assist people in picturing themselves or their situations in a concrete manner. For instance, abused children "typically portray the weather as disproportionate and/or excessive in size, and as falling on contents of the drawing" (Manning, 1987, p. 15). "Expressing one's thoughts through art is one way to externalize a distressing event and to prepare for healing and recovery" (Howe, Burgess, & McCormack, 1987, p. 35). Clients in such cases are more likely to be in positions to make changes depending on what they see. By employing the visual arts in counseling, a visible trail is created.

A third reason for using the visual arts in counseling is that they inspire and help people become more connected with the transcendent and growth sides of their personalities (Mills & Crowley, 1986). Clients who can envision through paintings, drawings, and sculptures what they have accomplished over a period of time or what they could be are more likely than not to stay with the process of change until they are satisfied with their progress. Thus, through the use of the visual arts hope is created, as is a chance for new growth that might not be achieved through traditional verbal counseling. The visual arts in counseling help "increase self-esteem by facilitating self-awareness" (Tibbetts & Stone, 1990, p. 140).

A fourth premise behind using the visual arts in counseling is that many art tasks, especially those with children, are "usually perceived as nonthreatening and self-interpreted" (Riley, 1987, p. 21). Yet they engage clients from the very first session and help them identify goals for counseling. The arts are helpful also in revealing client problems that are sometimes difficult to talk about, such as family violence and abuse (Brooke, 1995; Trowbridge, 1995).

A final reason for using visual arts in counseling is that they can easily be combined with other creative arts such as movement, creative writing, and imagery (McNiff, 1997; Steinhardt, 1985). The flexibility of this medium is outstanding, and the results can be kept mentally or physically as reminders of time and circumstance. Indeed, movements, visuals, and sounds can become elements of an art piece no longer static but living (Moon, 1997).

Practice of the Use of Visual Arts in Counseling

Visual arts are used in counseling throughout the life span. Despite the fact that many people claim that they cannot draw, the visual arts appeal to numerous clients. Many standard psychological projective tests, such as the Draw-A-Person test (Machover, 1949) and the House-Tree-Person test (Buck, 1948), make use of clients' artistic abilities to express how they perceive and feel about the world. In addition, other projective tests, such as the Rorschach and the Holtzman ink blots, make use of artistic forms.

In setting up situations for using the visual arts in counseling, the best quality art materials should be purchased so that clients who might otherwise be intimidated by the use of these media will become more relaxed and creative (Makin, 1994; Nadeau, 1984). Other qualities important to visual art counseling sessions are adequate space, quiet, freedom of movement, encouragement, and time. It is essential for those who assist in visual art therapy to be patient, too. Just as great art takes time, so does psychosocial change. It may take several sessions before clients actually begin to enjoy and benefit from visual art experiences. Even more delayed at times is the ability of clients to integrate art into their lives in a productive way through owning what it symbolizes as a part of themselves.

Most counselors who use visual art in their work have received special training. Those who earn a master's degree with a concentration in art therapy from a program approved by the American Art Therapy Association are eligible to become art therapists registered (ATRs) provided they accumulate a 1,000 hours of paid art therapy experience (Wadeson, 1987b). As professionals, art therapists work to set up conditions in which clients can explore underlying emotional issues and perceptions by using a rich source of artistic materials and methods (Kaiser, 1996). Other professionals who do not want this credential compensate for the lack of overall training in using the visual arts by concentrating their practice on specific areas in which they are competent to work. Almost all clinicians who use the arts make use of perceptual strategies employed by the client artist including these:

- negative spaces,
- relationships and proportions,
- lights and shadows,
- edges, and
- the gestalt or total product (McClure, Merrill, & Russo, 1994).

Visual arts practitioners participate in many activities, and the following types are merely general examples.

Published Pictures

One way of introducing and using the visual arts in counseling is through making the most of already existing artwork. This approach arouses minimal anxiety, and it encompasses a variety of artwork that looks like clients expect artwork to look. In addition, "there is an inexhaustible storehouse and variety of such images in this world: published pictures that appear in magazines, newspapers and other periodicals, in books, on greeting cards and postcards, and as posters and art prints" (Comfort, 1985, p. 245). Such "found" images provide an excellent basis for familiarizing clients with ways of understanding and communicating "how it feels to be a certain unique human being who holds an idiosyncratic worldview" (Comfort, 1985, pp. 245–246).

Body Outline

Body Outline Drawings

Another universal way visual arts can be introduced in counseling is through body outline drawings. These drawings are made when a person lays spread out and his or her body is traced on paper. After the drawings are completed, individuals can decorate them in any way they wish, from a literal to a figurative form (Steinhardt, 1985). Sometimes in such an endeavor, persons, especially children, reveal indirectly troublesome aspects of their lives that can later be discussed.

Serial Drawing

The idea behind the use of serial drawing is that through daily unstructured drawings clients will symbolically represent themselves and their problems to counselors. By working in a positive transference manner that involves a talk component, a positive self-concept emerges in these individuals, and behavior change occurs (Allan, 1978). This approach is Jungian and requires patience and an intuitive timing as to what to say or do and when.

Paint and Clay

Being able to use a variety of paints and clay is essential to the process of employing the visual arts in counseling. Colors make pictures come alive and the type of materials selected for artworks is crucial because of its impact or lack thereof on the creator of the work and others. An important element in using the visual arts is getting a feel for the materials and what they can do. Working in clay promotes this and in addition fosters cooperation between clients. Clay can also provide a safe medium with which individuals can regress or gain insight by manipulating the malleable material (Makin, 1994).

Photography

"Photographs are footprints of our minds, mirrors of our lives, reflections from our hearts, frozen memories we can hold in silent stillness in our hands—forever, if we wish. They document not only where we may have been but also point the way to where we might perhaps be going, whether we know it yet or not" (Weiser, 1993, p. 1). According to Weiser, photography, or as she calls it "phototherapy," is a way to capture and express feelings and ideas in a visual-symbolic form across the life span. It has many similarities to art therapy and works "particularly well for people who find other visual arts too demanding or too risky to try" (Weiser, 1993, p. 13).

The basic techniques of using photography in counseling are those related to relationships:

1. photos taken of the client
2. photos taken by the client
3. photos of the client by the client (self-portraits)
4. biographical pictures, which may or may not include the client, of groups of friends and family

In all procedures involved in using photography in counseling, there is also a project process, that is, an emotional response (Weiser, 1993).

Visual Arts in Counseling With Specific Populations

Specific ways that the visual arts can be used in counseling with certain populations are highlighted here. The visual arts, like other of the arts, cover the life span.

Children

"There is a way that children commonly share their stories with an adult, one that is both spontaneous and laden with content. They draw" (Riley, 1997, p. 2). "The art work of children, when it is an expression of their simple and honest feelings, is almost always beautiful" (May, 1953, p. 190). However, children are many times the victims of abuse or mistreatment. In these situations, their art may reflect more pain than pleasure. Regardless, children's art "is a safe way to 'tell' what has been forbidden to be talked about, a language of its own" (Riley, 1997, p. 2). Through art, children forge a vital link between themselves and helpers, such as counselors, and from such a relationship they regain their health and build constructive lives.

There are several ways to use visual arts to gather information from children about their mental health. One is through standardized psychological instruments (i.e., the Draw-A-Person and House-Tree-Person), but counselors are prone to use more informal approaches in most situations. For instance, children may be asked to draw a circle and then to color different parts of the circle to represent various feelings, such as "smart," "dumb," "good," or "bad" (Hughes, 1988). Drawing in such a manner helps children become more aware of how they see themselves and opens up concrete avenues for them to use in talking about their feelings.

A second type of preventive approach that can be used by most counselors is to have children display feelings in sculpture, clay, or other art projects (Gerler, 1982). In this exercise counselors team up with art teachers. The results may vary from ripped up paper spread across the floor to represent anger to a drawing of a sad face with paper clip tears to symbolize sadness, to decorated bags with string, ribbons, candy, and cotton balls pasted on to show happiness.

A third technique, mentioned previously, that is based on Jungian theory (and usually carried out by an art therapist) is "serial drawing. . . a therapeutic approach whereby the counselor meets on a regular basis with the child and simply asks the child to 'draw-a-picture' " (Allan, 1988, p. 20). In this process, which takes place over an extended period of time (at least 10 sessions), a therapeutic alliance and rapport are developed between the counselor and the child, and a sanctuary where growth, development, and healing can occur are created as well (Jung,

1965, 1966). One variation of this approach is the "rose bush" (Allan & Crandall, 1986). In this exercise, the child is simply asked to draw a rose bush every time he or she meets with the counselor. The rosebush is symbolic of the child's mental health, and changes in the drawings indicate positive movement or distress within the child.

A final procedure that can help counselors and children understand family dynamics more readily through art is the family drawing–storytelling technique (Roosa, 1981). This procedure is used as part of a larger process and is employed with children under the age of 10 years. It has four steps:

1. Children draw their families, including themselves, on a sheet of white paper.
2. They make up a story of what the family is doing in the picture.
3. They draw on a separate sheet of paper any family member that may have been left out of the original picture (e.g., a divorced parent or a family pet).
4. After all of the drawings are photocopied and cut out, children (on a one-to-one basis) tell the counselor stories about small-group family interactions, using the cutoffs as symbolic representations.

Rosebush—Healthy

Overall, "art in therapy helps children better understand themselves and how they function" in a family and in society (Orton, 1997, p. 261). "As children draw, paint, or sculpt, they are communicating their thoughts and feelings in a form of 'art talk' that the counselor can listen to and understand" (Orton, 1997, p. 261).

Adolescents

The use of visual arts for adolescents varies depending on their age and the situation that needs addressing. Visual art has been found, however, to have a potency in many treatment situations, including working with juvenile sexual offenders (Gerber, 1994), with teens in group therapy (Rambo, 1996), and even with blind teens (Herrmann, 1995). The visual art experiences range from those that are primarily preventive to those that are mainly remedial. Art materials used with adolescents include clay, paints, and photo equipment.

For young adolescents structured art experiences related to counseling may be most appropriate. In fact, the National Career Development Association (NCDA) sponsors a positively directed program of this sort each year. It is a poster contest for children and young adolescents, for which they literally draw out pictures of various career opportunities and are encouraged through the awarding of prizes to think about their vocational futures. Two other activities for this age group include photography and the painting of dreams.

Photography

Photo counseling or phototherapy methods appropriate for use with adolescents have been formulated by Amerikaner, Schauble, and Ziller (1980); Gosciewski (1975), Schudson (1975), and Weiser (1993). They include active methods in which actual pictures are taken and talked about, and more passive processes in which already developed pictures are displayed and discussed. In both of these procedures, the photographs help personalize the counseling process while promoting self-awareness and increased sensitivity. In the active process adolescents actually take pictures of themselves, their friends, and their environments. They may display the pictures in many ways, such as by mounting them on poster board or putting them in a photo album. Through such a process and through their interaction with a counselor, adolescents describe their lives, including their feelings and plans for the future.

In the more passive approach, pictures that have already been taken are collected and displayed as adolescents reflect on the times these pictures represent. Both the counselor and adolescent look for missing moments and significant themes that may be represented or absent. For example, I once worked with an older adolescent using this procedure only to find that he had left out pictures of a significant portion of his life. When I inquired, he stated he had suffered a trauma at the beginning of that time and it had taken him years to work through it. This omission gave us more material from which we could work to help him come to a final resolution regarding his trauma.

Painting Dreams

In this visual arts approach, adolescents are encouraged to draw and paint troublesome dreams. In this way the covert nature of the dream becomes more overt, and adolescents who participate in this activity gain a mastery over the dream content. Especially helpful here is "spontaneous painting," which can be akin to a dream and during which one "abandons conscious control and allows the picture to appear" (Adamson, 1984, p. 37). A related activity that is not as threatening is painting daydreams. In such paintings art becomes "fossilized consciousness, vibrating with the life it once contained" and yet maintaining a life of its own as daydreams and visual representations of them continue to evolve (Roje, 1994, p. 375).

College Students

College environments expose students to a lot of different forms of art, but many students only see art in a distant and nonmeaningful way. In contrast to this type of stale atmosphere is the healthy and innovative visual arts programs for college students sponsored by the counseling center and the housing office of George Washington University (in the District of Columbia). These programs for different groups at different times during the semester are collectively known as "Artbreak" (Geller, Kwaplen, Phillips, Wiggers, Jordan, & Marcellino, 1986). The activities in Artbreak are held on campus, require a minimum of 1 hour of time, involve minimal equipment, and are centered around an open group experience. They are designed to "(a) help students relax and release stress; (b) develop a sense of community through shared group experience; (c) air concerns about issues such as adjustment to college, roommates, and studies; (d) gain self-awareness; and (e) awaken creative energies" (Geller et al., 1986, p. 230). Sometimes themes are suggested by professionals working with students; often they are not. The same is true for discussion about what students create.

Some of the various forms that Artbreak has taken are these:

1. a group mural, in which long pieces of paper are hung on walls and various art materials are distributed and used;
2. a clay group, in which students work in a structured small circle on individual clay pieces and then are encouraged by the group leader (an art therapist) to tell the group about their work and the experience as a whole;
3. individual drawings of situations, during which pressures that have built up can be therapeutically released in a harmless and sometimes humorous way.

In Artbreak and experiences similar to it, the creativity of students is released and revealed. Feelings accompany the expression and healthy interactions with oneself and others are promoted.

Adults

As a group adults are reluctant to use the visual arts outside of already published pictures. The reason is that most adults do not have very refined artistic skills, and they feel embarrassed trying to express themselves in such a way. Nevertheless, employing art as a part of a counseling treatment plan can be most beneficial. Introducing adults to classic paintings and having them reflect and sometimes write about how a particular piece of art affects them is an effective method for fostering insight and promoting growth. The inclusion of arts in counseling a mildly mentally retarded adult has also been shown to be positive by helping to reduce maladaptive behaviors and increase internal locus of control (Arnheim, 1994; Bowen & Rosal, 1989).

The artwork of adults can be useful to counselors working with this population to help them obtain the type of treatment they need. For instance, the drawings of depressed adults show more empty space, less color, less investment of effort, and either more depressive affect or less affect than the drawings of well-functioning adults (Wadeson, 1980).

Likewise, counselors can use art in a prosocial way to help their adult clients plan their lives better. For example, in career counseling adults are often helped if they gain a sense of direction about where they have been and where they are going. There are at least two types of pictures that can be drawn in such cases. One is in the form of a road map on which clients paint or draw their life path and career influences in the same manner that they map out directions to a specific destination (Liebmann, 1986). In this procedure the person who draws the line may also

Career Road Map

pencil or color in any scenes or particular moments along the way. The idea in this visual art exercise is to give adults free reign to evaluate the factors that have most heavily influenced them and then symbolize these events and people in a form that allows them to see the past, present, and future all together. In such an experience, adults can get a feel for what may lay ahead if they do not think through their plans (Campbell, 1974).

The second type of drawing that can be used in such situations is known as "windows." In this experience, a person is asked to draw a window. They are then asked to draw scenery in the window, either looking from the outside in (i.e., interiors) or from the inside out (i.e., landscapes). The type of window drawn and the view are then discussed between the counselor and client especially in regard to issues and directions in life (Gladding, 1991).

Elderly Clients

Using the visual arts in counseling is an excellent therapeutic approach to employ with many elderly persons. The visual arts with this population can take many forms, but two of the best are described here.

Photographs and Memories

The use of old photographs is an excellent way to help older adults participate in the life-review process that is so important to fostering a sense of ego integrity (Myers, 1989; Sweeney, 1988; Weiser, 1993). The procedure used in introducing this activity can vary depending on the counseling setting. For example, if the counselor is employed in an older adult day care center, he or she can ask members of the center to bring in photographs of their lives. On the other hand, the counselor may have to be more active and find some "representative photographs" if he or she is employed in an inpatient facility where clients do not have ready access to their personal possessions. Regardless, the idea is to accentuate the positive and help clients in this process recall early recollections while reframing negatives to promote self-esteem.

Art on Occasions

"Art on occasions" is the indirect suggestion of an elderly art therapist, Maxine Toch Frankenfelder (1988). She began an art therapy program at age 73 and upon graduation worked in a psychogeriatric day treatment center. Her description of the experience reflects a great deal of versatility in using the arts. For example, in introducing art to her participants she began by drawing a mandala and then drew circles within circles that she colored. The group she worked with followed her lead and improvised, too. On the occasions of members becoming ill, Frankenfelder had other members of her group make cards. At the termination of the experience she had members draw the "saddest pictures they could imagine, but add a ray of hope. The images ranged from a weeping willow with a bit of sunshine to a Madonna and child" (Frankenfelder, 1988, p. 253). Thus using the visual arts with elderly clients was a way to therapeutically help them show care for others and at the same time care for themselves.

Hospitalized Clients

Only about 2% of hospitalized individuals in psychiatric settings spontaneously undertake artistic activities (Esman, 1988). Those who volunteer or who participate involuntarily are helped in several ways, the most noticeable being the structure and control they gain through such endeavors. Through artistic expressions hospitalized persons are able to visualize more clearly their fears and feelings. They can then talk more concretely about the disturbing elements in their lives and ways they can overcome or neutralize them. Sometimes in this process clients draw themselves out as people and in the process devise strategies for becoming healthier.

Art therapy has been found to benefit patients hospitalized for severe burns who suffer psychological as well as physical trauma. Art can be of assistance at each stage in the recovery process (Russel, 1995).

Families and Couples

A number of structured ways exist to use the visual arts with families. "In the course of family therapy, a shared task such as a family drawing or mural" provides the counselor with an opportunity to "observe interactions, form a hypothesis about the family system, and plan interventions to alter dysfunctional sequences of behavior. By observing patterns of family behavior as well as the content of the art," counselors learn "about family members' relationships with each other and about the family system of which they are a part" (Riley, 1987, p. 21).

One way of working with families in an artistic endeavor is the "joint family scribble." Individual members of a family are asked to make scribbles and are then instructed to incorporate their scribbles into a unified picture (Kwiatkowska, 1967). Another technique is known as the "conjoint family drawing," for which the family is instructed to "draw a picture as you see yourself as a family." In this exercise, each member of the family draws a picture and then discusses the finished product with the rest of the family. Often family members are surprised by the results, and a lively discussion follows (Bing, 1970).

A third refined method of using the visual arts with families is the "symbolic drawing of family life space" (Geddes & Medway, 1977). In this procedure the counselor draws a large circle and instructs the family to draw everything that represents aspects of the family, including members in relationship to each other, inside the circle. Persons and institutions that are not a part of the family are drawn outside the circle. As with the other visual art exercises, the results of this procedure often get individuals within families talking to each other in new ways.

A final form of the family drawing is the Kinetic Family Drawing test (KFD), during which an individual "is asked to 'draw everyone in the family doing something.' In analyzing the drawing, the examiner looks for who is present and who is omitted or given a substitute. The relative size of the figures is important, in addition to their position and distance in relation to each other and any interaction" (Drummond, 1996, p. 154). The way a person portrays him- or herself is given special attention also.

The main drawback to using visual arts with families is that members may feel these experiences are artificial and gimmicky and thus have no real life value (Nichols & Schwartz, 1995). When such is the case, they experience a release of emotions within a session but no transferability of learning to situations outside.

Ethnic Minorities

Visual art is not limited by color. It is an art form in which people from all ethnic backgrounds and cultures can meaningfully participate. In working with clients from cultures other than one's own, it is important that counselors understand something about the cultural heritage of their clients' art. "For example, Hispanic and Latin American art is often more metaphorical in its use of imagery and color than majority counselors might be accustomed to. Cultures, such as many of the Indian subcultures, may use stylized imagery to express events and feelings. It might be necessary for counselors to become familiar with art history and folk art of a particular cultural group through research, reading, and museum visitations" (Kincade & Evans, 1996, p. 106).

Therefore, when working with clients who are culturally distinct from oneself, counselors must focus on two aspects of the experience. The first is the professional readiness of the counselor. Counselors who have an accurate and sensitive understanding of the cultures of their clients as well as of their own heritage will be more relaxed and ready to work artistically and therapeutically in an appropriate way. Along with such knowledge must come a concentrated focus on the creative process involved in particular arts activities and what clients report learning or questioning from their experiences. The second phase of counseling using the visual arts will only occur if the first task of preparation for the event takes place thoroughly.

Counselor Drawings

The visual arts are not only therapeutic for clients to employ in working through developmental and situational crises. They are also helpful for counselors either in working with clients to alter perceptions or in assessing various dimensions of their own personal lives. Milton Cudney (1975) was a leader in advocating for the use of counselor-made drawings. According to Cudney, pictures counselors might draw in sessions could help in understanding and objectifying counseling issues, increasing openness to oneself, promoting counselor-client conversation, and reaching nonverbal and nonreading clients. Cudney also believed that pictures could shorten the counseling process by clarifying problems and making them easier to address.

A way Cudney might work and that counselor drawings continue to work is to challenge a client perception through a drawing. For instance, if a client states that a problem is so large it cannot be overcome and yet solid evidence shows the contrary, the counselor might draw two pictures. Both would be of a mountain with the first mountain much higher and steeper than the other.

The counselor might then say to the client that he or she hears the client describing the problem in terms of the first mountain but that the counselor perceives that the difficulty is much more like the second, more gently sloping mountain. Such a challenge may help the client think through how he or she is presenting a situation and modify his or her outlook accordingly.

In addition to working with clients, counselor drawings may be helpful to the counselor in gauging his or her own mental health. For example, Mary Beth Edens, a school counselor in Winston-Salem, North Carolina, when drawing a picture of herself came up with a wide variety

Client Perception of Problem

Counselor Perception of Problem

of activities that helped her develop a strong self-concept. She entitled her picture "Me!"

In assessing her more difficult days, however, Edens found that she had self-defeating talk she could use to put herself down. Her picture of the use of that talk and its results can be seen in the picture she titled "Beating Myself Down."

The contrast between the two pictures is stark and significant. Eden has found that through looking at the pictures she can remind herself not only of her strengths but also of ways she might sabotage herself if she is not careful. Her situation, while unique in the way it is depicted,

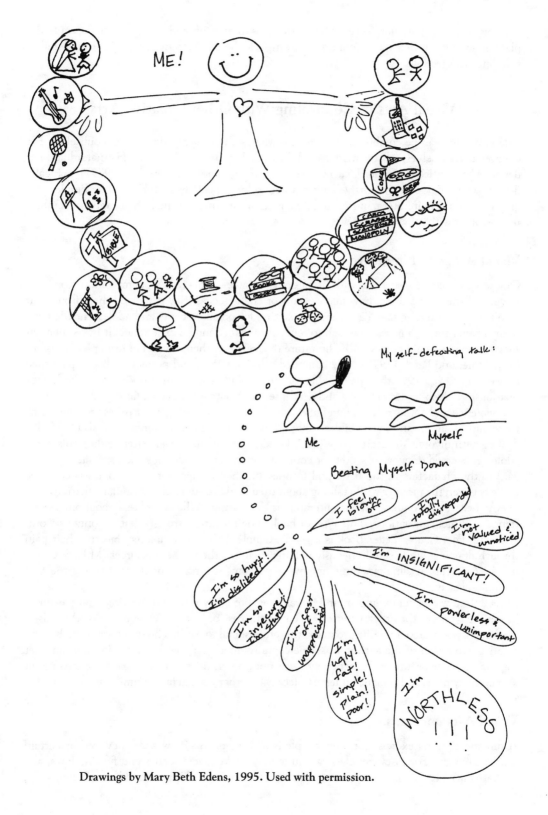

Drawings by Mary Beth Edens, 1995. Used with permission.

is common to all counselors—we all have strengths to draw on and bad times that seem to deplete or temporarily defeat us. Counselor drawings can help in tapping one's abilities and understanding one's feelings.

Visual Arts in Counseling With Other Creative Arts

The visual arts can be combined in numerous ways with other creative arts in counseling. For counselors themselves, a book written and illustrated by the late Mary Joe Hannaford and her daughter Joey, titled *Counselor Under Construction* (Hannaford & Hannaford, 1979) graphically depicts what life is like when becoming a counselor, especially in the schools. Besides this graphic approach, literature, music, and psychodrama are three of the primary ways of combining visual art with other creative arts.

Visual Arts and Literature

One way to link the visual arts with literature is to have clients read a poem, a short story, or a novel and then have them draw main events or characters as they perceived them from their readings. This exercise may be especially exciting for preadolescents and adolescents. It gives them a paper trail of images by which to remember a story and an experience. It helps them visually remember main points in the literature that relate to themselves. For example, Christenbury, Beale, and Patch (1996) have compiled a list of fiction and nonfiction books published between 1990 and 1994 that are suitable for use with adolescents in this kind of bibliotherapy relationship. Such topics as illness and death, self-destructive behaviors, family relations, identity, violence and abuse, race and prejudice, sex and sexuality, and gender issues are covered by these authors in an annotated bibliography. A book from the Christenbury et al. (1996) list dealing with divorce and secrets is Willey's (1993) *The Melinda Zone*. After reading this work, adolescents could draw what secrets or conflicts involving divorce look like, specifically in regard to the characters in the book and to oneself. Then comparisons and contrasts could be made between the pictures while talking about them and the adolescents' similar situation.

Another way to combine art with literature is by creating an illustrated text about one's experience in difficult situations. This type of book shows feelings strongly, but it contains words also. The *Pain Getting Better Book* is a good example. It has participants objectify their pain through drawings while simultaneously helping them tap their inner resources (Mills & Crowley, 1986). Thus, it simultaneously empowers participants and helps them discover the best within themselves.

Yet a third way of combining art and literature is through writing and painting simultaneously. Either the words or the art can come first, but in the case of Harriet Wadeson (1987a) words in the form of poetry about midlife prompted this professional to paint. The result was a graphic and creative expression of the author-artist's perceptions about making the transition into another stage of life. The beauty of the experience was not only in the meaning it gave the creator but also in the symbols and guidance it left as a legacy for other women facing similar situations.

Visual Arts and Music

A fun and exciting exercise for most people is to have clients draw images evoked by certain sounds in music. For instance, classical music may evoke placid scenes and flowing lines, and staccato music (e.g., rap or disco) may inspire action scenes or sharp, jagged lines (Fisher, 1989;

Witmer, 1985). One way to "draw to music" is for clients to arrange music they like in a certain order and then draw to the music they enjoy (Mills & Crowley, 1986).

Music and art may be used educationally, too, to document events and uplift spirits. A master of this procedure was Paul Fitzgerald at the University of Florida. Fitzgerald would take photographs at professional meetings, such as the conventions of the Association for Counselor Education and Supervision, and at the end of the conference he would display slides of his photographs set to the beat of contemporary music by such individuals and groups as Bob Dylan, Elton John, Barbra Streisand, the Beatles, and Styx.

Visual Arts and Psychodrama

Visual art is usually not combined with psychodrama, and the difficulty of linking these modalities is challenging. In an experimental program involving termination and transition for a psychiatric day treatment program, it was suggested that art activities be used as a focus for role-plays and psychodrama (Dallin, 1986). The nonverbal quality of producing visual art may serve as a "warm up" for enacting scenes connected with the act on a verbal level, as in psychodrama. The key bridge between these experiences is having participants verbally process their art experiences before acting on them.

The idea behind all of these varied experiences is that through combining visual arts with other artistic forms, clients come to see themselves more clearly, experience themselves in different ways, and talk about themselves with new understanding.

Summary

The visual arts have been a valuable asset to humankind throughout recorded history and even before. People represent their worlds visually, not just in their minds, but in drawings, sculpture, and photographs. When individuals come to face and understand the concreteness of what they have created, they are often awakened to a new sense of self and deeper understandings of their intra- and interpersonal relationships. Thus the arts stir up feelings and open up possibilities.

In this chapter several forms of the visual arts, including drawing, sculpture, and photographs, have been examined in regard to their therapeutic use in counseling with a number of specific populations. It is obvious that not everyone can be artistic in expression, but the visual arts lend themselves to being used in already completed forms. Thus, the change that comes about as a result of employing visual art methods is one that allows for versatility and not necessary ability. Overall, the use of the visual arts is open to a wide variety of expressive forms.

References

Adamson, E. (1984). Art as healing. London: Conventure.

Allan, J. A. B. (1978). Serial drawing: A therapeutic approach with young children. Canadian Counsellor, 12, 223–228.

Allan, J. (1988). Inscapes of the child's world. Dallas, TX: Spring.

Allan, J., & Crandall, J. (1986). The rosebush: A visualization strategy for possible identification of child abuse. Elementary School Guidance & Counseling, 21, 44–51.

Amerikaner, M., Schauble, P., & Ziller, R. (1980). Images: The use of photographs in personal counseling. Personnel & Guidance Journal, 59, 68–73.

Arnheim, R. (1994). Artistry in retardation. Arts in Psychotherapy, 21, 329–332.

Exercises

1. As an initial "icebreaker" in group or family therapy, spread a large sheet of paper on the floor and ask members to paint a cooperative picture with the materials you have provided, such as crayons or paint. After the group has worked on the project for about 20 minutes (tell them ahead of time how much time they have), have each member talk about the finished work and his or her part in it. Have members relate to one another during this time also. Try to link the feelings and experiences in the session project with parallel events in regular group or family life.

2. In between counseling sessions have clients make masks using a grocery bag as the main material. Discuss with clients the shapes, colors, and unique features of the masks, and then have them put on the masks and act in a way that they think represents the masks' spirits. Process the experience, especially in light of any new behaviors or emotions that clients display.

3. Make a collage of your life out of photographs and words from newspapers (or out of pictures and words from magazines if photographs and newspapers are not available). Allow 1 hour to complete the project, and on a second day allow another hour to reflect on or refine your work. Present your collage to a trusted friend or colleague and talk about what you have learned about yourself and how you think you might therapeutically use this method.

Bing, E. (1970). The conjoint family drawing. *Family Process, 9,* 173–194.

Bowen, C. A., & Rosal, M. L. (1989). The use of art therapy to reduce the maladaptive behaviors of a mentally retarded adult. *Arts in Psychotherapy, 16,* 211–218.

Brooke, S. L. (1995). Art therapy: An approach to working with sexual abuse survivors. *Arts in Psychotherapy, 22,* 447–466.

Buck, J. (1948). The H-T-P test. *Journal of Clinical Psychology, 4,* 151–159.

Campbell, D. (1974). *If you don't know where you're going, you'll probably end up somewhere else.* Niles, IL: Argus Communications.

Christenbury, L., Beale, A. V., & Patch, S. S. (1996). Interactive bibliocounseling: Recent fiction and nonfiction for adolescents and their counselors. *The School Counselor, 44,* 133–145.

Comfort, C. E. (1985). Published pictures as psychotherapeutic tools. *Arts in Psychotherapy, 12,* 245–256.

Cudney, M. R. (1975). *Self-defeating characters*. Kalamazoo, MI: Life Giving Enterprises.

Dallin, B. (1986). Art break: A 2-day expressive therapy program using art and psychodrama to further the termination process. *Arts in Psychotherapy, 13,* 137–142.

Drummond, R. J. (1996). *Appraisal procedures for counselors and helping professionals* (3rd ed). Englewood Cliffs, NJ: Prentice-Hall.

Esman, A. H. (1988). Art and psychopathology: The message of outsider art. *American Journal of Art Therapy, 27,* 13–21.

Fisher, P. P. (1989). *Creative movement for older adults*. New York: Human Sciences.

Frankenfelder, M. T. (1988). For later days—a fulfillment. *Arts in Psychotherapy, 15,* 251–254.

Freud, S. (1923). The ego and the id. In J. Strachey (Ed.) *The complete psychological works of Sigmund Freud, vol. 19*. London: Hogarth.

Geddes, M., & Medway, J. (1977). The symbolic drawing of family life space. *Family Process, 16,* 219–228.

Geller, S. K., Kwaplen, A., Phillips, E. K., Wiggers, T. T., Jordan, K., & Marcellino, I. (1986). "Artbreak": Innovation in student life programming. *Journal of College Student Personnel, 27,* 229–233.

Gerber, J. (1994). The use of art therapy in juvenile sex offender specific treatment. *Arts in Psychotherapy, 21,* 367–374.

Gerler, E. R., Jr. (1982). *Counseling the young learner*. Englewood Cliffs, NJ: Prentice-Hall.

Gladding, S. T. (1975). Twilight. *Personnel and Guidance Journal, 53,* 230.

Gladding, S. T. (1991, April). *The well counselor*. Paper presented at the annual convention of the American Association for Counseling and Development, Reno, NV.

Gosciewski, F. W. (1975). Photo counseling. *Personnel & Guidance Journal, 53,* 600–604.

Hannaford, M. J., & Hannaford, J. (1979). *Counselor under construction*. Atlanta, GA: Author.

Herrmann, U. (1995). A Trojan horse of clay: Art therapy in a residential school for the blind. *Arts in Psychotherapy, 22,* 229–234.

Howe, J. W., Burgess, A. W., & McCormack, A. (1987). Adolescent runaways and their drawings. *Arts in Psychotherapy, 14,* 35–40.

Hughes, J. N. (1988). Interviewing children. In J. M. Dillard & R. R. Reilly (Eds.), *Systematic interviewing* (pp. 90–113). Columbus, OH: Merrill.

Jourard, S. M. (1971). *The transparent self* (Rev. ed.). New York: Van Nostrand Reinhold.

Jung, C. G. (1965). *Memories, dreams, reflections*. New York: Random House.

Jung, C. G. (1966). *The collected works. Vol. 16, The practice of psychotherapy*. Princeton: Princeton University Press.

Kaiser, D. H. (1996). Indications of attachment security in a drawing task. *Arts in Psychotherapy, 23,* 333–340.

Kincade, E. A., & Evans, K. M. (1996). Counseling theories, process and interventions in a multicultural context. In J. L. DeLucia-Waack (Eds.), *Multicultural counseling competencies: Implications for training and practice* (pp. 89–112). Alexandria, VA: American Counseling Association.

Kramer, E. (1971). *Art as therapy with children*. New York: Schocken.

Kwiatkowska, H. Y. (1967). Family art therapy. *Family Process, 6,* 37–55.

Leary, D. E. (1992). William James and the art of human understanding. *American Psychologist, 47,* 152–160.

Liebmann, M. (1986). *Art therapy for groups*. Cambridge, MA: Brookline.

Machover, K. (1949). *Personality projection in the drawing of the human figure*. Springfield, IL: Thomas.

Makin, S. R. (1994). *A consumer's guide to art therapy*. Springfield, IL: Thomas.

Manning, T. M. (1987). Aggression depicted in abused children's drawings. *Arts in Psychotherapy, 14,* 15–24.

Maslow, A. H. (1991). How to experience the unitive life. *Journal of Humanistic Education and Development, 29,* 109–112.

May, R. (1953). *Man's search for himself*. New York: Norton.

McClure, B. A., Merrill, E., & Russo, T. R. (1994). Seeing clients with an artist's eye: Perceptual simulation exercises. *Simulation and Gaming, 25,* 51–60.

McNiff, S. (1997). Art therapy: A spectrum of partnerships. *Arts in Psychotherapy, 24,* 37–44.

Mills, J. C., & Crowley, R. J. (1986). *Therapeutic metaphors for children and the child within.* New York: Brunner/Mazel.

Moon, C. (1997). Art therapy: Creating the space we will live in. *Arts in Psychotherapy, 24,* 45–49.

Myers, J. E. (1989). *Infusing gerontological counseling in counselor preparation.* Alexandria, VA: American Counseling Association.

Nadeau, R. (1984). Using the visual arts to expand personal creativity. In B. Warren (Ed.), *Using the creative arts in therapy* (pp. 61–86). Cambridge, MA: Brookline.

Naumberg, M. (1966). *Dynamically oriented art therapy.* New York: Grune & Stratton.

Nichols, M. , & Schwartz, R. C. (1995). *Family therapy* (3rd ed). Boston: Allyn & Bacon.

Orton, G. L. (1997). *Strategies for counseling with children and their parents.* Pacific Grove, CA: Brooks/Cole.

Prinzhorn, H. (1922/1972). *Artistry of the mentally ill.* New York: Springer.

Rambo, T. (1996). The use of creative arts in adolescent group therapy. In S. T. Gladding (Ed.), *New developments in group counseling* (pp. 31–33). Greensboro, NC: ERIC.

Rhyne, J. (1973). *The gestalt art experience.* Belmont, CA: Wadsworth.

Riley, S. (1987). The advantages of art therapy in an outpatient clinic. *American Journal of Art Therapy, 26,* 21–29.

Riley, S. (1997, Winter). Children's art and narratives: An opportunity to enhance therapy and a supervisory challenge. *The Supervision Bulletin,* 2–3.

Roje, J. (1994). Consciousness as manifested in art: A journey from the concrete to the meaningful. *Arts in Psychotherapy, 21,* 375–385.

Roosa, L. W. (1981). The family drawing/storytelling technique: An approach to assessment of family dynamics. *Elementary School Guidance & Counseling, 15,* 269–272.

Rubin, J. (1980). Art in counseling: A new avenue. *Counseling and Human Development, 13,* 1–12.

Russel, J. (1995). Art therapy on a hospital burn unit: A step towards healing and recovery. *Art Therapy, 12,* 38–45.

Schudson, K. R. (1975). The simple camera in school counseling. *Personnel & Guidance Journal, 54,* 225–226.

Steinhardt, L. (1985). Freedom within boundaries: Body outline drawings in art therapy with children. *Arts in Psychotherapy, 12,* 25–34.

Sweeney, T. J. (1988). *Adlerian counseling: A practical approach for a new decade.* Muncie, IN: Accelerated Development.

Tibbetts, T. J., & Stone, B. (1990). Short-term art therapy with seriously emotionally disturbed adolescents. *Arts in Psychotherapy, 17,* 139–146.

Trowbridge, M. M. (1995). Graphic indicators of sexual abuse in children's drawings: A review of the literature. *Arts in Psychotherapy, 22,* 485–494.

Wadeson, H. (1980). *Art psychotherapy.* New York: Wiley.

Wadeson, H. (1987a). Pursuit of the image: Painting from poetry in a personal mid-life odyssey. *Arts in Psychotherapy, 14,* 177–182.

Wadeson, H. (1987b). *The dynamics of art psychotherapy.* New York: Wiley.

Weiser, J. (1993). *Phototherapy techniques.* San Francisco, CA: Jossey-Bass.

Willey, M. (1993). *The Melinda zone.* New York: Bantam.

Witmer, J. M. (1985). *Pathways to personal growth.* Muncie, IN: Accelerated Development.

6

Literature and Counseling

In the morning light I write of you
   as my dreams fade to memories
     in the midst of winter's chill
      and the smell of fresh-brewed coffee.
In the noonday rush I think of you
   as I log frail thoughts into a dog-eared journal
     during silence preceding the joining of friends
      for lunch and the taste of fresh insights.
At home, past dusk and after traffic, I read about you
   some words from my pen, some from more intimate admirers.
At bedtime as I lay down
   my head dances with plans and emerging feelings
In that knowledge which is your presence
   my life becomes more open
     like a book in progress
I live with you in lines through time.

(Gladding, 1990)

COUNSELING IS A PROFESSION directly related to personal and societal health. As such, it is informed by numerous artistic traditions that describe human nature. One of the most powerful means of comprehending human life to the fullest is found in the written words of poets, novelists, biographers, and clients. In essence, counseling is an art and "a science of experience, not only from formal research and case conferences, but from literature. . . . Without Shakespeare's plays, Dostoyevsky's novels, or James's short stories, our knowledge of anguish and conflict would be hollow, our self-revelations would be one-dimensional" (Kottler, 1986, p. 35).

Sometimes troubled individuals have been able to help themselves through selectively or systematically writing or reading. At other times these same people have needed guidance from counselors as to how to write or what to read. In both situations, the results have been manifested in the mending of broken spirits and the restoration of hope and wholeness. It is interesting to note that some of the primary writers and consumers of literature historically and contemporarily have been physicians, including John Keats, Anton Chekhov, A. J. Cronin, William Carlos Williams, Robert Seymour Bridges, Walker Percy, John Stone, and Rafael Campo (Barbour, 1991; Ingalls, 1997; Kolodzey, 1983). The connectedness between health, healing, and literature is significant.

This chapter examines the premise behind and practice of reading literature and writing in counseling. Suggested methods to employ when using these two traditions will be highlighted. Much of what is being done in the domain of the written word in counseling needs more verification. Making the written arts more uniform in practice is another area in which work is essential (Hynes & Hynes-Berry, 1986).

Premise of the Use of Literature in Counseling

The therapeutic use of literature as a healing tool in counseling is known by a variety of names. *Bibliotherapy, bibliocounseling, poetry therapy,* and *scriptotherapy* are the terms most often used to describe the employment of the written word in the therapeutic process. For simplicity's sake, the use of published literature in counseling will be referred to here primarily as bibliotherapy (from the Greek words *biblion* meaning "book" and *therapeio* meaning "healing"). Likewise, the process of having clients write will be referred to as scriptotherapy (from the Latin roots *scriptum* meaning "thing written" and *therapia* meaning "to nurse or cure.")

Regardless of what it is called, the concept of therapeutically employing literature and writing "is as old as Aristotle's discussion of catharsis" (Hynes & Hynes-Berry, 1986, pp. iii). Freud (1965) credited poets and writers as being the first to discover the unconscious and bring it into awareness. Regardless, published literature and writing have been used historically in a number of ways, such as working through grief (Berger, 1988; Bowman, 1994; Heninger, 1987), improving socialization, and increasing self-actualization (Gold, 1988).

Bibliotherapy

As opposed to reading done for diversion or practical purposes, "bibliotherapy is directed to disordered states" (Alekseychik, 1989, p. 19). It is aimed at assisting people to gain control over their lives and situations by identifying with others and finding unique and universal solutions. As such, it provides both inspiration and solace (Riordan & Wilson, 1989).

Bibliotherapy is practiced on one of three levels—institutional, clinical, or developmental (Rubin, 1978). At the institutional level, those who receive treatment are generally quite disturbed, and the material used is traditionally didactic and instructive. Such material can take many forms, from Edgar Guest's poem "It Takes a Heap of Living to Make a Happy Home" to selections from the "Big Book" of Alcoholics Anonymous (AA). The impact and status of bibliotherapy in hospitals is reflected in the fact that the Joint Commission for Accreditation of Health Care Organizations (JCAHCO) has approved this procedure as a professional modality (Lerner, 1997).

At the outpatient clinical level, persons receiving bibliotherapy services have moderate emotional or behavioral problems. The material presented to them is imaginative (Riordan, Mullis, & Nuchow, 1996). Examples of imaginative literature can range from Horatio Alger stories to Rudyard Kipling's poem "If." In these types of literature, insight is gleaned from reading what others have done or thought when faced with challenging situations or circumstances.

Finally, at the developmental level, the focus of the bibliotherapeutic experience is on "normal" people and the multitude of everyday problems and situations they face. Therefore, the materials used are flexible and cover a wide range of emotions (Gladding & Gladding, 1991). Judith Viorst children and adult books such as *Alexander and the Terrible, Horrible, No-Good, Very Bad Day* and *Necessary Losses* are examples of literature appropriate at this stage.

At its best, bibliotherapy is interactive. Thus, it is defined as "a therapeutic modality in which guided discussion of literature, other media material and/or creative writing by the participant or group is used to achieve prescribed therapeutic goals" (Rossiter & Brown, 1988, p. 158). The type of literature employed and the way it is handled depends on the problems to be resolved and the thoroughness with which clients wish to achieve certain outcomes. Often self-help, behaviorally based books, such as *Your Perfect Right* and *What Color Is Your Parachute?* are prescribed by counselors, because the results can be more readily measured than with works of fiction or inspiration (Riordan & Wilson, 1989). An important part of the bibliotherapeutic process is to personalize it so that materials are appropriate to clients in regard to reading level and situation handled. Therefore, to-the-point material in the form of articles from *Reader's Digest, Prevention,* and *Guideposts* may be appropriate for some clients, whereas such material would be unthinkable for others.

Basically, bibliotherapy involves a three-step process based on several nonexclusive premises. The first premise is that through reading literature the counselor can help clients realize more fully the multiple emphasis behind counseling as a profession. Furthermore, participating in this process can assist individuals in making significant discoveries about themselves as persons. For example, a great deal of poetry expresses subtle and overt psychological insights about life situations that are related to counseling themes (Chavis, 1986). By reading and discussing such material, counselors and clients may come to personalize aspects of the poetry into their own lives. Thus, they may "incorporate the Freudian insight about telling (their) story as it was, the Jungian insight of transforming it with a metaphor drawn from outside sources, and the Perlsian emphasis on the here-and-now action" (Gorelick, 1987, p. 94). Counseling theories have a place in human growth and development, but that focus is sometimes deemphasized. Literature, especially poetry, helps highlight the importance of counseling traditions in understanding life. Poetic literature ranging from John Donne to Gladys Wellington emphasizes the many roads to actual client change and the difficulty and thrill of getting to and through life stages.

Another premise behind the inclusion of literature in counseling is that "true self-knowledge" and a greater understanding of the world emerge (Hynes & Hynes-Berry, 1986, p. 1). Clients realize that their problems are universal as well as unique. Thus, they share a connectedness with many other people across time, gender, culture, and circumstance (Leedy, 1985; Lerner, 1994).

Such an experience gives comfort to individuals who may otherwise be naive or myopic in viewing their circumstances. For example, children may be unaware that other children face situations similar to theirs. Therefore, reading and discussing a book like Joy Berry's (1987) *Every Kid's Guide to Handling Feelings* may be helpful in getting such children to talk about everyday emotions from love and joy to anger and jealousy.

Yet another reason for including literature in counseling is that more constructive and positive thinking and creative problem solving are generated (Watson, 1980). Reading literature is relaxing and allows participants to become more engaged in using imagery while mentally developing divergent and novel ways of resolving difficulties.

In the bibliotherapy process a triadic connection is fostered between (a) literature (the primary tool), (b) participants, and (c) facilitators (counselors or developmental specialists who help participants process the insights and knowledge they have obtained for real-life situations). A "dual interaction" occurs: Participants' responses to a piece of literature are enhanced or expanded because of their dialogues with facilitators (Hynes & Hynes-Berry, 1986). An example of this process at work is the use of prescriptive literature. This idea has been advocated over the years for a wide variety of human ailments (Perakis, 1992), but it originated in a concrete form when Jack Leedy, a New York psychiatrist, started asking his patients to read specific poems in connection with certain disorders or problems. For insomnia persons might read "Hymn to the Night" by Henry Wadsworth Longfellow, or for anxiety, the poem "I'm Nobody! Who Are You?" by Emily Dickinson (Kolodzey, 1983). Overall, bibliotherapy is a popular way of working with clients. Research suggests it will continue to be used and assessed even more in the future (Riordan & Wilson, 1989).

Scriptotherapy

The term *scriptotherapy* is frequently used to refer to the process of writing in a therapeutic way (Riordan, 1996). Writing allows self-expression, acceptance of feelings, and sometimes increase in one's sense of spirituality. Writing also may relieve pain and allow clients to deal with emotions on a cognitive and objective level (Mercer, 1993). Counselors and clients who use scriptotherapy create their own literature, which may be quite personal and insightful. In addition to being a therapeutic release and relief, there may be secondary health benefits to writing. For example, James Pennebaker (1990) found that college students who wrote for 20 minutes a day about matters of concern to them stayed healthier than a control group whose members did not write.

Writers frequently begin expressing themselves because of a problem they have had in their own lives. Their desire is to find a resolution through writing. The results of their writing "consists of the deeper and wider dimension of consciousness" to which they are carried "by virtue of . . . wrestling with the problem" (May, 1969, pp. 170–171). Thus, what is produced is not only a literary and artistic work but "genuine self-realization" (May, 1969, p. 172) that carries writers past innocence and into an existential dimension of life from which they can never emerge again the same as before entering.

Often clients will express a desire to keep a journal or write but almost as frequently they will end up not doing so. Adams (1994) has suggested a number of ways to help clients help themselves to keep a journal. One of her ideas is for clients to prepare themselves to write before they start the process. Preparation includes physically locating oneself in a space that is physically and psychologically conducive to writing and where there will be no interruptions. Once such a space is found, clients should go through any needed rituals, such as deep-breathing exercises or lighting of candles, to further create a therapeutic mood. Finally, clients should limit themselves in regard to time spent in this activity.

One of Adam's favorite ways to get clients writing is called the "5-minute writing sprint." An egg timer is set to go off after 5 minutes, so the client does not have to continually keep track of time. Then the client begins writing about anything he or she wishes. The only rules are that the writing instrument has to constantly be in motion. Thus, if words do not come to mind, the writer should doodle or scribble on the paper in a flow that is similar to writing and that is continuous. When the egg timer goes off, the person stops writing. This approach to writing is practical; most clients can find 5 minutes to devote to writing. Following this exercise, I like to have clients write one day and read and reflect on what they have written the next. This practice helps clients stay motivated to write and gives them an opportunity to process what they are writing.

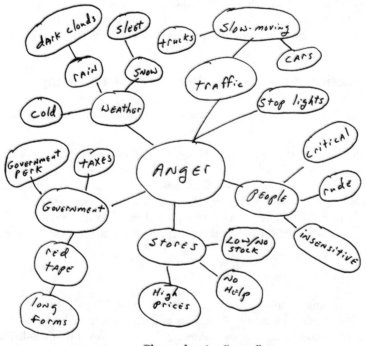

Cluster drawing "anger"

Adams (1994) also suggested that clients can be helped to learn how to write by doing a word cluster around a central word, such as *anger*, *anxiety*, or *distress*. Thus, the word *anger* might lead to people, places, times, or situations that have been associated with this feeling in one's life. Ways of constructively dealing with the intensity of the emotion may arise as well.

Clients can loosen up their writing skills (and their thought processes) simultaneously, too, by writing a character sketch on someone they have found interesting. When such an exercise is done, clients have a good opportunity to compare and contrast themselves with the admired person in a positive way.

Two forms of scriptotherapy that have become increasingly popular are what Riordan and Ketchum (1996) called "therapeutic correspondence" and the rewriting of personal stories. Therapeutic cor- respondence is the writing of notes and letters by clients or counselors after a session. It may take many forms, be done extensively, and follow a number of theories. For example, France, Cadieux, and Allen (1995) reported the case of a literary therapeutic encounter that lasted 5 months (15 letters) and that followed the principles of Morita therapy. The practice of therapeutic correspondence has been most noted and popularized on a clinical level by the narrative family therapists led by Michael White and David Epston (1990). These practitioners believed they should not write notes apart from those they would share with a family with whom they are working. Therefore, their clinical observations are often written in the form of letters that they send to client families. Session notes in the form of letters can stimulate client thought and help clients concentrate on particular issues. Letters of this type can test the accuracy of perceptions as well (Riordan & Ketchum, 1996).

The rewriting of stories is an emphasis of solution-focused family therapists led by two prolific theorists-writers, Steve deShazer and Bill O'Hanlon (Gladding, 1998). A key to solution-focused family work is for counselors to help clients find exceptions to the stories they tell or write. These exceptions are then examined and expanded to create new stories and break old, repetitive, nonproductive behaviors. The idea is based on the philosophy of constructivism, which states that reality is a reflection of observation and experience, not an objective entity.

Practice of the Use of Literature in Counseling

Literature is employed in counseling in numerous ways, but four main traditions will be highlighted here:

1. reading select prosaic works, such as novels, autobiographies, and self-help books
2. reading select poetic works, such as classic or modern poems
3. keeping a journal or writing an autobiography in whatever language form the writer wishes to use, such as telegraphic speech, poetry, reflective thoughts, or descriptions of events
4. paying attention to the literary way clients express themselves in counseling, such as the use of select metaphors, and expanding these literary devices to create something new

Prosaic Practices

Prosaic practices center around the reading of any type of literature that results in the formulation of new ideas, insight, or information. A number of different types of books can be read for either enlightenment or counseling purposes. Among the most frequently included works are short stories (fiction), biographies (nonfiction), self-help books, fairy tales, and picture books (Pardeck & Pardeck, 1993). Books that are selected to help clients should be chosen thoughtfully and with care. The age, stage, developmental level, and situation people are facing need to be considered. Some books, however, have a universal appeal. For example, *The Wonderful Wizard of Oz* (Baum, 1900), a children's book with adult themes about the meaning of life, is a work that can be used with persons throughout the life span. This book, when read and processed thoroughly, can help participants in the bibliotherapy process become more attuned to themes within their own lives about loss and identity (Reiter, 1988).

Other books that are helpful for adults in this prosaic but stimulating way range from Scott Peck's (1978) *The Road Less Traveled* to H. Jackson Brown, Jr.'s (1991) *Life's Little Instruction Book*. For children, prosaic books may cover general subject areas, such as the importance of making decisions, found in Richard Nelson's Stop-Think-and-Choose elementary and middle school novels like *In the Land of Choice* and *Incident at Crystal Lake*. The beauty of these books is that they contain broad themes that can be discussed with the counselor. In addition to encouraging insight in the process of discussion, they can also stimulate readers to write their own parallel or novel works and gain greater knowledge of themselves through the experience.

Counselors who need ready sources of self-help books, especially for adults, would do well to consult a resource such as *The Authoritative Guide to Self-Help Books* (Santrock, Minnett, & Campbell, 1994). Clinicians who wish to tailor literature to the developmental level and concerns of children and adolescents may find *The Bookfinder* (Dreyer, 1989) quite useful.

Poetic Practices

Poetic practices center on the use of poetry in the counseling experience. A group of counselor practitioners are certified by the National Association of Poetry Therapy (NAPT) to practice this specialization, and other professionals on occasions use poetry in their work but are not certified or registered by NAPT. The work of both may have considerable overlap, although the training of a registered or certified poetry therapist is usually more thorough.

The term *poetry therapy* is descriptive of the use of a wide variety of poetry in counseling, especially by trained poetry therapists (Lerner, 1997). "The poetry therapist is one who is committed to the appropriate use of language in the healing process" (Lerner, 1988, p.120). He or she is not interested in the creation of great literature (although classic poetry such as that by Yeats, Keats, Shelley, Wordsworth, Tennyson, Hughes, and Ferlingetti may be used). Rather, the poetry therapist is concerned with the proper expression of emotion. Thus, poetry that is written or used may not be exemplary, although such works are "vivid in imagery and emotional impact" and express universal feelings (Chavis, 1986, p. 121).

In choosing poetic works for counseling, special attention is given to both form and content (Gorelick & Lerner, 1997). Poetic form focuses on the rhythm of a poem and how compelling, appealing, and appropriate it is (Hynes & Hynes-Berry, 1986). "Verses tend to be clocked to a poet's body rhythms. . . and the poets we like best tend to be those whose body rhythms match our own" (Kolodzey, 1983, p. 67). Content is the "what" within the poem that makes it appealing or repelling to particular audiences. For instance, didactic content is rarely embraced by poetry therapists or counselors who use poetry because it has a way of turning people off due to its "preachiness."

Poems that are most open to discussion have a greater universal appeal (Lessner, 1974). The background of a poet can make a difference too, in whether the poem is pertinent or relevant to a particular population. For example, in working with ethnic minority at-risk youth using poetry, Gardner (1993) has employed Native American poet Joy Harjo's (1983) poem "I Give You Back" to express wisdom and strength in resolving fear. The African American poet Lucille Clifton's (1991) poem "Whose Side Are You On?" has also been used to describe the importance of community.

Journals and Autobiographies

Keeping a journal (or log) of one's life or experiences about particular events (such as counseling) is an excellent way to discover what has been learned over time and how much growth has taken place. Journals record "reflections on and feeling-responses to present, personal experiences" (Hynes & Hynes-Berry, 1986, p. 188). They can be written in many forms, from the intensive journal process of Progoff (1975) to the poetic reflections of Carroll (1970). Group members and leaders may use logs to relive and reflect on experiences, become active in the group process, and give feedback to one another (Valine, 1983). Some of the more common forms of journal work include these:

1. "The Period Log." People are encouraged to define a recent period of their lives, reflect on their experiences and life events during that period, and record their feelings, impressions, and descriptions.

2. "The Daily Log." This closely resembles a diary and serves as a running record of a person's subjective experience of his or her daily life.
3. "The Stepping Stones." The most significant points of movement in a person's life are listed. These can help people see overall patterns and unconscious goals and motivations.
4. "The Dream Log." This log is used to keep a record of dreams and dream themes and patterns.
5. "Twilight Images." Thoughts and images that occur just before falling asleep are recorded. (Weinhold, 1987, p. 10)

In keeping a journal, it is crucial that the material in it be reviewed on a regular basis so that reflection and insight can be used. A good method to employ in such a review is to read journal entries every 2 or 3 days and spend the time that would normally be used in writing by reflecting. Journaling may be an especially appropriate procedure for working with Asian Americans, whose cultural values are not to share issues about feelings or family relationships openly with a counselor, at least initially (Kincade & Evans, 1996). In such cases, the information written in the journal should be private and shared only if the client wishes to do so. Journaling may also be appropriate for clients who are not fluent in literary skills, because through journal writing these authors have time to reflect and edit their thoughts. In some extreme cases, an audiotaped journal may be used if the client is an auditory processor of information and lacks solid writing skills.

Writing an autobiography is usually a more formal and structured task than keeping a journal. A major advantage of writing an autobiography is that it "lets a person express what has been important in his or her life, to emphasize likes and dislikes, identify values, describe interests and aspirations, acknowledge successes and failures, and recall meaningful personal relationships. Such an experience, especially for the mature client, can be thought-provoking, insightful, and a stimulus for action. On occasion, the experience can also relieve tension" (Gibson & Mitchell, 1990, p. 278).

There is no best method that the writing of an autobiography should take, because each person's life is unique. Nonetheless, to be complete an autobiography should include as much information as possible from as many different times in the client's life as feasible. Early childhood memories as well as current events add to the significance of such a work, and the more material that is included the more likely that patterns will emerge and issues arise that can be discussed and resolved if needed.

Client Language and Metaphor

One of the main achievements of successful counselors is their ability to listen to and use the language of clients, a procedure known as "minesis." Such a process often involves hearing unique and universal metaphors employed by clients and then using these figures of speech in select ways to build rapport and foster change. "A metaphor is a figure of speech, containing an implied comparison—expressing an idea in terms of something else" (Meier & Davis, 1997, p. 30). It is common for Native Americans to express themselves in metaphorical stories either verbally or in writing (Kincade & Evans, 1996), but clients from all cultural backgrounds may use metaphors. Besides respecting and using a client's language, counselors can listen and encourage clients to tell their stories in a style that suits them best. The result is sometimes a wonder to behold both emotionally and literally.

Clients who speak in figurative language may weave a rich tapestry of tales focusing on such matters as being "wrapped up in rage" or "torn between two feelings." They may also give rich descriptions of themselves and their surroundings. In some cases, counselors can help clients "unravel" or "mend" their situations by speaking metaphorically themselves to clarify or amplify what the client is saying. In such situations they are primarily working to "problem set," that is, literally frame or reframe a problem so the client can deal with it. Thus, "a tidal wave of emotions" may be seen as "an abundant mixture of anxiety and depression." Then clinicians must work further with clients to employ additional metaphorical language in select ways to solve problems so that clients do not become literally or figuratively stuck in the situations. For example, the "abundant mixture of anxiety and depression" can be weakened and controlled through exercise, role plays, relaxation techniques, preparation, and prescription medicines, which act as "barriers to the mixture becoming toxic or disabling."

Literature in Counseling With Specific Populations

Children

Literature for children is usually written in the form of storybooks, fairy tales, and nursery rhymes (Bettleheim, 1976). Often these works are unique in their simultaneous presentation of a story through words and pictures (Coughlin, 1991). They frequently have accompanying video- or audiotapes, and thus children are exposed to the book content through a variety of stimuli. To be effective using literature with young children, counselors may employ as many complementary media devices as possible.

Children's literature often focuses on teaching lessons "about how to handle most of the problems of childhood" (Guerin, 1976, p. 480). Numerous books help instill courage and deal with the mastery of fears in this population, such as *The Little Prince, The Velveteen Rabbit, Where the Wild Things Are, The Tales of Peter Rabbit,* and *The Little Engine That Could.* Other texts, such as Dr. Seuss's *Yertle the Turtle* and *Gertrude McFuzz,* teach basic lessons about interpersonal relationships. In addition, Sesame Street books and videos promote cognitive, affective, and prosocial learning in a style that is appealing and digestible for children of a young age. An excellent source of 36 popular stories for elementary school children (i.e., kindergarten through 6th grade) is *Children Talking About Books* (Borders & Naylor, 1993).

Preschool children seem to benefit from mutual storytelling—a verbal means of written expression. This approach, devised by Richard Gardner (1971), involves a counselor and client who participate in the telling of a story together. The counselor begins the story with a phrase, such as "Once upon a time," and tailors his or her initial remarks to parallel the present situation of the client. The story is then turned over to the client for telling. The counselor intervenes only when the client becomes stuck or asks for help, at which point the counselor adds neutral descriptive material or asks a question. The idea behind this activity is for the young client to really hear and attempt to resolve areas in life that are presently troubling. Kestenbaum (1985), among others, has found this technique effective in highlighting issues in the lives of children and helping them work through these matters in a nonthreatening way. It seems effective for a wide range of ages.

Children of all ages benefit from writing also. Young children, for example, begin to see themselves and their worlds more clearly through written exercises. They mature in the process, and writing "seems to proceed hand in hand with psychological growth, to reflect and enhance it, to deepen and extend it, and often to quicken the process" (Brand, 1987, p. 274). One way of helping young children learn to write poetically about themselves and their problems is to use Kenneth Koch's (1970) book *Wishes, Lies, and Dreams.* This text has illustrations and exercises that help children write poems about events and objects in their lives. Older children benefit as well.

For example, journal writing has been found to be therapeutic in helping children whose lives have suffered the turmoil of war (Costello, Phelps, & Wilczenski, 1994).

Adolescents

Adolescence is a time of turmoil in the midst of a search for identity. Therefore, literature serves a useful function in helping adolescents realize possibilities and meaning for their own lives. Biographies and autobiographies are especially relevant to this population. Such books as *Margaret Mead: A Life* by Jane Howard, *The Rise of Theodore Roosevelt* by Edmund Morris, or *No Direction Home: The Life and Music of Bob Dylan* by Robert Shelton are excellent in giving teenagers insight into what they can be and how they can grow. Other works that deal with life difficulties such as *The Kids' Book of Divorce: By, For and About Kids* (Rofes, 1981), are helpful, too, in gaining a perspective on overcoming difficulties. This book offeres perspectives on divorce by kids who have watched their parents go through it. Suggestions for coping are given. Novels such as Robert Cormier's *I Am the Cheese, The Chocolate War,* and *After the First Death,* can not only be compelling as literary works but can help students understand what is happening to them during adolescence (Monseau, 1994). In short, reading good literature in a directed way is an excellent way of assisting teens in coping and even thriving during this time of transition from childhood to adulthood.

An interesting way of helping adolescents think through problem areas in their lives is through the use of fairy tales. According to Franzke (1989), fairy tales can be used therapeutically in a number of ways, such as through modification, invention, acting-out, or reading or reciting them. For example, Hill (1992) has used fairy tales such as Cinderella to treat persons with eating disorders. The model that Hill advocated has four phases: (a) identification of the fairy tale, (b) development of connection with the fairy tale, (c) introduction of conflict, and (d) problem resolution. "The fairy tale offers the client opportunities to experience novel thoughts, sensations, and behaviors by working with and through fairy tale figures" (Hill, 1992, p. 585).

An inventive example of a "therapeutic fairy tale" that clients create from the beginning has been formulated by Hoskins (1985). Adolescents are asked to participate in a pretend experience for a limited time. Specifically, they are asked to image and then do the following:

1. Set up a scene far from the "here and now" in time and place.
2. Within this setting, include a problem or a predicament.
3. Include a solution to the problem that is positive and pleasing.
4. Write their story within a 6- to 10-minute time period.

They begin their tales with "Once upon a time," as that is how all fairy tales begin, but after this standard opening they are on their own. After the tale is written, adolescents share their stories either individually or in a group setting, depending on the counseling format. Particular attention is paid to how thorough the fairy tale is, the qualities of the main characters, the nature of the pleasing and positive ending and what it depends on (e.g., skill, chance, luck), and the type of language used in creating the story. It is stressed to participants after this exercise that the limited amount of time is symbolic of life in general; they do not have unlimited time to work on life issues.

A third way literature is used with adolescents is by strategically discussing song lyrics and poetry related to life issues, especially careers. "Throughout the ages, poems and lyrics have moved people, and 20th-century youth have made lyrics a mainstay of their culture (Markert & Healy, 1983, p. 104). Thus, lyrics are "user friendly" for adolescents and can be employed to reach them in a way that other media cannot. A particular area in which such lyrical and poetic works are valuable is in career decision making. Song lyrics ranging from those of James Taylor's "That's Why I'm Here" to traditional songs such as "I've Been Working on the Railroad" address lifestyle and employment issues and can be arranged to fit particular groups in regard to ability, interest, and sophistication.

Adults

Adulthood is filled with opportunities and questions. The opportunities are especially prevalent in careers, and the questions are often difficult because they deal with making the most of limited time. As with adolescents, adults may find both comfort and direction in literature. Books that deal with midlife and beyond, such as *Everything to Gain* by Jimmy and Rosalynn Carter, *How to Prepare for Your High School Reunion and Other Midlife Musings* by Susan Allen Toth, and *Depression* by William Styron offer wisdom and sometimes wit to those in the midst of life's journey.

Two other bibliotherapeutic processes for adults are "writing the wrongs" and "writing the rights" (Gladding, 1991). In the first procedure, adults write out the wrong or disconcerting experiences they have had in life (e.g., unexpected death of a loved one, divorce, loss of physical or mental abilities). After the wrong has been described, clients write the situation right by not changing the facts but by simply writing out what they learned from the experiences and how they have benefited or been made right (or better) from it. Some excellent examples of this procedure appear in the October 1988 issue of the *Journal of Counseling and Development*, which was devoted to critical incidents in the lives of counselors. Another excellent example of this procedure is a brief article on loss and resolution by Sue Chance (1988) in which she has interwoven poetry, philosophy, and reality in a moving and dramatic way. Writing the rights is a similar experience, except it entails writing out the good or positive in one's life and assessing what was learned from these experiences.

Elderly Clients

Reading or writing is often quite therapeutic for elderly populations. It is an ancient healing art found throughout recorded history. One of the best non-Western personages to exemplify this therapeutic resource was Nezahualcoyotl (1402–1472), king of Texcoco (a city located approximately 20 miles northeast of modern Mexico City; Wasserman, 1988). In his struggle with his own mortality, Nezahualcoyotl wrote poetry as a way of working through despair and finding purpose in life.

In more recent history, the life-review process has become a popular therapeutic tool in helping elderly clients (Lewis & Butler, 1974). A life review involves having a person write his or her autobiography using family albums, old letters, personal memories, and interviews with others to gather and integrate life experiences into a meaningful whole. Ideally, this effort produces wisdom and satisfaction while alleviating pain and regrets.

Another literary way of working with elderly persons involves reading works by those within their age range. Books by Koch (1977), such as *I Never Told Anybody: Teaching Poetry Writing in a Nursing Home*, and by Kaminsky (1974), such as *What's Inside You It Shines Out of You* illustrate the creative potential of older adults and their insightful wisdom. Furthermore, reading these works helps to sensitize elderly clients and those who work with them to facts and feelings about aging, and thus they assist in creating understanding and empathy, as well as providing enjoyment.

Finally, in an experience that involves group work with elderly people, residents in nursing homes and other long-term care facilities can do reaction readings of poetry, during which they read poems aloud together as a group (i.e., a choral reading). They "then react to the content of the poems with their own knowledge, opinion, emotion, and imagination" (Asmuth, 1995, p. 415). In such an activity, residents become their own audience of their own performance. They are stimulated emotionally and intellectually. Furthermore, their self-concepts and cohesiveness as a group improves. Some examples of poems that have been found helpful in reaction reading include "Trees" by Joyce Kilmer, "They Have Yarns" by Carl Sandburg, and "Mother to Son" by Langston Hughes.

Groups

Groups are a popular setting for using literature. Creative writing exercises help heighten the use of language and emotion within a group (Wenz & McWhirter, 1990). "At the present time, group therapy seems to be the setting in which poetry is most frequently used as a therapeutic tool" (Chavis, 1986, p. 121). Psychiatric groups, which are usually open-ended and contain different people in each session, can use poetry and other literary works to generate a common bond at the start of the group session and to stimulate the expression of emotions. Self-help groups, such as AA, are settings in which other types of literature, for example, the "Big Book," are employed. (the "Big Book" focuses on implementing the 12 steps of AA). Usually poetry becomes a part of the group experience at the beginning or end of the process. In psychiatric and self-help groups, prosaic literature may be responded to throughout the process. In other types of counseling groups, however, literature is rarely referred to after the initial "forming" stage (Gladding, 1995).

One way of using a poem at the beginning of a group is as a catalyst. Lessner (1974) described this type of procedure: in her work with groups, she has read nondidactic poems—such as those by Langston Hughes, Maya Angelou, James Dickey, or A. R. Ammons—to group participants after they have been through a series of warm-up exercises. Each person in the group is asked to identify with an image in the poem and then talk about this image in regard to how it represents them. For example, a person might identify with grass and talk about how his or her life is growing.

In closing poems, group participants usually write couplets or lines and link them together in an interactive way that results in a collaborative poem (Yochim, 1994). Such a procedure requires involvement by everyone in a receptive (listening and reading) and expressive (creating) way (Mazza, 1988). It is usually an effective way to terminate a group experience permanently, or in the case of open-ended groups, to close the group for that session.

Life Skills

Besides being used with specific populations, literature can be employed in a guidance capacity to promote and foster general and specific life skills. In this type of arrangement, classic literary novels by such well-known writers as John Steinbeck, Toni Morrison, William Faulkner, Anne Tyler, Oscar Hijuelos, Ernest Hemingway, E. Annie Proulx, James Baldwin, Eudora Welty, and John Updike that deal with issues and problems of different age groups are included. Unique personal and universal developmental difficulties of primary characters are discussed along with ways employed by characters in a book to handle situations. Different ways of resolving dilemmas are highlighted by a helping professional, and other literary examples dealing with similar themes are presented. In this way, individuals of any age can learn from the insight of literature and discussions with others, especially in a group setting. The result is that those who participate in such a process often become better prepared to face issues in their own lives.

Such a life-style development approach complements and makes more relevant the theories of life development formulated by such well-known theorists as Erik Erikson (1968) and Carol Gilligan (1982). One way of promoting life skills using a reading approach is to have clients select relevant topics and chapters that deal with issues in their lives from a book such as Lerner and Mahlendorf's (1991) *Life Guidance Through Literature*. This text focuses on issues ranging from the establishment of personal identity to death as presented in novels, plays, short stories, and films. After reading, clients discuss their thoughts and struggles with the counselor as outlined previously in the bibliotherapy process. If a writing or scriptotherapy approach is chosen, it can take the form of writing poetry, which Bowman, Sauers, and Judice (1996) stressed as a way to anchor "insights into a context, physically as well as metaphorically" (p. 21) and thereby provide "a reference point for transforming experience" (p. 21).

Family Life Guidance

A similar approach to life-span guidance literature is family-life guidance literature. Three different styles have been taken with this focus. One is exemplified in the work of Rubinstein (1990), in which excerpts from different types of literature from poetry to novels are quoted as they relate to the developmental stages of marriage, such as newlyweds and midlife couples. A unique feature of this book is that it encompasses literature across the ages of civilization and thus combines the best of the old and the best of the new.

A second focus is taken by Chavis (1987); she has taken modern short stories depicting stages of family life and introduced the stages with a summary of the primary therapeutic issues involved. In this way an overlay is presented to readers before they read, alerting them to important elements to look for in particular passages. As in the life-span guidance approach, Chavis does not give answers, but has provided thought-provoking literature that stands on its own merits in addressing important family issues that must be successfully resolved. In this subtle, indirect manner, she has helped counselors and the lay public gain insight and chart directions for their own lives.

The third focus in family-life guidance is the autobiography. Few of these books have been written that focus on therapeutic issues, and by far the best in Augustus Napier's (1989) work *The Fragile Bond*. In his book, Napier details events of his own life that influenced his development as a professional and a person. His book is unique in its inclusion of marriage and family life in so detailed and vivid a manner. It offers behind-the-scenes accounts and insight into the difficulties and success of balancing a career with a marriage.

Graduate Counseling Students

A unique way to help graduate students resolve issues in their own lives involves having them write a 15- to 20-page family autobiography. They are instructed to describe the dynamics of their families of origin "utilizing the terminology and theoretical rationale" (Piercy & Sprenkle, 1986, p. 11) of major family theorists, such as Murray Bowen and James Framo. This type of assignment is biased in favor of students' perceptions of their families, yet it personalizes family theory and gives students an opportunity to think about issues within their own families.

Another way to help graduate students is to have them read about the lives of noted professionals. A resource in this area is *Pioneers in Counseling & Development* (Heppner, 1990), which highlights the achievements and setbacks of some of the most prominent counselors of the 20th century. *The Journal of Counseling & Development*, along with other American Counseling Association journals, and the *American Psychologist* publish current biographies and obituaries of leading figures in the helping professions, too.

Literature in Counseling With Other Creative Arts

Many creative arts complement the use of literature in counseling. For example, words may be acted out in formal or informal dramas, in which they are seen as well as heard. Counseling approaches to working from a literary point of view may take the form of movement or dance, too, as individuals express in a dynamic motion the essence of poetic or prosaic words. Two of the most widely used ways of integrating literature with other creative arts in counseling are by using music and art. These two media are covered here.

Literature and Music

Music can be employed in various ways with literature, and in some cases literature, especially poetry, is music. It is next to impossible to recite a poem without some "rhythmic pauses, vocal inflections, and interline harmonies as in music" (Masserman, 1986, p. 61). In other cases music is used to set a mood for a story or to heighten emotions. In these situations, instrumental or lyrical music may be played in the background before or during reading of literature. Similarly, music may be played before a select writing exercise. In such circumstances music helps stir up feelings and words that otherwise would have remained dormant. An example of such a process is the playing of John Denver's song "Poems, Prayers, and Promises" as a backdrop for a writing exercise entitled "What I Believe In" (Berger & Giovan, 1990).

An auditory complement to literature need not always be musical. For instance, in conducting bibliotherapy, special-effects tapes, such as sounds of the wind, a waterfall, or a crackling fire may be useful in setting a type of atmosphere conducive to reading or writing. Participants in a bibliotherapy session may make music of their own too (Hynes & Hynes-Berry, 1986). In the latter activity, clients either reflect in sound what they have experienced on the written level, or they anticipate what they believe will occur because of the title of a story or the focus of a writing assignment.

Literature and Visual Art

Art serves a special function when it is combined with literature. In such cases, pictures are thousand-word representations that are either realistic or distorted. Self-portraits, free form drawings, and classic paintings can be a prelude to, or complement to, writing assignments or other literary ways of expression that promote self-awareness and personal development (Creskey, 1988; Hageman & Gladding, 1983).

Drawing a personal logo and then describing it in a story is a creative and effective method for combing art and literature (Wenz & McWhirter, 1990). In this exercise, the logo is developed through playing with doodles until a symbol emerges that feels "just right" for the participant. Writing a story to accompany the art is similar to writing a therapeutic fairy tale as described previously. In hospice settings, terminally ill patients have benefited from the combined use of poetry and art (Hodges, 1993). In uniting these two art forms therapeutically, hospice residents were able "to gather new thoughts and ideas, to reflect upon past memories and experiences, and to enjoy the fellowship of others" who truly understood and cared about them (p. 28).

Another art and literature exercise is known as "lines of feelings." In this procedure, clients are asked to draw and color lines that represent their feelings about certain situations or people. The lines vary in length and shape, but often jagged, rough lines in red or orange are used to signify anger or discontent, and smooth, flowing lines in blues and greens are more often us to display calmness and contentment. After the lines are drawn, clients can expand on them by writing about what the lines represent, how it feels to draw them, or to whom or what they are directed.

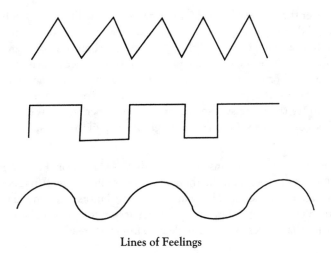

Lines of Feelings

The employment of modeling clay can be helpful because of the hands-on experiences participants obtain from shaping it. Often working in clay gives clients a feel for life experiences that may be expressed in writing. Likewise, photography can inspire reading or writing of the highest caliber and thus make the process of counseling more enjoyable and rewarding (Amerikaner, Schauble, & Ziller, 1980). In short, music and visual art contribute an added dimension to the main treatment modality of integrating literature into the counseling process.

Summary

Literature is used in numerous ways in counseling and with many different types of clients. Individuals gain insight and are able to release emotions through reading and writing exercises that are prosaic or poetic in nature. These processes are known as bibliotherapy and scriptotherapy and are practiced on an interactive level. By participating in prosaic or poetic reading and writing activities, including keeping journals and autobiographies, clients gain a perspective on their lives that helps them establish meaning and purpose. By following the language of clients, counselors are able to offer them additional assistance for helping themselves.

Literature can be used in counseling with other media devices such as video- and audiotapes, pictures and drawings, and music. Storytelling may also be included and is quite effective with children as well as adults. When chosen properly, literature can offer life guidance for people of all ages. It depicts possible futures while energizing clients and offering them ways of integrating their experiences.

Exercises

1. Over the course of a week's time, reflect on the literature you have experienced that has made a lasting impact on your life. Write down the titles and authors of these works and the age you were when you discovered them. Look for any age- or stage-specific patterns in your choices and how the literature you read or had read to you made a difference. After you have made your list, discuss this experience with a close friend or colleague. Invite that person to try the exercise also. Compare your experiences. What literature from both of your lists do you think might be helpful to others?

2. Examine recent counseling journals and American Library publications for recent articles on the therapeutic use of literature. What books and writings are recommended? How do these contributors recommend using literature in counseling? Draw up a guidance lesson for a particular group you work with that makes use of ideas gleaned from your readings.

3. Consult a reference librarian in your local community about the literature currently being read. Survey these materials and think of ways you might incorporate them into your counseling sessions.

References

Adams, K. (1994). *The way of the journal.* Lutherville, MD: Sidran.

Alekseychik, A. (1989). Bibliotherapy: An effective principal and supplementary method of healing, correcting, and administering relief. *Journal of Poetry Therapy, 3,* 19–22.

Amerikaner, M., Schauble, P., & Ziller, R. (1980). Images: The use of photographs in personal counseling. *Personnel and Guidance Journal, 59,* 68–73.

Asmuth, M.V. (1995). Reaction reading: A tool for providing fantasy imagery for long-term care facility residents. *Gerontologist, 35,* 415–419.

Barbour, J. (1991, March 27). Doctors who become writers. *Winston-Salem Journal,* pp. W1, W4.

Baum, F. L. (1900). *The wonderful wizard of Oz.* New York: Hill.

Berger, A. (1988). Working through grief by writing poetry. *Journal of Poetry Therapy, 1,* 11–19.

Berger, A., & Giovan, M. (1990). Poetic interventions with forensic patients. *Journal of Poetry Therapy, 4,* 83–92.

Berry, J. (1987). *Every kid's guide to handling feelings.* Chicago: Children's.

Bettleheim, B. (1976). *The uses of enchantment: The meaning and importance of fairy tales.* New York: Knopf.

Borders, S. G., & Naylor, A. P. (1993). *Children talking about books.* Phoenix, AZ: Oryx.

Bowman, D. O., Sauers, R. J., & Judice, R. P. (1996). Exploration of sexual identity through poetry therapy *Journal of Poetry Therapy, 10,* 19–26.

Bowman, T. (1994). Using poetry, fiction, and essays to help people face shattered dreams. *Journal of Poetry Therapy, 8,* 81–89.

Brand, A. (1987). Writing as counseling. *Elementary School Guidance & Counseling, 21,* 266–275.

Brown, H. J., Jr. (1991). *Life's little instruction book.* Nashville, TN: Rutledge Hill.

Carroll, M. R. (1970). Silence is the heart's size. *Personnel and Guidance Journal, 48,* 546–551.

Chance, S. (1988). Loss and resolution. *Journal of Poetry Therapy, 2,* 93–98.

Chavis, G. G. (1986). The use of poetry for clients dealing with family issues. *Arts in Psychotherapy, 13,* 121–128.

Chavis, G. G. (1987). *Family: Stories from the interior.* St. Paul: Graywolf.

Clifton, L. (1991). *Quilting.* Brockport, NY: BOA Editions.

Costello, M., Phelps, L., & Wilczenski, F. (1994). Children and military conflict: Current issues and treatment implications. *The School Counselor, 41,* 220–225.

Coughlin, E. K. (1991, February 13). A Cinderella story: Research on children's books takes on new life as a field of literary study. *Chronicle of Higher Education,* pp. A5–A7.

Creskey, M. N. (1988). Processing possible selves in possible worlds through poetry. *Journal of Poetry Therapy, 1,* 207–220.

Dreyer, S. S. (1989). *The bookfinder.* Circle Pines, MN: American Guidance Service.

Erikson, E. H. (1968). *Identity: Youth and crisis.* New York: Norton.

France, M. H., Cadieux, J., & Allen, E. (1995). Letter therapy: A model for enhancing counseling intervention. *Journal of Counseling & Development, 73,* 317–318.

Franzke, E. (1989). *Fairy tales in psychotherapy: The creative use of old and new tales.* New York: Hogrefe & Huber.

Freud, S. (1965). *The interpretation of dreams.* New York: Avon. (Original work published 1900)

Gardner, J. (1993). Runaway with words: Teaching poetry to at-risk teens. *Journal of Poetry Therapy, 6,* 213–227.

Gardner, R. A. (1971). *Therapeutic communication with children: The mutual storytelling technique in child psychotherapy.* New York: Aronson.

Gibson, R. L., & Mitchell, M. H. (1990). *Introduction to counseling and guidance.* New York: Macmillan.

Gilligan, C. (1982). *In a different voice: Psychological theory and women's development.* Cambridge, MA: Harvard University Press.

Gladding, S. T. (1990). *In lines through time.* Unpublished manuscript.

Gladding, S. T. (1991, April). *The well practitioner.* Paper presented at the annual convention of the American Counseling Association, Reno, NV.

Gladding, S. T. (1995). *Group work: A counseling specialty (2nd ed.).* Englewood Cliffs, NJ: Prentice-Hall.

Gladding, S. T. (1998). *Family therapy: History, theory & practice* (2nd ed.). Englewood Cliffs, NJ: Prentice-Hall.

Gladding, S. T., & Gladding, C. T. (1991). The ABCs of bibliotherapy. *The School Counselor, 39,* 7–13.

Gold, J. (1988). The value of fiction as therapeutic recreation and developmental mediator: A theoretical framework. *Journal of Poetry Therapy, 1,* 135–148.

Gorelick, K. (1987). Poetry therapy as therapeutic ritual in treating traumas from the past. *American Journal of Social Psychiatry, 7,* 93–95.

Gorelick, K., & Lerner, A. (1997, May). *Choice or chance: Choosing and using literature.* Paper presented at the annual conference of the National Association for Poetry Therapy, Cleveland, OH.

Guerin, P. J., Jr. (1976). The use of the arts in family therapy: I never sang for my father. In P. J. Guerin, Jr. (Ed.), *Family therapy: Theory and practice* (pp. 480–500). New York: Gardner.

Hageman, M. B., & Gladding, S. T. (1983). The art of career exploration: Occupational sex-role stereotyping among elementary school children. *Elementary School Guidance & Counseling, 17,* 280–287.

Harjo, J. (1983). *She had some horses.* New York: Thunder's Mouth.

Heninger, O. E. (1987). Poetry generated by stillbirth and livebirth: Transgenerational sharing of grief and joy. *Journal of Poetry Therapy, 1*, 14–22.

Heppner, P. P. (1990). *Pioneers in counseling & development*. Alexandria, VA: American Counseling Association.

Hill, L. (1992). Fairy tales: Visions for problem resolution for eating disorders. *Journal of Counseling & Development, 70*, 584–587.

Hodges, D. (1993). For every season . . . art and poetry therapy with terminally ill patients. *Journal of Poetry Therapy, 7*, 21–43.

Hoskins, M. (1985, April). *Therapeutic fairy tales*. Paper presented at the annual meeting of the National Association of Poetry Therapy, Chicago, IL.

Hynes, A. M., & Hynes-Berry, M. (1986). *Bibliotherapy: The interactive process*. Boulder, CO: Westview.

Ingalls, Z. (1997, February 28). A professor of medicine discovers the healing power of poetry. *Chronicle of Higher Education*, pp. B8, B9.

Kaminsky, M. (1974). *What's inside you it shines out of you*. New York: Horizon.

Kestenbaum, C. J. (1985). The creative process in child psychotherapy. *American Journal of Psychotherapy, 39*, 479–489.

Kincade, E. A., & Evans, K. M. (1996). Counseling theories, process and interventions in a multicultural context. In J. L. DeLucia-Waack (Ed.), *Multicultural counseling competencies: Implications for training and practice* (pp. 89–112). Alexandria, VA: American Counseling Association.

Koch, K. (1970). *Wishes, lies, and dreams*. New York: Harper & Row.

Koch, K. (1977). *I never told anybody: Teaching poetry writing in a nursing home*. New York: Random House.

Kolodzey, J. (1983, January). Poetry: The latest word in healing. *Prevention, 35*, 62–68.

Kottler, J. A. (1986). *On being a therapist*. San Francisco, CA: Jossey-Bass.

Leedy, J. (1985). *Poetry as healer*. New York: Vanguard.

Lerner, A. (1988). Poetry therapy corner. *Journal of Poetry Therapy, 2*, 118–120.

Lerner, A. (1994). *Poetry in the therapeutic experience*. Saint Louis: MMB Music.

Lerner, A. (1997). A look at poetry therapy. *Arts and Psychotherapy, 24*, 81–89.

Lerner, A. & Mahlendorf, U., (1991). *Life guidance through literature*. Chicago: American Library Association.

Lessner, J. W. (1974). The poem as catalyst in group counseling. *Personnel and Guidance Journal, 53*, 33–38.

Lewis, M. I., & Butler, R. N. (1974). Life review therapy. *Geriatrics, 29*, 165–173.

Markert, L. F., & Healy, C. C. (1983). The effects of poetry and lyrics on work values. *Journal of Career Education, 10*, 104–110.

Masserman, J. H. (1986). Poetry as music. *Arts in Psychotherapy, 13*, 61–67.

May, R. (1969). *Love and will*. New York: Norton.

Mazza, N. (1988). Poetry and popular music as adjunctive psychotherapy techniques. In P. A. Keller & S. R. Heyman (Eds.), *Innovations in clinical practice: A source book* (Vol. 7, pp. 485–494). Sarasota, FL: Professional Resource Exchange.

Meier, S. T., & Davis, S. R. (1997). *The elements of counseling* (3rd ed). Pacific Grove, CA: Brooks/Cole.

Mercer, L. E. (1993). Self-healing through poetry writing. *Journal of Poetry Therapy, 6*, 161–168.

Monseau, V. R. (1994). Studying Cormier's Protagonists: Achieving power through young adult literature. *ALAN Review, 22*, 31–33.

Pardeck, J. T., & Pardeck, J. A. (1993). *Bibliotherapy: A clinical approach for helping children*. Landhorne, PA: Gordon & Breach.

Peck, M. S. (1978). *The road less traveled*. New York: Simon & Schuster.

Pennebaker, J. (1990). *Opening up: The healing power of confiding in others*. New York: Avon.

Perakis, C. R. (1992). Prescriptive literature: Story and lyric as therapy. *Journal of Poetry Therapy, 6*, 95–100.

Piercy, F. P., & Sprenkle, D. H. (1986). *Family therapy sourcebook*. New York: Guilford.

Progoff, I. (1975). *At a journal workshop*. New York: Dialogue House.

Reiter, S. (1988). The Wizard of Oz in the Land of Id: A bibliotherapy approach. *Journal of Poetry Therapy, 3*, 149–156.

Riordan, R. J. (1996). Scriptotherapy: Therapeutic writing as a counseling adjunct. *Journal of Counseling & Development, 74*, 263–269.

Riordan, R. J., & Ketchum, S. B. (1996). Therapeutic correspondence: The usefulness of notes and letters in counseling. *Georgia Journal of Professional Counseling*, 31–40.

Riordan, R. J., Mullis, F., & Nuchow, L. (1996). Organizing for bibliotherapy: The science in the art. *Individual Psychology, 52*, 169–180.

Riordan, R. J., & Wilson, L. S. (1989). Bibliotherapy: Does it work? *Journal of Counseling & Development, 67*, 506–508.

Rofes, E. E. (Ed.). (1981). *The kids' book of divorce*. Lexington, MA: Lewis.

Rossiter, C., & Brown, R. (1988). An evaluation of interactive bibliotherapy in a clinical setting. *Journal of Poetry Therapy, 1*, 157–168.

Rubin, R. J. (1978). *Using bibliotherapy: A guide to theory and practice*. Phoenix, AZ: Oryx.

Rubinstein, H. (1990). *The Oxford book of marriage*. New York: Oxford University Press.

Santrock, J. W., Minnett, P. M., & Campbell, B. D. (1994). *The authoritative guide to self-help books*. New York: Guilford.

Valine, W. J. (1983). Intensifying the group member's experience using the group log. *Journal for Specialists in Group Work, 8*, 101–104.

Wasserman, M. (1988). Poetry as a healing force in later adulthood: The case of Nezahualcoyotl. *Journal of Poetry Therapy, 1*, 221–228.

Watson, J. (1980). Bibliotherapy for abused children. *The School Counselor, 27*, 204–208.

Weinhold, B. K. (1987). Altered states of consciousness: An explorer's guide to inner space. *Counseling and Human Development, 20*, 1–12.

Wenz, K., & McWhirter, J. J. (1990). Enhancing the group experience: Creative writing exercises. *Journal for Specialists in Group Work, 15*, 37–42.

White, M., & Epston, D. (1990). *Narrative means to therapeutic ends*. New York: Norton.

Yochim, K. (1994). The collaborative poem and inpatient group therapy: A brief report. *Journal of Poetry Therapy, 7*, 145–149.

7

Drama and Counseling

At 35, with wife and child,
    a Ph.D., and hopes as bright
        as a full moon on an August night,
He took his place as a healing man
Blending it with imagination, necessary change,
    and common sense
To make more than an image on an eye lens
    of a small figure running quickly up steps;
Quietly he traveled
    like one who holds a candle to darkness
        and questions its powers,
So that with heavy years, long walks,
    shared love, and additional births,
He became as the seasoned actor,
    who, forgetting his lines in the silence,
        stepped upstage and without prompting
        lived them.

(Gladding, 1974, p. 586)

DRAMA FOCUSES ON COMMUNICATION between people and the roles that individuals take in their daily lives. "In therapy, as in all human activity, drama is both inevitable and necessary. It is inevitable because, during the human lifecycle, people are constantly confronted with dramatic changes, and it is necessary because all transitions occur as a result of more or less dramatic experiences-in-action" (Kedem-Tahar & Felix-Kellermann, 1996, p. 27). Therefore, as Jaques eloquently remarks in Shakespeare's *As You Like It* (Act 2, Scene 7), "All the world is a stage." Roles vary as persons develop and face new challenges at different times and in various situations.

Joseph Campbell (1949) took the view that much of human life and drama is similar to patterns found in myths throughout the ages. Unhealthy individuals often act out in rigid and stereotyped ways, such as being placaters, distracters, computers, or blamers (Satir, 1972). In such roles they fail to be straightforward and honest with their thoughts and feelings. Through default they act in an uncaring manner such as many characters on television soap operas do in relationship to issues of intimacy (Lowry & Towles, 1989).

Healthy people, on the other hand, are able to change their behaviors in response to environmental demands. They are open, flexible, and communicate in a congruent manner. Sometimes they become stuck and dysfunctional, too, but in these cases they seek assistance. Drama or drama-related approaches to counseling, such as psychodrama, may be helpful to these individuals in gaining a "greater understanding of social roles" and a clearer perspective on their lives in "relationship to family, friends, and past life" (Warren, 1984, p. 133). It is on the formal and informal use of drama, psychodrama, and drama-related techniques that the material in this chapter focuses.

The employment of drama as a part of the healing process extends far back in history. One of its most important times was in fifth century B.C. Athens, where dramatic traditions originated and flourished for years. The tragic drama, the older of the Greek drama forms, "depicted the unthinkable and unspeakable in ways that allowed members of the audience to participate in the dual roles of sufferer-participant and empathizer-observer" (Gorelick, 1987, p. 38). Dramatic productions dealt with the eternal struggle between individual strivings and realistic limitations and engaged observers in asking existential questions regarding self-identity and purpose in life. The works of Sophocles, Aeschylus, and Euripides are examples of dramas that fostered audience identification, catharsis, and insight in such a way that what was personally felt at the time of a performance "would carry over to personal life beyond the theatrical space" (Gorelick, 1987, p. 40).

Even in modern times, dramatic art forms continue to be very powerful and widespread. "The female shamans of Korea, the Taoist priests of China, the masked dancers at Owuru Festivals in Nigeria and the celebrants at Mardi Gras in Louisiana and Carnival in Brazil, all enact a form of cathartic healing through assuming archetypal roles and working their magic" (Landy, 1997, p. 5). Basically, dramatic activities include rituals, plays, improvisations, storytelling, masks, puppetry, and festivals, as well as theater performances.

Premise of the Use of Drama in Counseling

As a profession, counseling has many parallels with the type of drama practiced by the ancient Greeks and practiced worldwide today. In both endeavors, those involved learn to experience a whole range of emotions and appropriately express them. Counselors and dramatists then and now practice being sensitive to the parts they are called to play and to become likewise attuned to those with whom they interact. Besides learning and expressing emotions, persons involved in both processes become consciously aware that what they do and how they do it will have an effect on the audiences before whom they perform. In essence, people who practice these two professions become heavily involved in all aspects of life and experience life on its deepest levels (Friedman, 1984). They become role models in their search for deeper understanding (Bandura, 1977). Their behaviors have either a positive or negative effect on others with whom they closely deal.

In addition to the qualities mentioned, another parallel in drama and counseling is timing (Okun, 1997). It is essential in both that events be timed to have a maximum impact. "Good drama is not a function of clever words. And like all process, whether it is baking, gardening, or healing, it is a child of the experience of time. Time is the father of joy and pathos, tragedy and seriousness, irony and mischievousness, paradox and madness, and absurdity and love. Most comparisons of theater and therapy overlook this common organizing principle so essential to the flowering of human creativity" (Friedman, 1984, p. 29).

In drama, impact moments are staged and involve three factors: the characters, the audience, and information about what is going to happen. Several incidents build up to a dramatic climax. Usually, the creation of such a scene is due to these elements:

1. mystery (when a character in a story has information unknown to others),
2. suspense (when someone else knows something is about to happen but a character is un-suspecting), and
3. shock or surprise (when something happens that simultaneously surprises everyone; Lankton & Lankton, 1983).

These scenes are staged in such a way that everyone involved is aware of their importance.

Likewise, in counseling, certain dramatic movement is a natural part of the process. Family therapist Salvador Minuchin conducts family treatment as though he were a theatrical director, and insists that interpersonal enactments are essential for capturing the real drama of family life (Nichols & Schwartz, 1995). In reality, counselors and clients may be in the midst of mystery, suspense, or even shock at times. At other times, less dynamic events occur. For instance, on occasions counselors withhold insights and ideas until they feel assured that clients will be able to hear and use this information to the fullest. Overall, drama and counseling often mimic each other.

A fourth premise behind the use of drama in counseling is that life difficulties are reflected in counseling through dramatic means. Therefore, the language and action of counseling should be expressed in dramatic terms. This idea is most manifest in the theoretical underpinnings of transactional analysis. Clients enact the roles of parent, adult, and child by playing games such as "if only" and "kick me," and living by scripts that either enable or inhibit them in establishing healthy life styles (Berne, 1964). The most dysfunctional way individuals play games is through engaging in "drama triangle" interactions, in which all involved unconsciously agree to rotate being in the destructive positions of victim (the oppressed), rescuer (the savior) and persecutor (the punisher; Karpman, 1968).

Another premise of using drama in counseling is that through enacting different roles clients will become more attuned to their full range of feelings and become enabled to exercise all parts of themselves in an integrated and holistic way (Irwin, 1987). The idea behind this view is represented well in the work of gestalt therapy (Perls, 1969). In the gestalt approach, clients play many roles, some of which are more comfortable for them to enact than others. Ultimately, clients are introduced through role plays to those aspects of themselves that they have repressed or denied.

A sixth premise in using drama in therapeutic settings is the concept that through witnessing or participating in spontaneous plays or staged productions, participants gain insight into themselves by identifying with certain emotions that are expressed. Thus, the focus of drama therapy is on the problems of specific individuals or groups, although the format of any one drama may seem universal in scope (Blatner, 1989). If all goes well, the level of feeling in particular persons is increased to the point that repressed or denied affect is recognized and eventually worked through.

For example, minorities are often stereotyped by majority populations and consequently have difficulties being treated as equals. The power of drama highlights such unequal and unjust action and can lead toward greater sensitivity and fairness. *Guess Who's Coming to Dinner*, a film about racial equality, *Coming Into Passion: Song for a Sansei*, a play about the stereotyping of Asian women, and *Dances With Wolves*, a film about the lives of Native Americans, are three examples of dramatic productions that have made a positive impact on individuals in their audiences and society as a whole.

Yet another rationale behind using drama in counseling is that powerful drama, like effective counseling, is relationship-oriented and based in a climate of creative spontaneity. In other words, methods and techniques are secondary to personalization and imagination. By reminding themselves that the elements of change and resistance are found in authentic people encounters, counselors can productively set the stage for newness. Such a premise is exemplified in the universal principle that "people hear you when they are moving towards you, never when they are being pursued" (Friedman, 1984, p. 29). Any dramatic approach to counseling or life includes both involvement and distancing (Snow, 1996).

Practice of the Use of Drama in Counseling

Several counseling traditions advocate either participation in or observation of dramas. The most notable are drama therapy and psychodrama, which share a common territory but are distinctive (Casson, 1996; Snow, 1996). In addition, drama is used in therapeutic settings in conjunction with gestalt therapy, rational-emotive behavioral therapy, and Adlerian counseling approaches (Gladding, 1995).

Drama Therapy

Drama therapy involves the "intentional use of creative drama toward the psychotherapeutic goals of symptom relief, emotional and physical integration, and personal growth" (Johnson, 1982, p. 83). It deals with hypothetical situations and uses projective techniques that tend to distance the performer from the material being enacted. In drama therapy, "the dramatic action part of the process is unlike traditional theatre performance in that the action is not scripted but improvised, a return in some ways to the earliest known forms of drama when the actor and the dramatist were one" (MacKay, 1987, p. 201). Through the enactment of fantasy and hypothetical situations participants realize more fully the wealth of emotions within themselves and ideally translate this knowledge into their own life events. People who chose a drama therapist for treatment are generally open to, if not skilled in, acting (Landy, 1997). Many times they have developmental deficiencies, but they are usually not in a life crisis. "Drama therapy, as it is practiced today, is oriented specifically toward creative expressive learning of roles" (Kedem-Tahar & Felix-Kellermann, 1996, p. 34).

Drama therapy consists of three stages: (a) warm-up, (b) enactment, and (c) growth (Dunne, 1988). "The uniqueness of drama therapy is that it proceeds through role" and "through role-playing, storytelling, mask, and puppetry" (Landy, 1991, p. 39). Thus, it helps clients come in contact with internalized roles and allows the manifestation of these roles outward for a further extension of personal awareness.

Drama therapists registered by the National Association for Drama Therapy have a background in the theater. They are skilled in assessing the themes and potential impact of dramatic productions and hold at least an entry level degree (B.A.) from a college or university that offers a program in drama therapy with at least an internship in this specialty before they begin practice under supervision (Emunah, 1989). Because of this education, drama therapists are able to help a wide range of clients, including schizophrenic adults, autistic and developmentally disabled children, homeless persons, war veterans, and prisoners, among others (Landy, 1997).

Psychodrama

The term *psychodrama* comes from the Greek words *psyche*, meaning soul or spirit and *drama* meaning action. Thus, psychodrama means "presenting the soul in action" (Kedem-Tahar & Felix-Kellerman, 1996, p. 27). The practice of psychodrama "involves the integration of imagination and action with verbal expression and self-reflection. Because it involves movement and speech, psychodrama, like drama therapy, can readily integrate the related creative and expressive modalities of dance, music, poetry, and art" (Blatner, 1997, p. 23). The practice was originated by Jacob L. Moreno during the early part of the 20th century. He called psychodrama "a science which explores the 'truth' by dramatic methods" (Moreno, 1993, p. 53). Through his observation of children, Moreno was convinced of the "importance of spontaneity as part of the creative and vitalizing processes of life" (Blatner, 1989, p. 562). Moreno hoped to influence the mental health of mainstream society by forming a group of nontraditional actors into the Theater of Spontaneity in Vienna. Because of economic conditions, however, Moreno was forced to move his attention away from the masses to the treatment of the mentally ill and to move to the United States. By the 1960s, through his writings and workshops, he introduced psychodrama techniques to professionals in North and South America, Asia, and Europe (Hug, 1997).

Psychodrama emphasizes encounters in the present. Individuals act out their problems in creative, spontaneous, and productive ways with a full expression of feelings. The emphases in these circumstances is on the enactment of nonverbal events through which new realizations occur, thus enabling and empowering people in their growth and development. In these situations, it is vital that natural barriers of time and space be obliterated (Greenberg, 1974). Catharsis and insight must take place, too, through the total communication of feelings between individuals (Moreno, 1945).

Three phases occur within any psychodrama: (a) warm-up, (b) action, and (c) integration (Blatner, 1997). In the warm-up, everyone is emotionally and technically readied for the psychodrama by arranging the stage and engaging in affectively based activities such as sensory awareness (Blatner, 1989).

In the action phase, the psychodrama is actually performed, with a protagonist assigning others within the group various "auxillary ego roles of significant others or things in the protagonist's life" (Gladding, 1995, p. 391). Sometimes a protagonist is assigned to do a soliloquy. This person gives a monologue about his or her situation as he or she is acting it out. At other times, a "monodrama" (autodrama) technique is used, in which the protagonist plays all the parts of the enactment. A protagonist may be asked to literally switch roles with another person in the psychodrama and through this role reversal he or she can gain insight into conflict, as well (Corey,

1990). The protagonist may also be assigned the activity of watching from offstage while some-one else plays his or her part (the mirror technique). A final technique used in this action phase is the double or multiple double (in the case of ambivalence), during which a protagonist's alter ego helps express true inner feelings more clearly (Blatner, 1988).

In the integration phase, the protagonist is helped to process what happened in the psy-chodrama emotionally and intellectually. The counselor should emphasize "understanding and integration so the protagonist can act differently if any similar situations arise" (Gladding, 1995, p. 391). Thus, "the essential process of psychodrama occurs not in the action itself, but more when the participants in the event can pause, stand back, perhaps consciously play out some al-ternative scenes and endeavor to respond to the problem with greater awareness and for the pur-pose of more authentic and inclusive effectiveness" (Blatner, 1997, p. 23).

Drama in Counseling

Not all professionals who use drama in counseling are drama therapists, and not all use of drama constitutes psychodrama. Some are specialists in other helping professions who have interest and knowledge about the power and potential of drama in influencing change and have devel-oped skills to go with their awareness. For example, Philip Guerin (1976), a pioneer in the mar-riage and family counseling field, has included a number of movies in his work with families, such as Robert Anderson's *I Never Sang for My Father* and Ingmar Bergman's *Scenes From a Mar-riage*. He has used these films to prod families into thinking about their own problems. In a vari-ation on this technique, family therapist Frank Pittman (1989) has used select dramatic scenes from movies as diverse as *Gone With the Wind* and *Steel Magnolias* to illustrate aspects of interper-sonal relationships present off the screen. His intention is to emphasize the therapeutic inter-ventions connected with such situations when they are dysfunctional.

To highlight values and decision making in life, counselors can also use a number of other movies that teach and challenge one's thinking. Among those I have used are: *The Autobiography of Miss Jane Pittman, Brian's Song, Chariots of Fire, E. T.—The Extraterrestrial, The Elephant Man, Gandhi, Inherit the Wind, Judgment at Nuremberg, Mask, Pinocchio, Stand and Deliver,* and *To Kill a Mockingbird*. Before using dramatic videos, like these for so-called "cinematherapy" (Newton, 1995) counselors should view the films and decide what aspects they wish to highlight and why.

In discussing the importance of drama in promoting mental health in schools, Sylvia (1977) pointed out five essential elements common to both drama and counseling (problem, choice, crisis, climax, and resolution) that may be used in the helping process.

Problems may be presented in many ways, but usually a trademark of their appearance in a play or in a real life situation is a certain amount of emotional discomfort or incongruence on the part of the person(s) involved. For example, Hamlet is troubled by the sudden death of his father and the quick remarriage of his mother to his uncle. He agonizes over whether to pursue the matter further (choice) but eventually feels duty bound to the spirit of his father and con-fronts his mother, his uncle, and others involved by having actors perform a play paralleling his situation (crisis). The climax of the drama is the death of several leading characters, including Hamlet, and the final resolution is that the court in Denmark changes in regard to the primary players involved and its psychological climate.

When using drama in counseling, care must always be taken to see that clients feel connected with this form of treatment and that they benefit from it. Drama in counseling will occur on covert or overt levels regardless of whether a drama medium is used. It is up to the counselor in collaboration with clients to make the decisions that lead to or away from dealing with drama on a conscious level.

Gestalt Therapy and Drama

Gestalt therapy has emphasized drama techniques in its implementation ever since its inception. Gestalt means the formation of an organized meaningful whole, and "the main thrust of gestalt therapy is to help people develop their faculties of awareness in order to make choices, determine their existence, and become self-sufficient. . . . Gestalt psychodrama reflects the existential, experimental, and experiential nature of Gestalt therapy" (Coven, Ellington, & Van Hull, 1997, p. 17). Some of the dramatic methods used in this approach include role-playing, exaggerating, intensity, becoming aware of bodily senses, staying with feelings, and closure (James & Jongeward, 1971). In role-playing, clients enact scenes or situations they would otherwise describe. For instance, in reporting dreams, clients are directed to role-play all aspects of their dreams (Perls, 1970). If clients have complaints, they are encouraged to exaggerate their discontent and thus get the complaint in perspective.

Regardless of what clients are working on, they are instructed to be aware of what their body is telling them as well as what they are saying. A closed body posture in the midst of a conversation during which someone reports being open is a glaring contradiction. Finally, while they are focusing on themselves, clients are reminded to stay with their feelings and not option out of a situation by intellectualizing ("head tripping"). Like a sophisticated actor knows how to feel a wide range of emotions and respond to them appropriately, so clients learn to become more attuned to their feelings and act on them accordingly.

The empty-chair technique is unique in Perls' version of gestalt therapy, and an emphasis is placed on owning one's emotions. In this approach, which may also be employed in gestalt psychodrama, there is a "hot seat" for the person who wants to work and an empty chair into which troublesome emotions may be projected. Each individual who chooses to work will reflect and project emotions onto the empty chair as needed and dialogue with the polar parts of themselves until some integrated resolution results. Use of the word *I* is encouraged in this type and other types of transactions to increase a sense of personal responsibility (Coven et al., 1997).

Rational-Emotive Behavioral Therapy and Drama

Rational-emotive behavioral therapy (REBT) uses a number of behaviorally based and dramatic exercises to help clients become more rational and functional. Among the most dramatically creative is what is known as a "shame attack." In this assignment, clients first mentally and then actually practice, in role-plays and in real life, a particular behavior that they have always feared or dreaded. The action might be as simple as going into a restaurant and asking for a glass of water, or it might involve pretending to faint in a crowd and trusting the best behaviors of those around to prevail in offering help. As in any drama, learning how to enact a certain part is difficult at first, but as practice continues the part becomes an integrated aspect of the personality until acting a certain way becomes a habit of the heart.

Adlerian Therapy and Drama

Before Ellis devised his theory and emphasis on the practice of integrating thoughts with behaviors, such as in shame attacks, Alfred Adler was stressing behavioral change through a process known as "acting as if" (Adler, 1963). In this procedure, clients discuss how they would like to behave. Then they are simply instructed to act as if they were the persons they wish to be. The technique is one that is usually met with protests because clients think they are being "phony," but stress is lowered when individuals involved know they are simply acting and that their new behaviors in effect are no different from trying on new clothes to see how well they fit and feel (Mosak, 1989).

Drama in Counseling With Specific Populations

Drama is employed in different ways and at various levels of sophistication in counseling, depending on the age and stage of clients. It is critical that counselors be sensitive to developmental aspects of those with whom they work so that the drama work in which they engage will have a maximum impact.

Children

Preschool children live a life that is usually rich in fantasy and pretend. Thus, getting them to "act out" dramas with toys or talk to puppets is usually safe and fun for them and revealing for counselors (Hughes, 1988). Dramatic play in young children is related to creativity as well. Both involve alternative symbolic constructions and flexibility (Mellou, 1995). Therefore, children benefit in multiple ways through participating in drama activities.

One technique that has been successful with young children is the family puppet interview. Children make up stories about the family by using puppets (Irwin & Malloy, 1975). These stories usually highlight conflicts and alliances within families, but may be of limited usefulness—asking direct questions is often more productive in obtaining information. Nevertheless, by using objects such as dolls or puppets familiar to children, the opportunity to learn or promote conflict resolution is maximized (James & Myer, 1987). In such situations, counselors must be sure to focus on issues at hand and not become too involved in manipulating the props or puppets. An alternative to using puppets is for clinicians to have children watch select segments of popular television programs such as "Sesame Street," "Shari Lewis," and "Mr. Roger's Neighborhood." Professionals who produce these shows frequently emphasize socially appropriate ways of dealing with troublesome situations of childhood.

A similar developmental opportunity for dramatic impact, insight, and growth is present with older children (ages 6 to 12 years). These children live between young childhood and adolescence. They often daydream and fantasize about their futures, and therefore drama techniques such as role-playing or staging guidance plays are an excellent technique to employ with this group (Wilson, 1983). Children in this age bracket may enjoy writing and producing their own plays, too. Such an activity helps them gain a perspective on their values and become more sensitive to the way they handle complex problems or people.

For counselors in need of a source for creative drama activities, especially for elementary school children, Renard and Sockol (1987) have compiled a book containing guidance lessons for building healthy self-esteem. These lessons are based on dramatic activities and each lesson contains the same format—a focus, introduction, preparation, warm-ups and cool-downs, directions and activities, discussion, and summary.

Adolescents

Adolescents are often dramatic in their actions. Their participation in a number of ritualistic activities, such as sports, provides them with an opportunities to play out parts of life in a highly charged and physical way and to keep their impulses in check. Drama can be used to assist adolescents in gaining greater control over their lives, as well as in learning new roles. For instance, Shaffer (1996) has used a psychodrama technique based on Shakespeare's play *Hamlet* to help middle schoolers learn to become more aware that what they do has an impact on others as well as themselves and that they have choices in what they do. His approach works on both an experiential and cognitive level. The adolescents first warm up (by reading or viewing a video version of *Hamlet*), and then examine the wants and needs of each character. This is followed by a role-play in groups of three, in which one student plays the protagonist and is flanked by the other two students, whose roles are that of revenge and caution, action and inaction. In these role-plays, which last for 15 minutes, each of the flanking actors tries to passionately persuade the prince (or princess) to chose his or her point of view. After time is called, the protagonist shares with the others in the group thoughts and feelings that emerged during his or her decision making. The process is repeated until each of the trio (and ultimately everyone in a group) has an opportunity to actively participate as the protagonist.

Videotaped improvisational drama has been found to significantly increase the ability of adolescents to maintain internal locus of control (Dequine & Pearson-Davis, 1983). In most cases, videotaping therapy with adolescents helps them do one or more of the following:

- receive instant feedback about their behaviors (especially in groups);
- gain limited control over their therapy through operating some of the equipment, such as cameras and playback units;
- deal with transference issues realistically because of being able to see their conduct;
- overcome resistance to adults more easily because of a focus on equipment; and
- become more involved in formulating their identities through objective observations of their behaviors, both verbal and nonverbal (Furman, 1990).

When dramatic exercises are not videotaped, it is critical that a structured environment be set up in which adolescents still maintain a feeling of autonomy. This type of setting can be constructed by allowing adolescents to enact situations dealing with aggression, flight, conflict, and rebelliousness (Emunah, 1985). Using such a method avoids struggles between counselors and adolescents because primary issues are acknowledged in advance and dealt with therapeutically. Overall, adolescents, especially those who are prone to act out, benefit from drama therapy because of the differentiated tasks they are given and the role structures provided within each drama therapy session (Johnson & Eicher, 1990).

Adults

In prison populations, drama therapy is quite effective in reducing rates of recidivism. Ryder (1976) reported a recidivism rate of about 15% for inmates who participated in a drama project he conducted. Such a rate is far below the national level.

Marriage and family counselors and therapists have found drama techniques to be quite effective too. Enactment is a major dramatic tool of most marriage and family counselors. In this process, a counselor "constructs an interpersonal scenario in the session in which dysfunctional transactions among family members are played out," such as those involving yelling or fighting. In this scenario the therapist can observe "the family members' verbal and nonverbal ways of signaling to each other and monitoring the range of tolerable transactions. The therapist can then intervene in the process by increasing its intensity, prolonging the time of transaction, involving other family members, indicating alternative transactions, and introducing experimental probes" (Minuchin & Fishman, 1981, p. 79). The drama, which occurs in presenting the problem and in finding successful resolutions, decreases the power of symptoms and empowers the family to be innovative.

Elderly Clients

The most recent trend in working with elderly persons through drama is developmental drama therapy. In this approach, counselors work to help disoriented or depressed older adults connect with their past and their present, and with each other—all in a positive way. A group format is used to implement this process, and group members are actively engaged in a sustained manner (Johnson, 1986). The developmental nature of drama progresses from greeting, to unison activities, to expression of group themes, to personification of images, to playing, to closing rituals. Members are encouraged to interact with their fellow group members and to recognize and own their emotions in structured exercises such as "phoning home," in which a group member calls a significant person is his or her life and either resolves difficulties or expresses gratitude. Overall, drama therapy and the use of drama in counseling are just beginning to emerge in a sophisticated form for the elderly population.

Families

Families are often the source of life's most dramatic scenes. Part of the reason is the presence of considerable affect among family members. Another reason is the physical proximity of family members to each other in space and time. Issues related to distance and closeness also make families a forum in which drama is enacted passionately.

One dramatic way of helping families help themselves is through family sculpting, which has been briefly covered previously. This drama technique originated in the 1960s from the work of David Kantor and Fred and Bunny Duhl at the Boston Family Institute. It was an attempt "to translate systems theory into physical form through spatial arrangements" (Papp, 1976, p. 465). In family sculpting, members of a family are asked "to arrange one another as a living statue or tableau" (L'Abate, Ganahl, & Hansen, 1986, p. 166). In this way, people are given the chance to actively and concretely convey their impressions of the family in a nonverbal yet potent manner.

"Sculpting is a way of visualizing the closeness or distance experienced in a family" (Foley, 1989, p. 459). It involves all members of the family unit and basically enables the family to work with the counselor in a collaborative fashion. Sometimes sculpting is used to disengage family members from emotional experiences and "thus facilitate insight into the past and present situations" (Piercy & Sprenkle, 1986, p. 57). At other times it is employed to "bring about an affective experience that will unblock unexpressed emotions" (Piercy & Sprenkle, 1986, p. 57).

Sculpting is usually appropriate at any time during the treatment of a family, because it stimulates interaction and promotes insight (L'Abate et al., 1986). At a minimum, sculpting should include the following:

1. selecting a sculptor;
2. choosing sculpture content (event, problem, or process);
3. sculpting individual members of the family unit;
4. detailing the sculpture;

5. adding the sculptor into the scene;
6. choosing to give the sculpture a descriptive title, a resolution, or a ritualistic motion;
7. sculpting other relevant situations until a pattern emerges;
8. deroling and debriefing all involved; and
9. processing the results (Constantine, 1978; L'Abate et al., 1986).

Initially, sculpting and psychodrama resemble each other, yet they are not the same. "The difference between sculpting and psychodrama . . . is that the latter is used to relive and resolve a traumatic event, whereas sculpting is more concerned with closeness and space as a means of understanding emotional involvement" (Foley, 1989, p. 459). It is crucial that counselors who wish to use these techniques understand the advantages and limitations of each. Both processes may lead to change, but by design they address different aspects of life.

Drama in Counseling With Other Creative Arts

Drama has a natural connection with dance, music, art, and literature. Each of these arts complements the others in a way that highlights therapeutic aspects of change for counselors and clients.

Drama and Dance

Dance can be seen as drama enacted in ritualized and accentuated ways. For example, in Native American culture dance is a dramatic way of invoking the favor of the spiritual world. In middle-class U.S. culture, dramatic exercises may help dance therapy participants become more relaxed and less resistant to the therapeutic process of change (Johnson & Eicher, 1990). Dance in such cases is an extension of drama and leads past itself and into greater self-awareness. Regardless of the circumstances, the techniques of drama and dance both focus on the integration of multiple aspects of people. Once persons dramatically act out a role in a scene, they feel freer to express themselves in more nontraditional ways in dance, movement, or life.

Drama and Music

Music and drama also share much common ground. For instance, music and drama both require self-organization and discipline to master lines and feelings. Music and drama enhance the process of helping people become more realistic "by requiring time-ordered and ability-ordered behavior" (Wager, 1987, p. 137). Each may complement the other, too, as is demonstrated in music being played in the background of a dramatic scene or dramatic enactments of musical compositions (such as those seen on music videos). As with dance, music accentuates drama and increases the likelihood that participants and the audience will remember what they experienced.

Drama and Visual Arts

Art and drama are natural companions, too. In drama there is frequent discussion of "drawing out" a scene. On a concrete level, there is such an experience as "pictorial dramatization," where "clients draw pictures of an important moment, person, conflict, or fantasy. These pictures reveal inner feelings and give important data on self-esteem. Clients go on to act out short pantomimes or improvisational scenes based on the pictures" (Dunne, 1988, p. 141). In this method, people see and feel simultaneously and become more aware of themselves and their environments.

Drama and Literature

Literature and drama are combined in acting situations for which the script is already written, which is the case in plays. This process occurs also when clients pantomime scenes that counselors create to parallel their lives (Dunne, 1988, p. 141). For elderly or physically impaired clients, literature and drama may be united when they read and discuss tragic or humorous plays or movies such as those written by Eugene O'Neill, George Bernard Shaw, Luigi Pirandello, Langston Hughes, and Neil Simon. In their discussions of these works, individuals who cannot act out the scenes can imagine them or feel their impact and share these types of experiences with either the counselor or a therapeutic group.

Summary

The use of drama as either a primary or adjunct technique in healing and change is one that has a strong historical tradition. Human drama is staged in both formal and informal ways and insight into who we are as people is fostered through participating in drama-based experiences on many levels. Counselors share with dramatists the use of some techniques, such as staging, asides, scripting, and creating catharsis. The essence of what these two traditions share goes beyond technique to "a common impulse—an attempt to go beyond the everyday forms of communication to shift people's basic notions of themselves and their world. Both represent a revolt against the normal use of discourse. . . and a recognition that communication is at least as much an emotional phenomenon as a linguistic one" (Friedman, 1984, p. 24). Thus, from the ancient Greeks to today we see a promotion of drama for the common good and sensitivity it instills and promotes.

In this chapter, the historical context of drama in counseling has been explored along with the parallels and processes that dramatists and counselors share. In addition, the primary types of drama found in traditional counseling approaches have been examined along with the groups most amenable to drama-focused treatment and ways in which drama may be combined with other creative arts. The thrust of the chapter is that drama is an affective and effective approach to working with a variety of populations as long as the counselor uses theoretically sound methods (whether a drama therapist or not). Treatment from this perspective involves creativity, openness, and a willingness to be authentic and empathetic. Like the last line of the poem that introduced this chapter, this type of experience demands that counselors forget their lines (professionally distant roles) and instead live their lives congruently and courageously.

References

Adler, A. (1963). *The practice and theory of individual psychotherapy*. Patterson, NJ: Littlefield, Adams.

Bandura, A. (1977). *Social learning theory*. Englewood Cliffs, NJ: Prentice-Hall.

Berne, E. (1964). *Games people play*. New York: Grove.

Blatner, A. (1988). *Foundations of psychodrama: History, theory, and practice* (3rd ed.). New York: Springer.

Blatner, A. (1989). Psychodrama. In R. J. Corsini & D. Wedding (Eds.), *Current psychotherapies* (4th ed.; pp. 560–571). Itasca, IL: Peacock.

Blatner, A. (1997). Psychodrama: The state of the art. *Arts in Psychotherapy, 24*, 23–30.

Campbell, J. (1949). *The hero with a thousand faces*. New York: Pantheon.

Casson, J. (1996). Archetypal splitting: Drama, therapy and psychodrama. *Arts in Psychotherapy, 23*, 307–309.

Constantine, L. (1978). Family sculpture and relationship mapping techniques. *Journal of Marriage and Family Counseling, 4*, 13–23.

═══ **Exercises** ═══

1. Make a list of dramatic productions you have seen or participated in that have had a major impact on your life. Examine these dramas in regard to characters you identified with and emotions conveyed. Look at your own development as a person and the issues you faced then and now. What interconnections, if any, do you see?

2. Ask a client to play the role of someone with whom he or she is having difficulty dealing. Enact the role of the client. After about 10 or 15 minutes of role-play, process the experience and take special note of any changes in perceptions or attitudes that either of you have.

3. Videotape a session with colleagues or your own family during which you demonstrate the art of sculpting. As you and your participants review the videotape, stop it periodically and discuss what is occurring within you now as opposed to what you experienced during the actual sculpting. How different or similar are your thoughts and emotions in these situations?

Corey, G. (1990). *Theory and practice of group counseling* (3rd ed.). Pacific Grove, CA: Brooks/Cole.

Coven, A. B., Ellington, D. B., & Van Hull, K. G. (1996). The use of gestalt psychodrama in group counseling. In S. T. Gladding (Ed.), *New developments in group counseling* (pp. 17–19). Greensboro, NC: ERIC/CASS.

Dequine, E., & Pearson-Davis, S. (1983). Videotaped improvisational drama with emotionally disturbed adolescents: A pilot study. *Arts in Psychotherapy, 10,* 15–21.

Dunne, P. B. (1988). Drama therapy techniques in one-to-one treatment with disturbed children and adolescents. *Arts in Psychotherapy, 15,* 139–149.

Emunah, R. (1985). Drama therapy and adolescent resistance. *Arts in Psychotherapy, 12,* 71–80.

Emunah, R. (1989). Dramatic enactment in the training of drama therapists. *Arts in Psychotherapy, 16,* 29–36.

Foley, V. D. (1989). Family therapy. In R. J. Corsini & D. Wedding (Eds.), *Current psychotherapies* (4th ed.; pp. 455–500). Itasca, IL: Peacock.

Friedman, E. H. (1984, January/February). The play's the thing. *Family Therapy Networker,* 24–29.

Furman, L. (1990). Video therapy: An alternative for the treatment of adolescents. *Arts in Psychotherapy, 17,* 165–169.

Gladding, S. T. (1974). Without applause. *Personnel and Guidance Journal, 52,* 586.

Gladding, S. T. (1995). *Group work: A counseling specialty* (2nd ed.). Englewood Cliffs, NJ: Prentice-Hall.

Gorelick, K. (1987). Greek tragedy and ancient healing: Poems as theater and Asclepian temple in miniature. *Journal of Poetry Therapy, 1,* 38–43.

Greenberg, I. A. (1974). Moreno: Psychodrama and the group process. In I. A. Greenberg (Ed.), *Psychodrama: Theory and therapy* (pp. 11–28). New York: Behavioral.

Guerin, P. J., Jr. (1976). The use of the arts in family therapy: I never sang for my father. In P. J. Guerin, Jr. (Ed.), *Family therapy: Theory and practice* (pp. 480–500). New York: Gardner.

Hug, E. (1997). Current trends in psychodrama: Eclectic and analytic dimensions. *Arts in Psychotherapy, 24,* 31–35.

Hughes, J. N. (1988). Interviewing children. In J. M. Dillard & R. R. Reilly (Eds.), *Strategic interviewing* (pp. 90–113). Columlus, OH: Merrill.

Irwin, E. C. (1987). Drama: The play's the thing. *Elementary School Guidance & Counseling, 21,* 276–283.

Irwin, E., & Malloy, E. (1975). Family puppet interview. *Family Process, 14,* 179–191.

James, M., & Jongeward, D. (1971). *Born to win*. Reading, MA: Addison-Wesley.

James, R. K., & Myer, R. (1987). Puppets: The elementary school counselor's right or left arm. *Elementary School Guidance & Counseling, 21,* 292–299.

Johnson, D. R. (1982). Principles and techniques of drama therapy. *Arts in Psychotherapy, 9,* 83–90.

Johnson, D. R. (1986). The developmental method in drama therapy: Group treatment with the elderly. *Arts in Psychotherapy, 13,* 17–33.

Johnson, D. R., & Eicher, V. (1990). The use of dramatic activities to facilitate dance therapy with adolescents. *Arts in Psychotherapy, 17,* 157–164.

Karpman, S. (1968). Fairy tales and script drama analysis. *Transactional Analysis Bulletin, 7,* 38–43.

Kedem-Tahar, E., & Felix-Kellermann, P. (1996). Psychodrama and drama therapy: A comparison. *Arts in Psychotherapy, 23,* 27–36.

L'Abate, L., Ganahl, G., & Hansen, J. C. (1986). *Methods of family therapy*. Englewood Cliffs, NJ: Prentice-Hall.

Landy, R. J. (1991). The dramatic basis of role theory. *Arts in Psychotherapy, 18,* 29–41.

Landy, R. J. (1997). Drama therapy—The state of the art. *Arts in Psychotherapy, 24,* 5–11.

Lankton, S. R., & Lankton, C. H. (1983). *The answer within: A clinical framework of Ericksonian hypnotherapy*. New York: Brunner/Mazel.

Lowry, D. T., & Towles, D. E. (1989). Soap opera portrayals of sex, contraception, and sexually transmitted diseases. *Journal of Communication, 39,* 76–83.

MacKay, B. (1987). Uncovering buried roles through face painting and storytelling. *Arts in Psychotherapy, 14,* 201–208.

Mellou, E. (1995). Review of the relationship between dramatic play and creativity in young children. *Early Child Development and Care, 112,* 85–107.

Minuchin, S., & Fishman, H. C. (1981). *Family therapy techniques*. Cambridge, MA: Harvard University Press.

Moreno, J. L. (1945). *Group psychotherapy: A symposium*. New York: Beacon House.

Moreno, J. L. (1993). *Who shall survive? Foundations of sociometry, group psychotherapy, and sociodrama*. Roanoke, VA: Royal (Original work published 1934)

Mosak, H. H. (1989). Adlerian psychotherapy. In R. J. Corsini & D. Wedding (Eds.), *Current psychotherapies* (4th ed.; pp. 65–116). Itasca, IL: Peacock.

Newton, A. K. (1995). Silver screens and silver linings: Using theater to explore feelings and issues. *Gifted Child Today,* pp. 14–19.

Nichols, M., & Schwartz, R. (1995). *Family therapy* (3rd ed.). Boston, MA: Allyn & Bacon.

Okun, B. F. (1997). *Effective helping* (5th ed.). Pacific Grove, CA: Brooks/Cole.

Papp, P. (1976). Family choreography. In P. Guerin, Jr. (Ed.), *Family therapy: Theory and practice* (pp. 465–479). New York: Gardner.

Perls, F. S. (1969). *Gestalt therapy verbatim*. Lafayette, CA: Real People.

Perls, F. S. (1970). Four lectures. In J. Fagan & I. L. Shepherd (Eds.), *Gestalt therapy now* (pp. 14–38). New York: Harper & Row.

Piercy, F. P., & Sprenkle, D. H. (1986). *Family therapy sourcebook*. New York: Guilford.

Pittman, F. (1989, October). *The secret passions of men*. Paper presented at the annual conference of the American Association for Marriage and Family Therapy, San Francisco.

Renard, S., & Sockel, K. (1987). *Creative drama: Enhancing self-concepts and learning.* (ERIC Document Reproduction Service No. ED 345164)

Ryder, P. (1976). Theatre as prison therapy. *Drama Review, 20,* 60–66.

Satir, V. (1972). *Peoplemaking.* Palo Alto, CA: Science & Behavior.

Shaffer, W. (1996). Psychodrama technique in the middle school or meanwhile back at Elsinore Castle. In S. T. Gladding (Ed.), *New developments in group counseling* (pp. 35–36). Greensboro, NC: ERIC/CASS.

Snow, S. (1996). Fruit of the same tree: A response to Kedem-Tahar and Kellermann's comparison of psychodrama and drama therapy. *Arts in Psychotherapy, 23,* 199–206.

Sylvia, W. M. (1977). Setting the stage: A counseling playlet. *Elementary School Guidance & Counseling, 12,* 49–54.

Wager, K. M. (1987). Prevention programming in mental health: An issue for consideration by music and drama therapists. *Arts in Psychotherapy, 14,* 135–141.

Warren, B. (1984). Drama: Using the imagination as a stepping stone for personal growth. In B. Warren (Ed.), *Using the creative arts in therapy* (pp. 131–155). Cambridge, MA: Brookline.

Wilson, N. S. (1983). "What can school do for me?" A guidance play. *School Counselor, 30,* 374–380.

8

Play and Humor in Counseling

She smiles gently on cool spring nights
that remind her of a youthful season
when children played quietly within small groups
and boys were timid in her presence.
Amused, she laughs at recollections
letting the lines around her eyes
display the grace of older years
in the acceptance of fun and growth.

(Gladding, 1991)

What did the math book say to the counseling book?
"I've got lots of problems!"

What did the counseling book say back to the math book?
"I'm solution focused!"

PLAY AND HUMOR are arts of the highest order, but because of their lack of concreteness and structure they are often underused, unappreciated, or misunderstood (Ness, 1989; Schaefer & Reid, 1986). Perhaps the reason for this neglect is that counseling is considered to be serious work, quite the antithesis of fun and enjoyment. Yet, play and humor are multidimensional, flexible, and associated with creativity and the promotion of mental health (Witmer, 1985). Therefore, it is important that clients and counselors learn to play and laugh in many situations.

Play and humor share numerous similarities, such as an emphasis on spontaneity, pleasure, and active mental or physical participation by those so engaged. Play and humor are also dissimilar. One of the distinguishing qualities of play is that it "comprises many kinds of activity, linked by an attitude of nonliteralness and enjoyment known as 'playfulness'" (Liebmann, 1986, p. 13). The most salient characteristics of this venue are these:

1. Play is pleasurable and enjoyable.
2. Play has no extrinsic goals; it is inherently unproductive.
3. Play is spontaneous and voluntary and freely chosen.
4. Play involves active engagement on the part of the player.
5. Play is related to what is not play (Liebmann, 1986, p. 13).

A primary need of well-functioning human beings is play. Counselors and clients often complain or confess that they do not incorporate play into their lives often enough. "It is play that is the universal, and that belongs to health: playing facilitates growth" (Winnicott, 1974, p. 48). Too often play in counseling is structured in the form of close-ended activities such as board and card games (Crocker & Wroblewiski, 1975), whereas in more natural environments, play is open-ended in its content and implementation.

Humor as a unique art form combines the elements of reality and absurdity with surprise and exaggeration. Laughter is often accompanied by insight into the essence of what it means to be human (Arieti, 1976). At its best, "humor is a remarkable gift of perspective by which the knowing function of a mature person recognizes disproportions and absurdities" (Allport, 1955, p. 57). Comedians and cartoonists such as Mark Russell, Dick Gregory, and Gary Trudeau focus attention on specific political subjects that are absurd; generalists such as Bob Hope, David Letterman, and Charles Schulz concentrate on broader areas of human life that are fraught with imperfections. Depictions relayed by such artists remind us that "subjects for humor abound: our unfounded fears, endless primping, exaggerated story telling, and inflated self-importance" (Burke, 1989, p. 281).

When individuals do not play or laugh enough they become overly serious and mentally distraught (Ellis, 1977). The manifestations of this unhealthy behavior are displayed in uncontrolled anger, displacement, abuse, and depression—upsetting and unproductive states. Therefore, one of the primary tasks of counseling is to assist clients in learning how to appropriately play or be more playful with their words and actions, consequently having more fun.

Premise of the Use of Play and Humor in Counseling

Play

The idea behind the use of play in counseling is that play has a nonliteral quality about it which "means it can be done in safety" and "without fear of real consequences. By representing a difficult experience symbolically and going through it again, perhaps changing the outcome, a child [or an adult] becomes more able to deal with the problems of real life" (Liebmann, 1986, p. 13). This type of activity as described by Erik Erikson (1963) and seen in the dramatic play of children from age 2 years and older is one way individuals master their environments, including person-to-person interactions (Smilansky & Shefatya, 1990).

The use of play techniques in counseling is based on many theories (Landreth, 1987). For instance, behaviorists use play to help clients relax and learn to enact more adaptive behaviors. Psychoanalytic theories, on the other hand, use play to try to foster insight and call unconscious conflicts into greater awareness (Cochran, 1996). Three of the dominant theories used in play are Jungian (Allan & Brown, 1993; Jung, 1964), Rogerian (Rogers, 1951), and Adlerian (Kottman & Johnson, 1993). According to the Jungian viewpoint, "the process of play and dramatization seems to release blocked psychic energy and to activate the self-healing potential . . . embedded in the human psyche (Allan, 1988). The Rogerian point of view likewise stresses the importance of self-expression and inner growth in a nonjudgmental environment (Axline, 1947, 1967). Adlerian theory focuses play on helping children understand the ways in which they gain significance in the world and make changes in the ways they act toward others. Thus, play in counseling is an active and integrated phenomenon that links mind and body together in a healthy way.

In addition to helping children and adults become more congruent and express themselves more clearly, play may also be used (a) "as a means for establishing rapport" (Thompson & Rudolph, 1988, p. 157), (b) as a way of understanding family and peer interactions, (c) as a tool for tapping unexpressed feelings, (d) as an outlet for the safe expression of feelings, and (e) as an "effective method for teaching socialization skills" (Thompson & Rudolph, 1988, p. 157). The annual International Play Therapy conference and the Center for Play Therapy at the University of North Texas (Denton), headed by Garry Landreth, focus on the multiple uses of play in therapeutic settings.

Essentially, the ability to play is connected with expanding one's imagination through pretending (Madanes, 1981). Pretending can be used throughout the life span. The art of make believe allows individuals to see situations differently and thus to solve problems by reframing situations in a more positive light (Levy, 1987). An example of reframing came in my own life, after the birth of our third child. My wife looked up at me and said, "The honeymoon's not over, there are just more people on it." Her wit and play at the time made me realize that our family life was still manageable. Regardless, an important aim of pretend and play methods is to give clients unique opportunities to engage in activities they may be unable or unwilling to do otherwise. Learning to engage clients in these activities is an achievable goal that counseling can foster through behavioral, cognitive, and affective means.

Humor

The use of humor in counseling is premised on several ideas. First, humor is associated with positive wellness. Research indicates that involvement in humor has a therapeutic effect on one's overall health (Cousins, 1979; Fry, 1991). "Humor, particularly when it is accompanied by laughter, creates physiological, psychological, and social changes. The skeletal muscles become more relaxed, breathing changes, and possibly the brain releases certain chemicals that are positive to our well-being" (Witmer, 1985, p. 169). Clients who are able to laugh at themselves or their situations are able to positively take charge of their lives (Mosak, 1987). Humor seems to be a factor in increasing attention spans, improving comprehension, and promoting recall, all of which are crucial to the fostering of mental health. In his book *Anatomy of an Illness*, Norman Cousins illustrated how laughter helped him eliminate physical pain and bring him healing pleasure. Cousins's book has led others to playfully credit him as the founder of "ho-ho-holistic health" (Napier & Gershenfeld, 1989).

A second rationale for using humor in counseling is that it can distance clients from too much subjectivity and enhance the vision clients have of themselves and the environment. A sense of humor is "connected with one's sense of selfhood" (May, 1953, p. 52). Unconscious urges and repressed thoughts become conscious and expressed (Thompson & Rudolph, 1988). Clients basically gain an "aha" experience from their "ha-ha" perspective and achieve insight into problems that have heretofore perplexed them (Mosak, 1987, 1989). Often, the first slightly funny moment in counseling sparks the beginning of an emotional breakthrough and the start of resolution. People's abilities to "break free of symptoms with exaggeration and humor is an illustration of self-detachment" (Burke, 1989, p. 281) and allows clients to observe a situation from a distance. "One cannot laugh when in an anxious panic . . . hence the accepted belief in folklore that to be able to laugh in times of danger is a sign of courage" (May, 1953, p. 54). It is in such crises that opportunities for genuine heroism are created as individuals realize that their lives are not hopeless (Watzlawick, 1983).

Third, humor is an excellent predictor of creativity. It is expressed in many forms—laughter, comedy, kidding, joking, clowning, mimicking, and teasing (Robinson, 1978). A comic such as Woody Allen achieves success due to his ability to see ordinary relationships in extraordinary ways by making light of them or viewing them from different angles (Lax, 1975). Successful clients and counselors are similarly creative (but not nearly as neurotic) in their perceptions of people and issues. Thus, they achieve an ability to laugh as well as cry.

A fourth reason for employing the art of humor in counseling is past research. It has been only recently that the concept of humor "has been taken seriously as a subject worthy of scientific investigation" (Newton & Dowd, 1990, p. 668). Yet, many studies show promising aspects of humor that make it relevant for counseling. For instance, humor helps initiate and promote communication in social relationships and increases the "likability" of those who use it (Kane, Suls, & Tedeschi, 1977; Martineau, 1972). Couples who share a similar sense of humor are significantly more attracted to each other than those who do not (Murstein & Brust, 1985). In addition, managers and job candidates who are seen as possessing good senses of humor are more likely to be viewed positively (Duncan, 1985; Machan, 1987). Indeed, humor correlates with problem-solving ability, and it may be employed to probe into difficult subject areas, diffuse anger, and circumvent resistance (Adams, 1974; Gladding & Kezar, 1978; Haig, 1986). Joseph Dunn has developed a Humor and Health Institute (P. O. Box 16814, Jackson, Mississippi 39236-6814) and a periodical titled *Humor and Health Journal* that is dedicated to examining research related to humor and various aspects of health including medical, psychological, social, and spiritual. Likewise, Joel Goodman founded the HUMOR Project, Inc. (110 Spring Street, Saratoga Springs, New York 12866) and acts as editor of a funny and scholarly journal, titled *Laughing Matters*.

Practice of the Use of Play and Humor in Counseling

Play

Play approaches to counseling have traditionally been directed at children under the age of 12 years who have limited cognitive and verbal abilities. As such, play has often been structured as "play therapy," which Schaefer (1993) defined as "an interpersonal process wherein a trained therapist systematically applies the curative powers of play to help clients resolve their psychological difficulties" (p. 3). International associations and conferences specialize in play therapy. Within play therapy are a number of theories, among the most prominent of them being those that are child centered, psychoanalytic, cognitive-behavioral, Jungian, gestalt, filial, Adlerian, Ericksonian, developmental, dynamic, ecosystemic, and strategic (O'Connor & Braverman, 1997). Clinicians can become skilled in learning the theories and procedures involved in this specialty.

Play may be employed successfully in situations outside of formal play therapy sessions and with adults and adolescents as well. Many individuals, regardless of age, "have trouble expressing their feelings or attitudes verbally or artistically but can express themselves in play through manipulative materials such as puppets, toys, or play dough or clay" (Drummond, 1992, p. 177). In these situations, play becomes a projective technique and counselors observe clients in distraction-free situations with selective materials such as matchbox cars, dolls, or artistic materials. Those who use such media in creative and fun ways are most likely to be successful in resolving developmental dilemmas and situational aspects of their lives.

Two of the primary ways play is manifest in counseling include the use of sand play (a play therapy process) and a variety of different "games." Sand play is the more highly developed of these two procedures and is appropriate for "children as young as 2 years old and with adults of all ages" (Allan, 1988, p. 221). Games are universal, fluid, and diverse in nature. Based on needs and knowledge, counselors and clients are entrusted to discern which types of play are to be used and how they will be incorporated into any level of counseling.

Sand Play

The British pediatrician Margaret Lowenfeld (1939; 1979) is credited with the initial establishment of the counseling technique known as sand play, which she called "the world technique." The method was refined by the Swiss Jungian analyst Dora Kalff (1981), who formulated theoretical principles and began training practitioners. Kalff centered her ideas around the importance of a healthy ego and the repairing of impaired ego functions for children who experienced trauma early in their development. In sand play, clients have "the opportunity to resolve traumas through externalizing [their] fantasies and by developing a sense of relationship and control over inner impulses" (Allan, 1988, p. 213).

The basic equipment in sand play includes two sand trays of approximately $20 \times 30 \times 3$ inches, one of which contains dry sand and the other wet sand. The trays are waterproof and the insides are painted blue to simulate water when the sand is pushed back. In addition to this environment, numerous miniature toys and objects are made available to children in categories including people, buildings, animals, vehicles, vegetation, structures, natural objects, and symbolic objects (such as wishing wells; Allan & Berry, 1987; Orton, 1997).

The process of sand play begins when counselors invite persons "to play with the sand and to choose from the assortment of minatures" (Allan, 1988, p. 214). In this process of invitation, a safe, protected, and nonjudgemental environment is offered. Counselors witness individuals' symbolic working through of issues and offer encouragement and support through a consistent presence.

People move through predictable stages in the enactments they create. The three most dominant are (a) chaos, (b) struggle, and (c) resolution. To capture the essence of how persons are progressing, counselors either photograph or sketch the outcomes of each play therapy session. These pictures are later reviewed with individual clients. A typical pattern of treatment is around 8 to 10 sessions.

Games

The appeal of games covers the life span. Some healthy games are made up spontaneously and last only a brief time. I have been amazed at the number of games my children have made up with tennis balls that they have played only once and soon forgotten, such as "wall ball," "step ball," and "roof ball." Most productive games in people's lives have rules and are meant to be enacted for longer periods of time. There are basically two types of games with rules—"table games (dominos, cards, dice and board games) and physical games (hide and seek, jump rope, ball games of various types)" (Smilansky & Shefatya, 1990, p. 2). From childhood games of Candyland, jacks, and fox and hounds to adulthood games of Monopoly, basketball, and chess there are always people willing to participate. Playing games is inviting, exciting, and fun for most individuals. Games challenge "one's wits and afford an opportunity to do something with others besides engage in conversation that may not be challenging" (Jourard & Landsman, 1980, pp. 367–368).

Humor

In a more spontaneous way than play, the introduction of humor into counseling can originate from counselors or clients, depending on readiness and timing. Counselors from any theoretical position are often quite effective with clients if they introduce a measured amount of humor into their sessions. Humor at selective points in the counseling process helps promote joining and breaks down clients' resistance (Minuchin & Fishman, 1981). To be effective in such circumstances, however, humor must be spontaneous. For example, if counselors humorously point out their own faults or weaknesses as appropriate, clients usually feel more open and comfortable. This type of gentle self-effacement is associated with strong and admired personalities, including Abraham Lincoln, who joked about his height, or blues singer Eddie "Cleanhead" Vinson, who refers to his baldness as proof that that he is so desirable that women have rubbed his hair away (Moreno, 1987). In counseling, humor might come out if a counselor who misunderstood or misinterpreted a remark paused and said: "Let's try again. I really didn't hear what you were saying. Let me make sure these things (pointing to ears) are more receptive this time."

Humor is almost always unexpected and acts as an atypical way of structuring a seriously sanctioned relationship by altering the way individuals or families view distress (Beier, 1966). "Psychologically, humor overrides negative emotions, dissipating them at least for the time being, and then (leads) to perceptual changes in . . . thinking (Witmer, 1985, p. 169). The result is a reframed atmosphere in which "people can consider themselves more objectively than if they are 'out of control'" (Barton & Alexander, 1981, p. 431).

One of the outstanding proponents of the use of humor in counseling has been Albert Ellis. His REBT approach advocates the use of humor to help clients understand their absurd and self-defeating behaviors more clearly. Humor from this perspective may take many forms, but most often it is manifested in the employment of "paradoxical intention, evocative language, irony, wit, cartoons, and rational humorous songs" (Ellis, 1986, p. 34). The last technique—rational humorous songs—is an especially creative and enjoyable contribution to helping. Ellis (1981) recommended that his clients sing these songs on a regular basis to allow them to laugh at themselves and see their situations more realistically. Although some of the songs contain offensive language, many of them do not, and all of them are imbued with a large amount of fun.

Existentialists such as Viktor Frankl (1985) and Rollo May (1953) have also used humor. They use it to help their clients gain increased self-awareness of their lives and identify what they can do to become less anxious and more accepting of themselves and situations. Humor in such cases may take the form of present-oriented storytelling when counselors ask clients to try to see the absurdity in a situation as if they were someone from a different culture or planet. Thus, a person who is anxious about meeting people might make up a story or enact a minidrama depicting him- or herself nervous and upset to the point of silliness. The anxious person may do things such as say nonsense syllables to a new acquaintance or simply stare at their own shoes. In a parallel way, existential counselors might share their own stories about comparable situations to illustrate pertinent points. These brief stories have funny endings that may or may not be true.

At other times, clients are asked to focus on historical or projected humorous moments in their lives. This exercise helps clients concentrate on an area they have usually forgotten or neglected. Once clients begin to see funny aspects of their lives depicted, they are no longer able to be so serious or overinvolved in current difficulties. In such cases, humor enlightens clients, and they leave these sessions as transformed people. For example, a client who had become depressed over the unalterable loss of an opportunity in young adulthood took on a more optimistic attitude by making up a joke about the end of his life, at which time he was being held accoutable for the choices he has made. When asked in the afterlife what he had learned from all his suffering over the years, the client replied: "I'll never do that again."

Humor is an excellent tool for making or emphasizing a point in a therapeutic or educational setting. Most individuals remember amusing stories more easily than prosaic facts. For example, in illustrating the concept of making changes in one's life, I often tell my students the following true and humorous story:

"As a novice counselor I once had to make a telephone call from a pay phone. The cost of a call in those days was a dime, and all I had was a quarter. I wondered if I would get 15 cents back if I deposited the quarter into the coin slot. As I was thinking, I noticed that the phone company had written above the coin receiver these words: 'This phone does not give change,' to which another person (I am sure a client) had scribbled: 'It doesn't even try!!' "

The point of the story, that change is difficult, is enhanced by the punch line at the end. It helps students remember that despite their best efforts, some individuals will not move past their current state of "stuckness" no matter how well intentioned the counselor may be (Meier & Davis, 1997).

Using humor also results in the uniting of people who share a common experience. Bonding is encouraged by the employment of almost all the creative arts, but humor is especially powerful because of the enjoyment with which it is associated. Examples of the effect of humor on bonding continually emerge at college class reunions when former classmates remind each other of fun times. They are also present when a group speaking one language, such as Italian, listens for the first time to someone speaking a similar language, such as Spanish. In such moments, differences and similarities are exaggerated and group identities solidified (Arieti, 1976).

Play and Humor in Counseling With Specific Populations

Play and humor differ across the life span and among various cultures. Thus, no universal jokes or playful behaviors appeal to everyone. For example, adults prefer structured games such as baseball or football much more than children, who engage in solitary or parallel play in a free-form fashion. Puns (humorous plays on words) are not understood by young children but may be relished among adults. On a cultural level, the British and French often find "slapstick" humor such as that displayed by the comedian Jerry Lewis much more funny than do Americans. Likewise, the humor of Robin Williams as a radio talk show host in the movie *Good Morning Viet Nam* was embraced by troops in the field but hated by the military hierarchy. Despite personal and cultural differences, play and humor have many applications with various groups.

Children

Play

One of the most direct ways that children express their feelings is through play. "Children who cope effectively with stress are able to enjoy play. They become involved. They smile and laugh, and their bodies are relaxed. They use play to symbolically reenact their problems, solving them and overcoming imagined aggressors" (Brenner, 1984, p. 175). Therefore, play environments are often employed to assess the mental health of children because children feel comfortable in them (Drummond, 1992). Through play, children overcome barriers that may impede good mental health. "Play is a healing and growth process that children are able to use naturally and independently" (Cochran, 1996, p. 288). Overall, "imaginative play in young children . . . appears to be a manifestation and expression of the human tendency to create, transcend the immediate, and be aware of the possible" (Shmukler, 1985, p. 39).

The creativity, energy, and awareness that are part of the nature of play are also the basis for structured activities that incorporate play. Through play, children are provided with the opportunity to develop and practice more productive behaviors that may be applied to everyday life (Campbell, 1993). For example, Robert Bowman has developed an experiential exercise called "test busters" to help children overcome test anxiety in a playful manner. Material in the test buster kit comes in the form of songs, chants, and supportive group activities. Through participation in a test buster rally children learn to overcome anxieties about tests by essentially playing through their fears. In line with Bowman's ideas, Cochran (1996) has suggested that play can be used to help culturally diverse children overcome educational and social barriers in schools, thereby achieving greater success and self-esteem. For example, in the "anger ball" activity, a child's anger is released by hitting a ball that momentarily represents something or someone the child has anger towards.

Virginia Axline (1947, 1967) found that when children are encouraged to own their emotions in an accepting and unstructured environment that involves the use of play, they grow and become more positive in their relationships with others. Axline thus set up situations in which children were free to act out their fantasies in a trusting relationship with a nonjudgmental counselor. These environments allowed children to safely expose their innermost thoughts and feelings in symbolic ways, and these expressions could later be interpreted and treated. This child-centered play therapy (CCPT) approach has been used in a number of ways since its inception, including in the successful treatment of abused children (White & Allers, 1994) as well as in the treatment of childhood enuresis and encopresis (Cuddy-Casey, 1997). In CCPT, it is the child and not the problem that is the point of focus (Landreth, 1993).

Special populations of children, such as those with Down's Syndrome, have also been worked with therapeutically using play. For example, play dough has been used as an entertaining medium "for emotional expression on a basic level" (O'Doherty, 1989, p. 174). Angry sounds may be orchestrated when pounding the play dough, and whining sounds may accompany the squeezing of the material. Dry, clean materials should be used with these children to heighten their curiosity and promote learning.

An interesting example of this approach is found in the "paper and box" stimulus reported by O'Doherty (1989). A large packing box filled with various types of paper is kept in the counselor's office, and children are allowed to climb in it and play. The idea behind the box and the games it spontaneously inspires is that through this medium children encounter the creation of rapport, the skill of reciprocity, and the art of pretend. By fixing the box with multiple entrances and exits, counselors can heighten play and social interaction among these children.

In general, children enjoy game activities that can have an educational as well as a fun side to them. These activities add reinforcement to counseling sessions. Games are safe and relatively nonthreatening. In addition, "game play avoids an overuse of 'talk therapy,' which may force the child into acting like a miniature adult" (Friedberg, 1996, p. 17). A number of games are appropriate for children. One of the earliest was the Talking, Feeling, and Doing Game (Gardner, 1983) during which children are interviewed in the context of a game with a game board, dice, and movement along squares from start to finish. Children are encouraged to talk and acknowledge their emotions and actions in a positive and productive way. This game is won by moving their game piece to the finish square and gaining greater insight into themselves. A number of newer games for children that are based on cognitive-behavioral theory include the Assertiveness Game (Berg, 1986), the Anger Control Game (Berg, 1989), the Anxiety Management Game (Berg, 1990a), the Depression Management Game (Berg, 1990b), and the Self-Control Game (Berg, 1990c). Vernon (1989a) has also developed an emotional educational curriculum for children in grades 1 through 6 that is presented in the form of games.

Humor

Humor also has a powerful effect in counseling. It provides a way for children to cope and to make their environments safe. Humor can take many forms including storytelling, use of puppets, and word games. Although much humor for children is specific to the environments in which they live, humor has the wonderful ability to transcend cultures. For instance, Herring and Meggert (1994) have found humor to be a useful counseling strategy when working with Native American Indian children because of the emphasis on humor among the various tribes of this population.

One of the ways to foster cathartic laughter in children is to "exaggerate routine actions and expressions" (O'Doherty, 1989, p. 175). Children seem to enjoy seeing many of their daily situations mimicked. Humor creates a distancing effect and gives children a clearer perspective on what they are doing and how they and others look in social interactions.

The marriage and family therapist Cloe Madanes (1981) illustrated how having fun in a serious situation can eliminate dysfunctional behavior. In one case, for example, a boy pretended to have a temper tantrum and his mother pretended to comfort him. Although the enactment was "just pretend," the boy and his mother had fun together, and the behavior disappeared after that. Basically, humor is more physically displayed in young children and more verbally and intellectually manifested in older children (Figley, 1989).

Adolescents

Play

Play activities are a natural for use with adolescents (Nickerson & O'Laughlin, 1983). Most counselors who work with this age group include play activities for their clients. In hospital settings, play with teenagers may center around the "use of toys, amputation dolls, clay, and checkers" (Keith & Whitaker, 1991, p. 109). It may also include the use of Nintendo games, basketball, volleyball, and other games that involve eye-hand motor skills and a sense of achievement or teamwork. An interesting game created for high school freshmen is called Frustration (Teeter, Teeter, & Papai, 1976). In this group game, entering students are exposed to some of the hazards of high school and the effects that chance circumstances may have on their lives. They may draw a card that places them in a class with exceptionally bright or mediocre students, or they may find that in a school assembly they are seated next to either a popular or unpopular classmate. If they choose to think about such situations while playing the game, they have gained insight and understanding about themselves as well as their upcoming environment.

One of the most frequently used types of play with adolescents is an Outward Bound experience in which teenagers are challenged to individually and collectively overcome a number of obstacles in a wilderness setting (Bacon, 1984). In such a program the activities themselves become physical metaphors that help bring isolated individuals together as a unit. Often an act of play in the midst of adventure will help solidify the connectedness that increases everyone's sense of their own human qualities as well as those qualities in others.

When an outdoor experience is not possible, Vernon (1989b) has developed an emotional education curriculum for adolescents in grades 7 through 12. This curriculum, similar to her curriculum for younger children mentioned previously, is presented in the form of games that engage adolescents in learning while they are having fun. Such simulations make it possible to help teens develop their individual and group skills in an educational setting.

Humor

Often adolescents, in the words of Cyndi Lauper, "just want to have fun." They do this by teasing, mimicking, or acting out. Although such light moments may be enjoyed individually and collectively, it is crucial to make sure that fun and laughter are used positively and the topics that inspire the laughter are adequately addressed. One way to do this is to work with librarians to keep popular and prosocial humor on display at schools and in community settings. These books, periodicals, and even cartoons can be the subject of guidance lessons or other public presentations.

Another way to work with teenagers is to have them make up skits that humorously address subjects they have concern over, such as the environment, war, dating, and drugs. A type of cooperative "stunt night" activity can be the result of such an effort in schools, and the skits can be videotaped and shown to participants again at a party following the event. Through a combination of action and process involving humor such as the ones described here, teenagers gain a sense of empowerment and empathy that gives them more freedom to constructively operate within societal boundaries.

Adults

Play

Adult development is usually conceptualized in terms of intimacy and generativity issues (Erikson, 1963; Gilligan, 1982). In both domains, the concept of play is seldom stressed. However, adults "need to develop a sense of play, which can give them a much-needed 'space' away from the constraints of normal living, and helps them to renew their capacities for tackling life's problems and opportunities" (Liebmann, 1986, p. 13). One way of providing this opportunity is through counseling sessions and homework assignments.

Two of the best examples of playful counseling techniques for adults that are often humorous include "shame attacks" and the singing of humorous rational songs. Both approaches have qualities that exemplify the philosophy of their originator Albert Ellis (1977), who has advocated that therapeutic interventions can and should be fun at times. In shame attacks, people are encouraged to display behaviors they have been previously fearful of enacting, to see that the world does not collapse or fall apart if they make a mistake or do not get their desired outcome. For example, a person might ask for a glass of water in a restaurant without ordering food or might fall down at a shopping mall and see what happens.

With humorous rational songs, clients play with words and thoughts in a way that makes many of their problems less serious and therefore resolvable (Watzlawick, 1983). As mentioned previously, Ellis has numerous songs he has written to familiar tunes, but creative individuals can also write their own words or music. For example, to the tune "I've Been Working on the Railroad," a client once wrote:

> I've been working on my problems
> All the live long day
> I've been working on my problems
> Just to pass the time away
> Can't you hear the problems growing
> Rise up so early in the morn
> Can't you hear me as I'm shouting
> "This is how I blow my horn."

Regardless of the artistic nature of play by adults, actions that encourage playfulness can be essential in helping them gain perspective. Counseling with a playful quality is healthy and helpful for mature individuals who are often squeezed between too many demands and inadequate time or resources. Play, especially role-plays, can also be instructive in helping novice counselors "actively learn about the issues and challenges of the counseling process" (Rabinowitz, 1997, p. 216).

Humor

Most adults appreciate good humor and are open to laughter. They even appreciate a counseling joke such as the following:

> How many counselors does it take to change a light bulb?
> Just one, but the light bulb really has to want to change.

Some adults, especially those who are depressed, can actually be therapeutically helped through experiencing amusement pertaining to their life situations (Corey, 1991; Ellis, 1977). Thus, humor is an excellent approach to use with these individuals.

Most humor with adults in counseling takes the form of verbal exchanges and is often couched as an exaggeration, such as with a person who is overeating: "Wow! It sounds like your lunch attacked you and forced you into eating every bite," or with someone who just got fired again for insubordination: "You certainly have gotten to be an expert at shooting yourself in the foot. I admire a good shot but you may be too good." A danger that exaggerations may become sarcastic does exist, but the best contain a good mixture of truth and sensitivity.

Elderly Clients

Play

Far too little work has been done on how to use play with elderly people. Nevertheless, older people are diverse in their enjoyment of different forms of playfulness and fun. Because play is sometimes dependent on physical mobility, older adults may be confined to activities that involve less strenuous exertion, such as blowing bubbles; bouncing balloons; playing sensory-awareness games; or participating in sedentary interactions with cards, checkers, or dominos (Mayers & Griffin, 1990). On the other hand, many elderly persons enjoy the same playful events as do other age groups. Regardless, play is helpful in maintaining health and vigor within this population, and the types of play used are quite varied.

One fun example of play used in groups is known as "passive-active"(Fisher, 1989). Part of a group is passive and the other part active. The active members make statues out of the passive members (within reason), but the passive members may "come alive" at any time, and likewise the active members may become passive at any time. The enjoyment of this type of play is found in creating the statues and in the element of surprise. (It is important for counselors to make sure that the entire group does not become active or passive all at once.)

Humor

Humor is also much appreciated in this age group, and the wits of clients are often quite keen (Nahemow, 1986). One general advantage elderly persons have over other age groups is their appreciation of more diverse forms of humor since they have more experiences from which to draw. Certain themes are joked about more than others, such as sexuality, wisdom, and death.

In addition to verbally encouraging and using humor, nonverbal actions on the part of counselors who work with elderly populations can bring out the best and the lightest within members when warranted. For instance, if an elderly person takes the role of a "doormat" in a relationship with others, a counselor might literally have the client lay down and act out this helpless part (Raber, 1987). Such humorous enactments create an impression on clients using fun and laughter so that they are put in positions of change (Watzlawick, 1983).

Groups

Play

Play can be used in groups in many ways, but one of the best and most structured is in the form of games, if they are not overused. Games can make individuals in groups more aware of themselves and others. Elizabeth Mintz (1971) has devised a number of games based on gestalt therapy, a couple of which will be mentioned here. In "name game" two individuals carry on a conversation using only their names and no other words. In a variation of this game called "yes-no," they have a similar conversation, but in this case only the words *yes* and *no* can be used.

In addition to the gestalt literature, pragmatic practitioners such as Pfeiffer and Jones (1980) have devised group games in the form of exercises that are helpful in moving groups along to appropriate stages of development. These games can be gimmicky if not implemented with purpose and theoretical knowledge; however, in the hands of skilled practitioners they are stimulating and provide opportunities for personal growth and interpersonal interaction that would otherwise fail to take place.

Humor

Humor also may have a positive effect on groups. Groups that last frequently contain a humorous component (Scogin & Pollio, 1980). Humor gives members a "shared history" and a bonding experience and often helps them look forward to group sessions. In addition, it eases tensions, distills hostility, and promotes creativity and positive communication (Baron, 1974; Fine, 1977; LaGaipa,

1977; Murstein & Brust, 1985). "Groups able to laugh at their failures will be able to take risks together, will be prone to communicate openly and without fear, will be sensitive to the membership needs of the participants, and will be open to change" (Napier & Gershenfeld, 1989, p. 408).

Overall, the lighter moments in a group help enlighten and enliven the group process when they are expressed in humorous ways. At such times everyone in the group "wins" by having fun and feeling more connected. For example, if a group is stuck in a stagnant stage during which members talk only on a superficial level, the group leader may urge members to communicate only on that level and in as nonsensical a way as possible. Thus, one person may talk to the group about the weather while another describes the latest fashions. In such situations, group members begin to have fun with their surface conversations and kid each other about topics such as "windy moments" or "long hemlines." The point is that such silliness can be a road to realness and risk-taking by group members as they gradually cast off their limited roles and discuss topics that are of genuine concern to them.

Humor within groups can be cultivated also by "taking advantage of paradoxes within the group, discrepancies, the unpredictable, the unanticipated, universal truths, the absurd, and the familiar and the memorable" (Napier & Gershenfeld, 1989, p. 408). Humor is a way of helping group members resolve difficulties within themselves, differences they have with others, and outside situations. For instance, in regard to dealing with the death of a parent, Moore and Herlihy (1993) found that students they worked with not only needed to talk about their grief but were also helped when they learned to recognize and laugh appropriately at humorous moments in the grief process. In short, group leaders need to employ humor in a nonhostile way and help their members see the lighter moments of intense situations. Groups that develop in this way are more harmonious, and as a result individual tolerance is fostered.

Families and Couples

Play

Our society has an adage that the "family that plays together stays together." The saying has an intuitive appeal but is too simple. Although playing can be fun and bonding, it has to be fair and based on a "win-win" format to be therapeutic. In game theory, a fundamental distinction is made between two types of games that occur in human interaction. The first is a "zero-sum" game in which if one person wins another loses. Zero-sum games set up competitive situations and may be necessary in some situations such as sports that have the goal of crowning a champion. The second type of game is "non-zero-sum" and is based on the principle that "losses and gains do not cancel each other out. This means that their sum may lie above or below zero" (Watzlawick, 1983, p. 118). In such games everyone may win or lose simultaneously.

Intimate human relationships are always non-zero-sum situations, so that if one member of a couple or family gains self-esteem by putting down another member, then everyone loses. Too often couple and family members do not realize this aspect of deep relationships, and they discount each other and make life more difficult for themselves by playing zero-sum games. In healthy and functional marital and familial relationships, it is vital to establish fairness, tolerance, and trust. "Without them, the game becomes a game without end" (Watzlawick, 1983, p. 121). Counselors who work with couples and families have opportunities to help them learn to avoid zero-sum games by setting up cooperative situations in and outside of counseling sessions in which the good of everyone is promoted at no one's cost. An example of this cooperation is sharing household tasks so that everyone gets a chance to relax and more time is gained for family unity activities such as picnics and recreational outings.

A way to help parents and children learn how to improve their relationships is filial therapy (Guerney, 1982; Guerney & Guerney, 1989). In this procedure, based on person-centered theory, parents of young children meet in groups to learn how to conduct play sessions with their own children. The idea is to break down communication barriers and feelings that get in the way of parent-child communications while creating positive perceptions and experiences. Filial therapy focuses on two programs: child relationship enhancement therapy and parenting skills training. Separately or together they help families and individuals gain more feelings of self-worth and competence.

Humor

In addition to play and games, humor is frequently used in family counseling. "By deliberately understating or overstating a perception, humor clarifies intent, nudges a family member in a new direction, or encourages a little movement or change. . . . It serves as a strengthening agent for families, giving them a new way to experience their joint difficulties" (Satir & Bitter, 1991, p. 33). Veteran family therapists such as Salvador Minuchin and Charles Fishman (1981) use humor as a way of joining with families and helping everyone relax in the opening moments of the counseling process. "Part of the process of joining is to arrive with the family at that point where humor replaces helplessness and despair" (Morawetz & Walker, 1984, p. 61). An example of this occurred once with the existential therapist Virginia Satir: a mother brought her 8-year-old child in for treatment because he was still eating with his fingers. The mother worried that her son would continue this bad habit and at age 21 would embarrass himself at important social gatherings. Satir's response in the opening session was to look at the mother in a little disbelief and say in an incredulous way: "You mean in 13 years, he won't learn this?" Her response caused both women to laugh, and the mother called back 16 years later to inform Satir of her son's success as a psychologist (Satir & Bitter, 1991).

The use of humor with families is "a very personal thing" (Barker, 1986, p. 189), and it depends on the counselor's skills in reading verbal and nonverbal messages and in timing an appropriate witty response. If presented well, humor may relieve tension at any point of the counseling process, such as when a completely disorganized spouse who is the subject of complaint is described as a person who gives the organized spouse "a wonderful opportunity . . . to learn patience!" (Carter & Orfanidis, 1976, p. 200). Overall, using healthy humor during family counseling can increase the number of positive experiences a couple or family shares. As such, humor serves as a means of strengthening relationships (McBrien, 1993).

Play and Humor in Counseling With Other Creative Arts

Play and humor appear in many forms. Silly songs, absurd actions, structured activities, jokes, and stories have already been mentioned. In addition to these primarily verbal and musical forms, play and humor are found in combination with other creative arts, such as drama and visual art in the form of cartoons.

Humor and Drama

Humor and drama are displayed in many ways. Since ancient times, comedies have been a favorite form of entertainment for humankind. In modern times, this type of play continues to be popular as witnessed by the number of comedy clubs in most major cities as well as the number of television shows that are situational comedies or comically oriented. On any given night,

American television hosts a variety of comic entertainers from the legendary, gentle humor of "The Tonight Show" to the outrageous skits of "Saturday Night Live" and "Seinfeld." A great majority of the most frequently aired television productions often center on comic themes too, such as the classic "I Love Lucy" series to "M*A*S*H," "The Cosby Show," and "The Bob Newhart Show." Regardless of the form, humor segments are geared toward helping viewers take themselves and the world less seriously.

Counselors as a group are avid comedy consumers because of the power humorous play has in helping them to switch gears in life and enjoy it to the fullest. Some counselors make good use of humor and play with it constructively. One easy way to become involved in employing humor is to assign clients a homework task of watching certain television shows or attending a specific comedy performance. This type of assignment must be tailored to the individual taste of the client and is usually not a first-session type of intervention. One way it can be encouraged is to have clients buy or rent certain comic material from video stores and see the material in the privacy of their homes or to view select works with clients in a counseling session. In either case, processing the material afterwards is a must.

A second way comic drama can be used in counseling is through enactment, such as mime. This form of nonverbal but humorous entertainment has excellent potential for stirring up emotions that are lighthearted and serious. Professional mimes such as Marcel Marceau can be watched before an actual enactment is attempted. The advantage of humorous mime in counseling is that while entertaining, it uncovers important unresolved issues. Humorous mime can be used with groups as well as with individuals. It helps clients feel their emotions more fully, and when the mime is completed these clients may be more verbal than usual.

Play and Visual Arts

As mentioned earlier, some comic strips and cartoons have a universal appeal because of their subject matter and focus. Comic strips and cartoons are concrete in conveying a visual message. In counseling, they can be used to illustrate points that either counselors or clients need to consider. For example, the following cartoon created by Nels Goud and Tom McAdam illustrates this point by showing the demands that counselors often face on a daily basis. It conveys this message in a way that words alone could not.

David and Tim Fennel have also illustrated situations in family therapy that show the nature of this endeavor for counselors and consumers. Like Goud and McAdam, they get to the essence of relationships in families mainly by picturing the serious in a funny but frank manner.

Besides being viewed informally this form of humor can also be used in counseling in the following ways (O'Brien, Johnson, & Miller, 1978). First, an anthology of selected cartoons or comic strips can be given to clients by counselors with the idea that they will be discussed in relationship to clients' problems. Through such a process, counselors hope clients will reconceptualize their concerns in a humorous way. A second method of using cartoons and comic strips is as homework. Clients are given cartoons they are to study and bring back for discussion in the next session. The main difference between these methods and the O'Brien et al. scheme is that more time is given in the second process for reflection on clients' situations.

A third way of using comic strips and cartoons in counseling is for clients to find comic strips and cartoons that relate to their situations and bring them to counseling sessions for discussion. Another way of using this creative art in counseling is to have clients either fill in the ballooned part of cartoon scenes or to draw their own picture or strip. In either case, clients reveal essential information about themselves that can be used in sessions as a mechanism for understanding and change.

The Counselor's World

Reprinted by permission of Nels Goud and Tom McCain.

NOW, WHAT SEEMS TO BE THE PROBLEM?

Reprinted by permission of Timothy and David Fenell.

Summary

This chapter has emphasized that although counseling is not a play or comic activity, various forms of play and humor can be used in a therapeutic way with children, adolescents, adults, elderly persons, groups, and couples and families. Play is especially powerful in helping clients gain perspective on their situations and in devising appropriate and creative strategies to address these concerns. It helps clients rehearse, gain mastery over themselves and their environments, and become more integrated on verbal and nonverbal levels. Play may help in establishing rapport and in understanding personal, group, and family dynamics as well. By humanizing counseling into a workable, enjoyable, and productive experience, at times "play is the thing" that will capture the imagination of clients and counselors and will help them ultimately to work in a theory-based, fun, and nonthreatening environment in which understanding and change may occur regardless of age or cultural differences.

Likewise, humor can be used in counseling sessions to help clients and counselors gain insight and perspective on their situations. Humor is an art in regard to its content and timing. When employed in counseling, humor can be used to probe difficult subject areas, diffuse anger, circumvent resistance, and make the counselor more likable and effective. It is important that the type of humor used in counseling not be hostile. When effective, it helps to promote physiological, psychological, and social changes, thus fostering more positive mental health. Different forms of humor appeal to various populations, and what may be funny to one individual at a particular age and stage in life may not seem humorous to someone else in another circumstance. Counselor sensitivity is essential to understanding the choice and timing of actions.

Overall, play and humor are resources for most counselors. The impact of employing these modalities in a sensitive and sensible manner has great potential.

=== **Exercises** ===

1. Many introductory counseling exercises are playful and humorous, for instance, having individuals pretend to be animals representative of themselves and then actually to behave like themselves. Invite members of a group with whom you work to begin a session by acting as if they were a significant historical figure. They should play their parts for at least 15 minutes, after which they should inform others of their role and as a group talk about what they learned from the experience in regard to themselves and others that can help them in their daily functioning.

2. Think of a development situation that individuals in society usually experience, for example, going to school, beginning a career, getting married, or having children. Based on your knowledge of these events, devise a board game with dice (similar to the game "Monopoly") for clients to play. The idea of the game is to learn about particular situations, not to compete. Try the game out with colleagues and then after you have made refinements, use it in your counseling setting as appropriate.

3. Consult local and national periodicals to find what comic materials are most widely read. Sample as many of these as you can and record your feelings about the humor they convey, whether positive, negative, or neutral. Make a presentation to your colleagues on "fun that can be used in counseling."

References

Adams, W. J. (1974). The use of sexual humor in teaching human sexuality at the university level. *The Family Coordinator, 23*, 365–368.

Allan, J. (1988). *Inscapes of the child's world*. Dallas, TX: Spring.

Allan, J., & Berry, P. (1987). Sandplay. *Elementary School Guidance & Counseling, 21*, 300–306.

Allan, J., & Brown, K. (1993). Jungian play therapy in elementary schools. *Elementary School Guidance & Counseling, 28*, 30–41.

Allport, G. W. (1955). *Becoming*. New Haven, CT: Yale University Press.

Arieti, S. (1976). *Creativity: The magic synthesis*. New York: Basic.

Axline, V. (1947). *Play therapy*. Boston: Houghton-Mifflin.

Axline, V. (1967). *Dibs in search of self*. New York: Ballantine.

Bacon, S. (1984). *The conscious use of metaphor in Outward Bound*. Denver: Colorado Outward Bound School.

Barker, P. (1984). *Basic family therapy* (2nd ed.). New York: Oxford.

Baron, R. A. (1974). The aggressive-inhibiting influence of nonhostile humor. *Journal of Experimental Social Psychology, 10,* 23–33.

Barton, C., & Alexander, J. F. (1981). Functional family therapy. In A. S. Gurman & D. P. Kniskern (Eds.), *Handbook of family therapy* (pp. 403–443). New York: Brunner/Mazel.

Beier, E. (1966). *The silent language of psychotherapy.* Chicago: Aldine.

Berg, B. (1986). *The assertion game.* Dayton, OH: Cognitive Counseling Resources.

Berg, B. (1989). *The anger control game.* Dayton, OH: Cognitive Counseling Resources.

Berg, B. (1990a). *The anxiety management game.* Dayton, OH: Cognitive Counseling Resources.

Berg, B. (1990b). *The depression management game.* Dayton, OH: Cognitive Counseling Resources.

Berg, B. (1990c). *The self-control game.* Dayton, OH: Cognitive Counseling Resources.

Brenner, A. (1984). *Helping children cope with stress.* Lexington, MA: Lexington.

Burke, J. F. (1989). *Contemporary approaches to psychotherapy & counseling.* Pacific Grove, CA: Brooks/Cole.

Campbell, C. (1993). Play: The fabric of elementary school counseling programs. *Elementary School Guidance & Counseling, 28,* 10–16.

Carter, E. A., & Orfanidis, M. M. (1976). Family therapy with one person and the family therapist's own family. In P. J. Guerin, Jr. (Ed.), *Family Therapy* (pp. 193–219). New York: Gardner.

Cochran, J. L. (1996). Using play and art therapy to help culturally diverse students overcome barriers to school success. *The School Counselor, 43,* 287–298.

Corey, G. (1991). *Theory and practice of counseling and psychotherapy* (4th ed.). Pacific Grove, CA: Brooks/Cole.

Cousins, N. (1979). *Anatomy of an illness as perceived by the patient.* New York: Norton.

Crocker, J. W., & Wroblewiski, M. (1975). Using recreational games in counseling. *Personnel and Guidance Journal, 53,* 453–458.

Cuddy-Casey, M. (1997). A case study using a child-centered play therapy approach to treat enuresis and encopresis. *Elementary School Guidance & Counseling, 31,* 220–225.

Drummond, R. J. (1992). *Appraisal procedures for counselors and helping professionals* (2nd ed.). Columbus, OH: Merrill.

Duncan, W. J. (1985). The superiority theory of humor at work: Joking relationships as indicators of formal and informal status patterns in small, task-oriented groups. *Small Group Behavior, 16,* 556–564.

Ellis, A. (1977). Fun as psychotherapy. In A. Ellis & R. Grieger (Eds.), *Handbook of rational-emotive therapy* (pp. 262–270). New York: Springer.

Ellis, A. (1981). The use of rational humorous songs in psychotherapy. *Voices, 16,* 29–36.

Ellis, A. (1986). Rational-emotive therapy and cognitive behavior therapy: Similarities and differences. In A. Ellis and R. Grieger (Eds.), *Handbook of rational-emotive therapy* (Vol. 2, pp. 31–45). New York: Springer.

Erikson, E. H. (1963). *Childhood and society* (2nd ed.). New York: Norton.

Figley, C. R. (1989). *Helping traumatized families.* San Francisco: Jossey-Bass.

Fine, G. A. (1977). Humor *in situ:* The role of humour in small group culture. In A. J. Chapman & H. C. Foot (Eds.), *It's a funny thing, humour* (pp. 315–318). New York: Pergamon.

Fisher, P. P. (1989). *Creative movement for older adults.* New York: Human Sciences.

Frankl, V. E. (1985). Paradoxical intention. In G. R. Weeks (Ed.), *Promoting change through paradoxical therapy* (pp. 99–110). Homewood, IL: Dow Jones-Irwin.

Friedberg, R. D. (1996). Cognitive-behavioral games and workbooks: Tips for school counselors. *Elementary School Guidance & Counseling, 31,* 11–19.

Fry, W. Jr., (1991, April). *Laughter for the health of it: Search for humor research.* Paper presented at the annual conference of the Humor Project, Saratoga Springs, NY.

Gardner, R. A. (1983). The talking, feeling, and doing game. In C. E. Schaefer & K. J. O'Connor (Eds.), *Handbook of play therapy* (pp. 259–273). New York: Wiley.

Gilligan, C. (1982). *In a different voice: Psychological theory and women's development.* Cambridge, MA: Harvard University Press.

Gladding, S. T. (1991). *In acceptance.* Unpublished manuscript.

Gladding, S. T., & Kezar, E. F. (1978). Humor in teaching family life education: Advantages of use and guidelines for preventing abuse. *Family Life Educator, 9,* 10–11.

Guerney, B. (1982). Filial therapy: Description and rationale. In G. L. Landreth (Ed.). *Play therapy* (pp. 342–353). Springfield, IL: Thomas.

Guerney, L., & Guerney, B. (1989). Child relationship enhancement: family therapy and parent education. *Person Centered Review, 4,* 344–357.

Haig, R. A. (1986). Therapeutic uses of humor. *American Journal of Psychotherapy, 40,* 543–553.

Herring, R. D., & Meggert, S. S. (1994). The use of humor as a counselor strategy with Native American Indian children. *Elementary School Guidance & Counseling, 28,* 67–78.

Jourard, S. M., & Landsman, T. (1980). *Healthy personality* (4th ed.). New York: Macmillan.

Jung, C. G. (1964). *Man and his symbols.* Garden City, NJ: Doubleday.

Kalff, D. M. (1981). *Sandplay: A psychotherapeutic approach to the psyche.* Boston: Sigo.

Kane, T. R., Suls, J., & Tedeschi, J. T. (1977). Humour as a tool of social interaction. In A. J. Chapman & M. C. Foot (Eds.), *It's a funny thing, humor* (pp. 13–16). New York: Pergamon.

Keith, D. V., & Whitaker, C. A. (1991). Experiential/symbolic family therapy. In A. M. Horne & J. L. Passmore (Eds.), *Family counseling and therapy* (2nd ed., pp. 108–140). Itasca, IL: Peacock.

Kottman, T., & Johnson, V. (1993). Adlerian play therapy: A tool for school counselors. *Elementary School Guidance & Counseling, 28,* 42–51.

LaGaipa, J. (1977). The effects of humour on the flow of social conversation. In A. J. Chapman & H. C. Foot (Eds.), *It's a funny thing, humour* (pp. 421–427). New York: Pergamon.

Landreth, G. L. (1987). Play therapy: Facilitative use of child's play in elementary school counseling. *Elementary School Guidance & Counseling, 21,* 253–261.

Landreth, G. L. (1993). Child-centered play therapy. *Elementary School Guidance & Counseling, 28,* 17–29.

Lax, E. (1975). *On being funny: Woody Allen and comedy.* New York: Manor.

Levy, T. M. (1987). Brief family therapy: Clinical assumptions and techniques. In P. A. Keller & S. R. Heyman (Eds.), *Innovations in clinical practice: A source book* (pp. 63–77). Sarasota, FL: Professional Resource Exchange.

Liebmann, M. (1986). *Art therapy for groups.* Cambridge, MA: Brookline.

Lowenfeld, M. (1939). The world pictures of children. *British Journal of Medical Psychology, 18,* 65–73.

Lowenfeld, M. (1979). *The world technique.* London: George Allen & Unwin.

Machan, D. (1987, November 2). What's black and blue and floats in the Monongahela River? *Forbes,* 216–220.

Madanes, C. (1981). *Strategic family therapy.* San Francisco: Jossey-Bass.

Martineau, W. H. (1972). A model of the social function of humor. In J. H. Goldstein & P. E. McGhee (Eds.), *The psychology of humor.* New York: Academic.

May, R. (1953). *Man's search for himself.* New York: Norton.

Mayers, K., & Griffin, M. (1990). The play project: Use of stimulus objects with demented patients. *Journal of Gerontological Nursing, 16,* 32–37.

McBrien, R. J. (1993). Laughing together: Humor as encouragement in couples counseling. *Individual Psychology, 49,* 419–427.

Meier, S. T., & Davis, S. R. (1997). *The elements of counseling* (3rd ed.). Pacific Grove, CA: Brooks/Cole.

Mintz, E. E. (1971). *Marathon groups: Reality and symbol.* New York: Appleton-Century-Crofts.

Minuchin, S., & Fishman, H. C. (1981). *Family therapy techniques.* Cambridge, MA: Harvard University Press.

Moore, J., & Herlihy, B. (1993). Grief groups for students who have had a parent die. *The School Counselor, 41,* 54–59.

Morawetz, A., & Walker, G. (1984). *Brief therapy with single-parent families.* New York: Brunner/Mazel.

Moreno, J. J. (1987). The therapeutic role of the blues singer and considerations for the clinical application of the blues form. *Arts in Psychotherapy, 14,* 333–340.

Mosak, H. H. (1987). *Ha Ha and Aha: The role of humor in psychotherapy.* Muncie, IN: Accelerated Development.

Mosak, H. H. (1989). Adlerian psychotherapy. In R. J. Corsini and D. Wedding (Eds.), *Current psychotherapies* (4th ed., pp. 65–118). Itasca, IL: Peacock.

Murstein, B. I., & Brust, R. G. (1985). Humor and interpersonal attraction. *Journal of Personality Assessment, 49,* 637–640.

Nahemow, L. (1986). Humor as a data base for the study of aging. In L. Nahemow, K. A. McCluskey-Fawcett, & P. E. McGhee (Eds.), *Humor and aging* (pp. 3–26). New York: Academic.

Napier, R. W., & Gershenfeld, M. K. (1989). *Groups: Theory and experience* (4th ed.). Boston: Houghton-Mifflin.

Ness, M. E. (1989). The use of humorous journal articles in counselor training. *Counselor Education and Supervision, 29,* 35–43.

Newton, G. R., & Dowd, E. T. (1990). Effect of client sense of humor and paradoxical interventions on test anxiety. *Journal of Counseling and Development, 68,* 668–672.

Nickerson, E. T., & O'Laughlin, K. S. (1983). The therapeutic use of games. In C. E. Schaefer & K. J. O'Connor (Eds.), *Handbook of play therapy* (pp. 174–187). New York: Wiley.

O'Brien, C. R., Johnson, J., & Miller, B. (1978). Cartooning in counseling. *Personnel and Guidance Journal, 57,* 55–56.

O'Connor, K. J., & Braverman, L. M. (Eds.).(1997). *Play therapy: Theory and practice.* New York: Wiley.

O'Doherty, S. (1989). Play and drama therapy with the Down's Syndrome child. *Arts in Psychotherapy, 16,* 171–178.

Orton, G. L. (1997). *Strategies for counseling with children and their parents.* Pacific Grove, CA: Brooks/Cole.

Pfeiffer, D. C., & Jones, J. E. (1980). *A handbook of structured experiences for human relations training* (Vol. 7) San Diego: University Associates.

Raber, W. C. (1987). The caring role of the nurse in the application of humor therapy to the patient experiencing helplessness. *Clinical Gerontologist, 7,* 3–11.

Rabinowitz, F. E. (1997). Teaching counseling through a semester-long role play. *Counselor Education and Supervision, 36,* 216–223.

Robinson, V. M. (1978). Humor in nursing. In C. Carlson & B. Blackwell (Eds.), *Behavioral concepts and nursing intervention* (2nd ed., pp. 191–210). Philadelphia: Lippincott.

Rogers, C. R. (1951). *Client-centered therapy.* Boston: Houghton-Mifflin.

Satir, V. M., & Bitter, R. (1991). The therapist and family therapy: Satir's human validation process model. In A. M. Horne & J. L. Passmore (Eds.), *Family counseling and therapy* (2nd ed., pp. 13–46). Itasca, IL: Peacock.

Schaefer, C. E. (Ed.). (1993. *The therapeutic powers of play.* Northvale, NJ: Aronson.

Schaefer, C. E., & Reid, S. E. (1986). *Game play.* New York: Wiley.

Shmukler, D. (1985). Imaginative play: Its implication for the process of education. In A. A. Sheikh & K. S. Sheikh (Eds.), *Imagery in education* (pp. 39–62). Farmingdale, NY: Baywood.

Scogin, F., & Pollio, H. (1980). Targeting and the humorous episode in group process. *Human Relations, 33,* 831–852.

Smilansky, S., & Shefatya, L. (1990). *Facilitating play.* Gaithersburg, MD: Psychosocial & Educational.

Teeter, R., Teeter, T., & Papai, J. (1976). Frustration—A game. *The School Counselor, 23,* 264–270.

Thompson, C. L., & Rudolph, L. B. (1988). *Counseling children* (3rd ed.). Pacific Grove, CA: Brooks/Cole.

Vernon, A. (1989a). *Thinking, feeling, and behaving: An emotional education curriculum for children (grades 1–6).* Champaign, IL: Research.

Vernon, A. (1989b). *Thinking, feeling, and behaving: An emotional education curriculum for children (grades 7–12).* Champaign, IL: Research.

Watzlawick, P. (1983). *The situation is hopeless, but not serious.* New York: Norton.

White, J. , & Allers, C. T. (1994). Play therapy with abused children: A review of the literature. *Journal of Counseling & Development, 72,* 390–394.

Winnicott, D. W. (1974). *Playing and reality.* New York: Pelican.

Witmer, J. M. (1985). *Pathways to personal growth.* Muncie, IN: Accelerated Development.

9

Trends in Counseling and the Creative Arts

Amid the cascade of thoughts
 reflections flow and like a river
  weave a path through changing vistas
   where there is room and time for growth
   and opportunities to settle.
At dusk I ponder the journey's end
 and in the spirit of transformation
  I quietly launch forth frail ideas
   into waters filled with hope and turmoil
Conscious I may never see their final form
 yet knowing inside, peacefully,
  that others will keep the best on course.

(Gladding, 1991)

I T IS DIFFICULT to predict the future and distinguish between trends and fads. Nevertheless, there is no shortage of futurists who are willing, although not always able, to focus on the probable and possible (e.g., Brooks & Gerstein, 1990). In examining the arts and counseling a number of issues and articles point toward new directions in the field. In this chapter, five of the most likely of these events will be briefly discussed—research, education, identity, interdisciplinary efforts, and technology and accessibility in regard to the promotion of the creative arts. These topics are examined from the perspective of those who identify themselves as primarily arts therapists, because professionals that distinguish themselves as such have organized efforts to bring each issue to the attention of others.

In all probability, none of these issues will dominate the field of counseling in the foreseeable future. Nevertheless all of them will have an impact that will probably change the way the arts in counseling are practiced and viewed.

Research

One of the most pressing needs confronting counseling and the creative arts is the generating of scholarship. This need stems from the demands of the public, professional associations, licensure boards, insurance companies, and clinicians. Counselors who employ the creative arts in their work must be accountable to their clients and to others connected with mental health services. They must be able to answer questions such as these:

1. How does improvement produced by creative arts methods compare to those produced by other methods?
2. Is one creative art therapy approach superior to another?
3. What client characteristics are related to maximal outcome with creative arts methods in a counseling context? (Mazza, 1993)

If the creative arts in counseling are to be uniformly respected, they must merit admiration based on more than anecdotal testimony (Gladding, 1996). In essence, to be used theraputically, the creative arts need to go "beyond riding piggy-back"(Lerner, 1992, p. 45) on the already established schools, theories, and research of other behavioral sciences.

Yet, conducting research on the effectiveness of the creative arts in counseling is not easy. One of the frustrations with counseling research in the creative arts is the difficulty of controlling or isolating variables that promote or hinder client growth. Traditional research requires that practitioners demonstrate how a factor, such as a particular piece of music or a specific movement exercise, makes a difference in the treatment of persons. This problem is not particular to the creative arts, and every counseling approach has had to deal with showing how its main techniques have made an impact on the outcome of the therapeutic process (Kirschenbaum & Henderson, 1989).

For some of the creative arts associated with research-based theories, the problem of empirical validation is not a high hurdle. For example, imagery has a strong link with behaviorism and research from the 1950s by Joseph Wolpe (1958) up to more recent studies by Arnold Lazarus (1982) and those in career counseling (Skovholt, Morgan, & Negron-Cunningham, 1989). These studies have shown that imagery is an effective approach to helping people change. Likewise, humor has an affiliation with cognitive-behavioral theories, such as rational emotive therapy, and has a history of proven effectiveness (Ellis, 1986).

Some of the other creative arts, approaches, especially those without an association to older counseling theories, struggle more with the question of research. For example, the major factors that are the basis for using literature in counseling have been delineated (Hynes, 1988); however, empirical data supporting how these qualities specifically impact the client and how they may be used in a verifiable way by different counselors in various settings is still lacking, except for behaviorally based reading materials (Riordan & Wilson, 1989). Progress has been made in this and other areas, but much work needs to be completed to determine the influence of select creative arts on the field of counseling either separately or in combination. One aspect that hinders faster development of research in this area is the lack of tradition among counselors who use the creative arts for conducting research, as well as the subjective nature of many creative arts experiences.

Nevertheless, McNiff (1986) believed the creative arts have an advantage in generating research due to the fact that they are not "exclusively identified with either art or science" (p. 281). McNiff further stated that because the creative arts are broad and encompass arts, psychology, education, religion, philosophy, and psychiatry, varied, cooperative, innovative, and interdisciplinary research is essential and may be forthcoming. Indeed, Rossiter (1992) has suggested that because creative arts therapies share much in terms of processes and products, collaborative approaches to researching them may be possible and quite productive.

For those conducting research on the process and outcome of using the creative arts in counseling, the opportunity emerges for new discoveries that may become a part of the field of assessment as a whole. The challenges of finding proper procedures and of being innovative are the primary obstacles facing scientific practitioners in the field. One way around this difficulty is for researchers to develop methods of investigation that do not necessarily follow empirical research traditions (Politsky, 1995). It will probably take a number of years before such models of inquiry are formulated but Mitroff and Kilmann (1978) have noted that, based on Jungian typology, four outer manifestations for research are based on the processes of thinking and feeling. First, two thinking typologies exist—the analytic scientist (AS) and the conceptual theorist (CT). Both AS and CT investigators seek to explain things in scientific, technical, and theoretical terms apart from human needs or concerns. They are quantitative scientific-practitioners. Opposite these thinking types are primary feeling typologies—the conceptual humanist (CH) and the particular humanist (PH). Feeling investigators are particularly sensitive to individual differences. These researchers aim toward qualitative investigations. Unless or until the creative arts therapies come to own a special way of doing research, they will parallel psychoanalysis in its early years as being looked on with suspicion (at least by some) but being heuristic as a field of study.

While waiting to develop more sophisticated research methods, creative arts therapists and counselors who use the arts will have to rely on tried methods. One such method is known as single-case research designs. "These designs are appropriate for the development of research hypotheses, testing those hypotheses in daily clinical practice and refining clinical techniques" (Aldridge, 1994, p. 333). Most appropriately, single-case research allows for the assessment of individual development and significant incidents in a therapeutic relationship. Another group-oriented method is is the Structural Analysis of Movement Sessions (SAMS), which "is a system of observation and research of groups-in-action" (Sandel & Johnson, 1996, p. 15). Using SAMS, creative arts clinicians, especially dance and movement specialists, can study how groups as a whole and members individually influence one another. They can also assess the relationship between spatial arrangements and action tasks.

Education

Since the 1970s, considerable movement has been made to set up educational programs for those who wish to specialize in the creative arts in counseling. The number of programs devoted to this type of specialization has grown at a steady pace. For instance, in 1967, one program in art therapy existed in the U.S. By 1989, there were 17 approved programs regulated by the American Art Therapy Association (AATA; Levick, 1989) and the number of AATA approved master's programs grew to 27 by 1997. Other associations devoted to the creative arts of music, dance and movement, drama, and poetry have likewise established training centers that are either university affiliated or free standing. The facilities and faculties connected with such programs are devoted to providing systematic information to new practitioners in a cohesive and comprehensive manner. Yet, educational endeavors in the creative arts therapies face several difficulties. Some of the major problems for the creative arts therapies have been identified as follows (Johnson, 1989, p. 1):

1. How should the educational tasks of clinical practice, research, and theoretical scholarship be distributed among undergraduate, masters, and doctoral programs?
2. What are the essential skills required of creative arts therapists, and what methods of training (e.g., didactic, experiential, research, internship, and thesis) should be employed to promote competencies in these skills?
3. How can those who wish to become creative arts therapists "maintain an integrated identity amidst the competing influences of. . . more established fields" such as "education, psychology, counseling, marriage and family therapy, and professional art or music schools" (Johnson, 1989, p. 1), in which training programs in the creative arts in counseling are presently housed?

As with other professions, we have no easy answers to these problems. Some of the solutions depend on the stages of development of particular creative arts and their history. For example, in regard to the distribution of knowledge, most of the creative arts approaches require advanced degrees. In addition, most of the creative arts therapies have one accrediting body that constantly reviews and updates educational standards.

Indirectly addressing the second question raised by Johnson about competencies, Levick (1989) stated that "knowledge transcends program orientation" (p. 58). Disorders and issues that are part of all counseling programs must be addressed in therapeutic creative arts programs. Educational institutions offering degrees in creative arts therapies must give their recipients the best of both the art and science of helping.

Finally, focusing on the third issue of Johnson's about the unique identities of professions, some of the creative arts approaches have been subsumed under other professional disciplines such as psychology, counseling, marriage and family therapy, and medicine (Drachnik, 1989). For instance, "the art therapy profession has been almost exclusively tied to the medical model" (McNiff, 1997, p. 40). Professionals who use the creative arts in these recognized areas of mental health services do not mind their identities being conveyed as psychologists, counselors, marriage and family therapists, or physicians, but graduates of programs with degrees specifically in creative arts therapies are sensitive to this type of labeling. Considerable effort has been mede by such graduates to be recognized as a unique force in the umbrella structure of mental health service providers. In recent years the federal government, through the Department of Labor, has included art therapy, music therapy, and dance therapy in the *Dictionary of Occupational Titles*. Furthermore, these three specialties are listed as related professions under occupational therapy in the *Occupation Outlook Handbook* (Kleinman & Gantt, 1997).

Overall, the state of education in the creative arts therapies is in flux. A general trend seems to be that more and better standards are being established for those who are interested in obtaining degrees or certification in these areas. Music, art, and dance and movement seem to be the most advanced of the special artistic approaches in regard to formatting comprehensive curricula. It will only be through the continued establishment of strong educational programs and growing numbers of practitioners that identity issues will be resolved.

Identity

Almost all effective treatment procedures have common elements. The arts in counseling are no exception. "The similarities in music, art, dance/movement, drama, psychodrama, and poetry" as therapeutic ways of working have commonalties and overlap "in theory, research, clinical practice, education, standards, and ethics of practice" (Summer, 1997, p. 77). Among the most common qualities they share are "attention to verbal and nonverbal expression, symbolism, use of sensory modes, vision, order, and balance" (Mazza, 1988, p. 485). Two aspects of the arts in counseling unite them regardless of anything else. These aspects are expressed in a "commonality of form and pattern" (Aldridge, Brandt, & Wohler, 1990, p. 189). In regard to form, the arts "are based on verbs and doing is important" (Aldridge et al., 1990, p. 193). This feature is quite different from scientific inquiry, which is premised on empirical data and stresses nouns (Bateson, 1978). In inquiry, there is talk about a dynamic but not enactment. The second crucial quality of the therapeutic arts is the pattern they display, which emphasizes creativity as much as or more than catharsis. This type of expression not only has the power to heal but to enhance. Creative arts in counseling concentrate on going beyond emotional release to the process of building self-concepts that are stronger and more congruent than before in recipients of these services.

This commonality of form and pattern both unites and frustrates those allied with the use of the arts in counseling. On one hand, this common bond promotes the continued growth of the National Coalition of Arts Therapies Associations (NCATA), which is an umbrella organization for those who wish to learn more about or promote the creative arts in counseling. On the other hand, the central features that unite the arts are the very qualities that different art therapy groups measure themselves against and stress to emphasize the uniqueness of their disciplines.

Different associations have specific identities that relate to their names, purpose, and emphasis. The arts in counseling are no exception, and approximately half a dozen major groups have formed to promote the arts or an art form in counseling. All of them stress knowledge, skill, training, and supervision as being of paramount importance. Among the best known of these groups are these:

- American Art Therapy Association (AATA)—The primary association in promoting visual arts therapies—1202 Allanson Road, Mundelein, IL 60060; telephone: 847-949-6064; fax: 847-566-4580
- American Association for Music Therapy (AAMT)—One Station Plaza, Ossining, NY 10563; telephone: 914-044-9244; fax: 914-944-9387
- American Dance Therapy Association (ADTA)—2000 Century Plaza, Suite 108, Columbia, MD 21044; telephone: 410-997-4040; fax: 410-997-4048
- American Society of Group Psychotherapy & Psychodrama—301 North Harrison Street, Suite 508, Princeton, NJ 08540; telephone: 609-452-1339; fax: 609-936-1659
- Association for Play Therapy (APT)—California School of Professional Psychology–Fresno, 1350 M Street, Fresno, CA 93721

- Center for Play Therapy—An outstanding educational center at the University of North Texas directed by Dr. Garry L. Landreth, a leader in the field—P. O. Box 13857, Denton, Texas 76203-3857
- National Association for Drama Therapy (NADT)—15245 Shady Grove Road, Suite 130, Rockville, MD 20850; telephone: 301-258-9210; fax: 301-990-9771
- National Association for Poetry Therapy (NAPT)—P. O. Box 551, Port Washington, NY 11050; telephone: 516-944-9791; fax 516-944-5818
- National Coalition of Arts Therapies Associations (NCATA)—the "super association" of art therapies, it has become increasingly active since 1985 in publicizing the benefits of all creative arts therapies to other helping specialists and to the general public—2000 Century Plaza, Suite 108, Columbia, MD 21044; telephone: 410-997-4040

Interdisciplinary Movement

A popular television snack food commercial in 1990s began by saying: "Some things just weren't made to go together, like poetry and power tools." The scene then focused on a man trying to read poetry while another man cut his way through a room with a power saw. It is an unforgettable scene, and the commercial is effective in illustrating its point. Although some combinations do not complement each other or synergize into a more powerful gestalt than each one taken separately, such is usually not the case with the creative arts in counseling and therapy. In fact, most creative arts harmonize well with one another, such as poetry and music or imagery and movement. A major trend in using the creative arts in counseling is to employ them in concert with one another. The metaphor for this type of collaboration of art forms is opera. In an opera all the arts are combined: "the drama of the story, the poetry of the libretto, the artistic design of the setting, and the theatric direction of the performers—musicians, singers, and dancers" (Summer, 1997, p. 77).

The history of education in the creative arts in counseling attests to their interrelated nature. Among the first graduate master's degrees in the field was an umbrella program encompassing art, dance, and music therapy at Hahnemann University (now Allegheny University of the Health Sciences) in 1976 (Levick, 1989). This program continues today, and students can specialize in any of the three creative arts approaches. At the end of their program, however, they are all awarded the same degree: a master of creative arts therapy (MCAT). The crossover courses, as well as common core courses, are encouraged explicitly. In a similar type of arrangement, Lesley College in Massachusetts and the California Institute for Integral Studies offer interdisciplinary master's degree programs. Such programs offer students "an opportunity to broaden their artistic horizons and to deepen their sense of themselves as creative people" (Watkins, 1990, p. A17).

The type of programs just described provide a chance for those enrolled to become more aware of their senses and to increase their flexibility and social skills. Basically, they put people together who might not meet each other otherwise and help them dialogue and collaborate in ways that are personally and professionally enriching. The professional community fostered in such interdisciplinary programs is reflected in other efforts too, such as the publication of the journal *Arts in Psychotherapy* and programs sponsored by the National Coalition of Arts Therapy Associations (NCATA). The common aspect of these collaborative endeavors is their inclusivity in their content, membership, and commitment.

Numerous other illustrations exist of interdisciplinary artistic-based counseling procedures. One of the most powerful examples of the integration of several creative arts therapies is an assessment procedure used at West Oak Hospital in Houston, Texas. Practitioners of art therapy, movement therapy, and music therapy pool their talents to determine if a physician-referred client is an appropriate candidate for any of these treatment procedures. The assessment takes two sessions in which all the creative arts therapists meet together as a team (as opposed to six individually conducted sessions as was previously the case). In this time, sample work in each of the specialty areas is solicited from the client, and then the team makes a recommendation about which creative arts approach, if any, to use. The advantages of this procedure are many, including "one modality may help present an aspect of the patient not elsewhere seen" (Pulliam, Somerville, Prebluda, & Warja-Danielsson, 1988, p. 77).

Another example of the interdisciplinary approach to using the creative arts in counseling is a gender-role workshop in which extensive use has been made of the creative arts such as guided imagery, movies, music, and music videos to underscore and "promote participants' learning in both the cognitive and affective domains" (O'Neil & Carroll, 1988, p. 193). For example, when discussing family socialization and life, workshop leaders employed film clips from the movies *On Golden Pond* and *Ordinary People*. In addition, they showed the "Motown Anniversary Video" and played music from recording artists Marvin Gaye ("What's Going On") and Diana Ross ("Missing You"). While it might be argued that these creative arts were adjunctive or tangential to the total workshop, the leaders of this experience and the participants did not rate these aspects of learning in such a manner.

Technology and Accessibility

The creative arts, like the helping professions in general, have been affected by technology. Computers, in particular, have made a difference in the accessibility of the creative arts to individuals and society at large. Creative arts therapies associations have world wide web pages, as do clinicians who use the arts in counseling. In addition, sites on the internet allow practitioners and patients to pick up information on each of the arts this book has covered. Some of these locations are better then others (Haring, 1997). By spending some time on the internet, you as a counselor can find and inform others about appropriate information on the uses of the creative arts in counseling. The following sites are examples of what is available on the world wide web and not an endorsement of any site, materials, or persons.

General Art and Art Therapies Sites

http://www.yahoo.com/arts/organizations/

This site lists in alphabetical order a number of the leading art organizations in the United States and internationally.

http://membrane.com/ncata

NCATA maintains this home page that includes information on all of the creative arts therapies that are members of NCATA.

http://www.io.org/~phansen/index.html

This page is maintained by Art Therapy in Canada. It lists art therapy workshops, conferences, and associations in Canada along with journals, books, and international art therapy links.

Music Web Sites

http://ncata.com/music.html

This page describes the people who benefit from music therapy and how music therapy is used.

http://www.bmts.com/~smacnay/camt/mt_info.html

The Canadian Association for Music Therapy hosts this page, which gives a history of music therapy. It tells what happens in a session and tells how music is used therapeutically.

Drama and Psychodrama Web Sites

http://ncata.com/drama.html

This page describes what drama therapy is and the educational requirements needed to become a drama therapist, along with methods used by drama therapists. It links with the National Association of Drama Therapy (NADT@mgmtsol.com).

http://ncata.com/psychodrama.html

This page describes what psychodrama is and the educational requirements needed to practice it.

Visual Arts Web Sites

http://ncata.com/art.html

This page describes methods and goals of art therapy and includes a brief history of the use of art as therapy.

http://www.arttherapy.org/

This home page of the American Art Therapy Association includes a definition of art therapy, resources, a code of ethics, and information on art therapy in individual states.

Dance and Movement Web Sites

http://ncata.com/dance.html

This page describes how dance and movement therapy is effective and details the areas in which this method is frequently used. It links with the American Dance Therapy Association (ADTA@aol.com).

Poetry Therapy and Bibliotherapy Web Sites

http://www.poetrytherapy.org

This is the home page for the National Association for Poetry Therapy. It includes a list of goals for poetry therapy.

http://scholar.lib.vt.edu/ejournals/alan/winter95/myracle.html

This site provides information on how bibliotherapy began. It also describes the use of bibliotherapy in more modern times.

Play Therapy and Humor Web Sites

http://www.coe.unt.edu/cdhe/cpt/index.htm

This is the home page for the Center for Play Therapy at the University of North Texas. It describes the programs and services offered there.

http://www.playtherapy.org/resources/reading.htm

The home page of the Canadian Play Therapy Institute, this site provides a list of books and articles on play therapy and other professional resources and contacts.

http://www.humormatters.com/

This web site is dedicated to educating, informing, and helping its visitors locate resources for learning about humor, health, and healing.

Summary

The creative arts in counseling are currently undergoing a transition that promises to be long term and productive. Major efforts are under way on a grass-roots level to have the creative arts therapies recognized as professions in a more positive way. These efforts include attempts to do the following

- upgrade research,
- strengthen educational standards,
- mold better identities for creative arts therapies individually and collectively,
- become more interdisciplinary in regard to practice, and
- promote and make accessible the creative arts therapies through the use of computers and technology, especially by means of websites.

These five trends will be important in the future as more research is conducted in the use of artistic endeavors in counseling and more refined theories and techniques in the creative arts therapies are generated. Efforts supporting empirical and pragmatic aspects of the creative arts in counseling have the potential to lead to recognition of creative arts approaches in interdisciplinary counseling endeavors and in state licensure or national certification. Educational programs in the creative arts therapies and the incorporation of the creative arts in counseling will most likely continue to evolve. Promotion of the creative arts therapies will also continue, and the employment of computer technology will become increasingly important in highlighting achievements in the creative arts in the helping field.

Outside of the previously mentioned efforts, counselors who enjoy being creative will, in the spirit of the pioneers of the counseling profession, most likely be artistic in their endeavors to help people change, heal, and achieve an integrated whole. The extent to which formal artistic therapies grow and develop is important to these clinicians and to the helping professions. Approaches and creative techniques that work must go beyond intuition and be empirically supported. In the future, counseling will most likely be an artistic practice with a scientific base, and the creative arts should remain a part of it.

References

Aldridge, D. (1994). Single-case research designs for the creative art therapist. *Arts in Psychotherapy, 21,* 333–342.

Aldridge, D., Brandt, G., & Wohler, D. (1990). Toward a common language among the creative art therapies. *Arts in Psychotherapy, 17,* 189–195.

Bateson, G. (1978). *Steps to an ecology of mind.* London: Paladin.

Brooks, D. K., Jr., & Gerstein, L. H. (1990). Counselor credentialing and interprofessional collaboration. *Journal of Counseling and Development, 68,* 477–484.

Drachnik, C. (1989). The history of the licensing of art therapists as marriage, family, and child counselors in California. *Arts in Psychotherapy, 16,* 45–48.

Ellis, A. (1986). Discomfort anxiety: A new cognitive behavioral construct. In A. Ellis & R. Grieger (Eds.), *Handbook of rational-emotive therapy* (Vol. 2; pp. 105–120). New York: Springer.

Gladding, S. T. (1991). *The launching.* Winston-Salem, NC: Unpublished manuscript.

Gladding, S. T. (1996). *Counseling: A comprehensive profession* (3rd ed.). Englewood Cliffs, NJ: Prentice-Hall.

Haring, B. (1997, May 22). Few sing praises of music sites. *USA Today,* p. 10D.

Hynes, A. M. (1988). Some considerations concerning assessment in poetry therapy and interactive bibliotherapy. *Arts in Psychotherapy, 15,* 55–62.

Johnson, D. R. (1989). Introduction to the special issue on education and training in the creative arts therapies. *Arts in Psychotherapy, 16,* 1–3.

Kirschenbaum, H., & Henderson, V. L. (Eds.). (1989). *The Carl Rogers Reader.* Boston: Houghton Mifflin.

Kleinman, S., & Gantt, L. (1997, March). *Historical record of recognition of the creative arts therapies.* Columbia, MD: National Coalition of Arts Therapies Associations.

Lazarus, A. A. (1982). *Personal enrichment through imagery* [audiotape]. New York: BMA Audio Cassettes.

Lerner, A. (1992). Poetry therapy corner. *Journal of Poetry Therapy, 6,* 45–48.

Levick, M. F. (1989). On the road to educating the creative arts therapist. *Arts in Psychotherapy, 16,* 57–60.

Mazza, N. (1988). Poetry and popular music as adjunctive psychotherapy techniques. In P. A. Keller & S. R. Heyman (Eds.), *Innovations in clinical practice: A sourcebook* (Vol. 7; pp. 485–494). Sarasota, FL: Professional Resource Exchange.

Mazza, N. (1993). Poetry therapy: Toward a research agenda for the 1990s. *Arts in Psychotherapy, 20,* 51–59.

McNiff, S. (1986). Freedom of research and artistic inquiry. *Arts in Psychotherapy, 13,* 279–284.

McNiff, S. (1997). Art therapy: A spectrum of partnerships. *Arts in Psychotherapy, 24,* 37–44.

Mitroff, I. I., & Kilmann, R. H. (1978). *Methodological approaches to social science.* San Francisco: Jossey-Bass.

O'Neil, J. M., & Carroll, M. R. (1988). A gender role workshop focused on sexism, gender role conflict, and gender role journey. *Journal of Counseling and Development, 67,* 193–197.

Politsky, R. H. (1995). Toward a typology of research in the creative arts therapies. *Arts in Psychotherapy, 22,* 307–314.

Pulliam, J. C., Somerville, P., Prebluda, J., & Warja-Danielsson, M. (1988). Three heads are better than one: The expressive arts group assessment. *Arts in Psychotherapy, 15,* 71–77.

Riordan, R. J., & Wilson, L. S. (1989). Bibliotherapy: Does it work? *Journal of Counseling and Development, 67,* 506–508.

Rossiter, C. (1992). Commonalities among the creative arts therapies as a basis for research collaboration. *Journal of Poetry Therapy, 5,* 227–235.

Sandel, S. L., & Johnson, D. R. (1996). Theoretical foundations of the structural analysis of movement sessions. *Arts in Psychotherapy, 23,* 15–25.

Skovholt, T. M., Morgan, J. I., & Negron-Cunningham, H. (1989). Mental imagery in career counseling and life planning: A review of research and intervention methods. *Journal of Counseling and Development, 67,* 287–292.

Summer, L. (1997). Considering the future of music therapy. *Arts in Psychotherapy, 24*, 75–80.

Watkins, B. T. (1990, September 19). In non-traditional, interdisciplinary study at Columbia College, artists get a chance to broaden their horizons, hone creativity. *Chronicle of Higher Education*, pp. A17, A20.

Wolpe, J. (1958). *Psychotherapy by reciprocal inhibition*. Stanford, CA: Stanford University Press.

Subject Index

A

abuse
  music and victims of, 16
  music for victims of sexual, 26
  visual arts and abused children, 68
"acting as if" exercise, 108
acupressure, 35
"Adagio and Rondo in C Minor" (Mozart), 27
Adlerian concepts
  collegial relationships, 9
  dance therapy and, 37
  drama and Adlerian therapy, 108
  play and Adlerian theory, 119, 121
adolescents
  African American male, 24
  bibliotherapy, 76
  dance and movement with, 39, 43
  drama and, 109
  imagery and, 55
  literature and, 87, 90–91
  music and, 22, 24
  play and humor with, 125–26
  visual arts and, 69–70
adults
  adult literature, 91
  dance and movement with, 39–40
  drama and, 109–10
  imagery and, 55
  music and, 23
  play and humor with, 126–27
  visual arts and, 71–72
Adverbs drama technique, 44
African Americans
  children, 8
  music and African American male adolescents, 24
  poetry, 87
  proverb, 7
  spiritual gospel and blues music, 16

African music, 4, 18
After the First Death (Cormier), 90
Alcoholics Anonymous (AA), 44, 83, 92
Alexander and the Terrible, Horrible, No-Good, Very Bad Day (Viorst), 83
Allegheny University of the Health Sciences, 144
American Art Therapy Association (AATA), 66, 142, 143
American Association for Music Therapy (AAMT), 19, 143
American Counseling Association journals, 94
  World Conference of 1997, 54
American Dance Therapy Association (ADTA), 6, 36, 143
American Music Therapy Association (AMTA), 19
American Psychologist, 94
American Society of Group Psychotherapy & Psychodrama, 143
analytic scientist (AS) typology, 141
Anatomy of an Illness (Cousins), 120
Anatomy of Melancholy (Burton), 4
ancient cultures
  and the arts, 3–4
  imagery in, 50
  music in, 16
anger, 11
anger ball activity, 124
Anger Control Game, 125
anorexia, incongruence and, 6–7
anxiety
  anxiety-reducing music, 25
  imagery and reducing, 54
  poems for, 84
  test anxiety, 124

Anxiety Management Game, 125
archetypes, 52
Areas drama technique, 44
art
  dance and movement and, 44
  drama and, 111
  general art and art therapies web sites, 145
  hospice residents use of, 94
Art on occasions, 72
Art Therapy (Canada), 145
Artbreak program, 70–71
artists, clients who are, 10
arts in counseling, 1–2
  advantages and limitations of the creative, 9–11
  ancient cultures and the arts, 3–4
  the arts in more modern times, 4–6
  creative arts in a multicultural context, 8
  history of the creative arts in the helping professions, 3–6
  nature of creativity, 2–3
  rationale for using, 6–8
Arts in Psychotherapy, The, 6
arts therapy associations, 6, 143–44
As You Like It (Shakespeare), 102
Asian Americans
  play about Asian women, 104
  using journaling with, 88
Asian art, early, 4
Assertiveness Game, 125
Association for Counselor Education and Supervision (ACES), 77
  Counselor of Tomorrow project, 54, 59
Association for Play Therapy (APT), 143
"At Seventeen" (song), 25
audiotherapy, 19
auditory images, 50, 51

Name Index